ASTROLOGICAL PERIODICITY

ASTROLOGICAL PERIODICITY

A BOOK OF INSTRUCTIONS, SHOWING MAN, BEAST AND PLANT

LYMAN E. STOWE

Published by

FacsiMile Publisher
12 Pragati Market
Ashok Vihar, Ph-2
Delhi - 110052, India
Phone: 011-47034999
Email: www.facsimilepublishers.com
info@facsimilepublishers.com

Distribution Network
gyanbooks.com
India, USA, Canada, UK, Australia

ISBN: 978-93-6896-967-9 (PB)
First Published, 1907

2nd Impression 2025

Printed at: Gyan Press, Delhi.

ASTROLOGICAL PERIODICITY A BOOK OF INSTRUCTIONS, SHOWING MAN, BEAST AND PLANT
Author: LYMAN E. STOWE

THE TWELVE SIGNS OF THE ZODIAC.

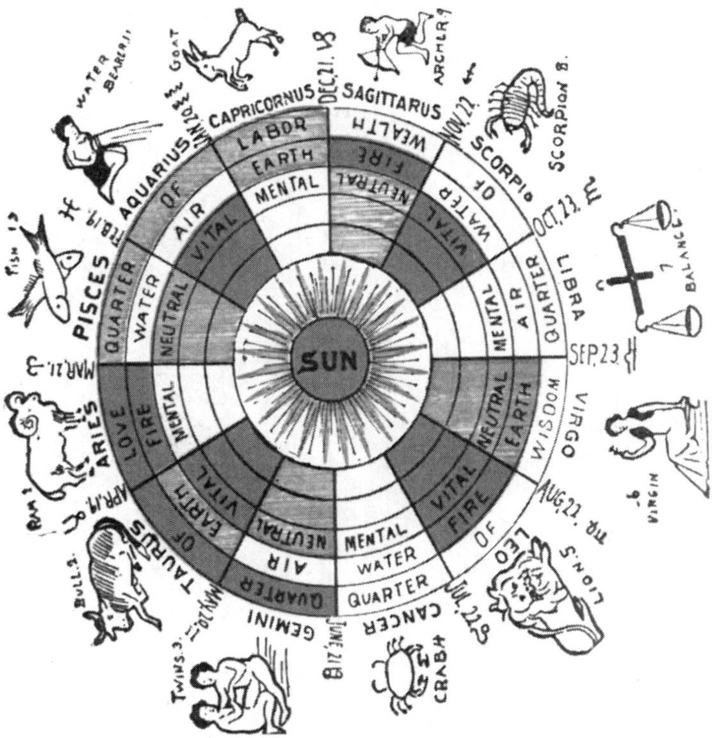

Yours Truly
Lyman E Stowe

TITLE PAGE.

ASTROLOGICAL PERIODICITY:

A book of instructions. showing man, beast and plant are subject to the influences of the planets, which gives good and evil periods, which can be taken advantage of and be a benifit, not only, to the individual, but to all classes of people.

Features too numerous to mention.

BY

LYMAN E. STOWE.

Author of many other astrological works.

Published by the Astrological Publishing Co.

133 Catherine st.

Detroit. Mich.

PREFACE OF PERIODICITY.

The author and publisher of astrological periodicity discovered, many years ago, that revolution and evolution are so closely connected that the life and destiny of man and, in fact, all organic bodies may be closely discribed, both before and after any period of life; in explaination let the author speak for him self,

I was born in the little vileage, now city of Flint, Mich. April 2nd 1843. Some men take pride in being a descendant of kings or other legal robbers, but I am proud I am a descendant of, an illustirous, legal beggar, John Stow, the Antiquarian of the 15th century. (see my Bible Astrology.) I was born and grew up in a period of my country's poverty, when money was so scarce that barter was the chief means of exchange, until wild cat money taught the people the great advantages of a stable currency. They soon learned, a more stable currency, and larger volume, was, not only, necessity to facilitate traide but to prevent national disaster. The late unpleasentness between the North and South came up when I was just 18 years of age. Naturally very patrotic, I was the first man, in my twon, to enlist for the war. The country had been doing business with a very unsetady banking system. The government knew no money, but gold and silver, which soon deserted us, and the government was compelled to issue the paper money so well known as "green backs." This, soon brout on the great financial controverasy. My own affairs, being much effected, both by my war experences and the fluctuating effects, the money question had, on business, caused me ot investigate along those lines, and to publish, my well known book, "What is Coming," and other works on finance.

My father was, a sort of, a lawyer and held some politcal office; post master, poor maste, judge, or other position. He was not in position to bring his boys up to any particular vocation. School privileges were very poor in those days, we acquired little education, but what we did acquire was practical, and experience was considered of more value than a stuffed brain.

Whether, or not, my war experiences were the greator injury or benefit to me it would be hard to say, but I will say my health is so under mined physical labor was out of the question, as a means of living, and to be a success in a business way dhmanded an education, and to get an education while making a living is a hard thing to do. I leave it to the reader to judge, whether, or not I lack natural ability. To make a long story short, I drifted into business and have conducted an extensive commercial business, of $ 50,000 a year; tho driven to the wall several times, I never failed in business, and owe no man a cent, yet it was during these active business periods that I noticed the commercial statements that 98 percent of all business men fail sooner or later. I also noticed the majority of these men were really not to blame for the failuers, but they were the result of unlooked for conditons. I also noticed that friends would urge the unfortunates on to greater activity and risk, and where such advice was acted upon, or greator risk taken, the results were disastrious. It was the investigation of those things that led me in-to the study of finance and astrology and this led in-to the literary field, in a general way, hence my first book "Poetical drifts of thot." Which treats of world building and evolution, and other topics done up in prose and verse. This work took so well it caused ma to continue in book makeing, so followed " What is Coming." Said to be the most perfect work, on finance ever written. Then followed "My wife Nellie and I." Another poetical work Then followed the " Universe." A book of condensed thot, on astrology, also a number of other astrological works, and works on the various branches of occult science, including my "Secrets of palmistry. This led in-to deeper study and investigation and I determined to be a benefit to my fellow man. The notoriety brout throu my general predictions, also brot me much horoscope work; I soon found, however, that to reach the many I must adopt a more general plan, which led to the work in hand. This has taken most of my time for ten years.

I noticed among the 98 percent of business failuers, attributed to business men came all at a given ,periods in life, according the month and day of month men are born in, and just as shure as history repeats its self so do these evil hours, days, months, years and cycles come at calculated periods. I reasoned, if these periods can be pointed out and acted upon many of the failuers, law suits, quarrels and divorces can, more easily be prevented.

Before these things could be treated of intelligently many inquiries had to be made in-to matters seemingly none of my business, which took much time and patience Of course I met with much opposition and biggotry; one man said "I think a man who is trying to know so much ought to be able to define the fourth dimension."

I at once replied " We are told the object of geometry is to investigate the properties of space, and we must assume Euclid purposely neglected to define thc 4th dimension. Proclus says Euclid wrote his 4th book, for the purpos of exercising beginers in the direction of erors in reasoning.

Euclid describes a point as' that which has no parts, or which has no magnitude.' The first dimension as 'a line which is length without breadth, or it is a space between two points. The 2nd dimension, is that which has has only length and breadith. but no thickness. The 3rd dimension is a solid, or that which has length breadth thickness, shape, size and position, of which its boundries are called' surfaces.'

We may assume a solid has three dimensions, a surface two, a line one and a point none. We now come to the 4th di mension, which may be summed up in these few words, a mass without length, breadth or thickness. This, necessarily, constitutes the eternal whole."

The gentelmans only reply to this was, "If astrology begets a line of reasoning like that I want to help it along." From that on he was a great help to me, but I was not always so successful in dispelling predjuice. As early as 1896 I called attetion to a planet beyond Neptune, giving my reasons why it will be discoverd in 1953, and called Celestia. This planet, lying beyond Neptune cannot be picked up without a powerful glass, even if it can before we get the more rarefied air the Sun's passag in-to Aquarius, in the great zodiac, is sure to bring, and we need not expect the great mogulls will ever let the honor of such a discovery go to a poor astrologer, only yestrdays paper, Jan. 24th 1909 gives credit to Harvrd for calling attention to what I have been calling attention to for twelve years.

•Many changes have peen made in this work hence the reader will pay no attention to the lower folio fiigures which are left for the convenience of the publisher.

INDEX TO ASTROLOGICAL PERIODICITY 1

INDEX OF ILLUSTRATIONS.

INDEX TO ASTROLOGICAL PERIODICITY 4

THE HEAVENLY BODIES AND THEIR INFLUENCE ON OUR EARTH AND ITS INHABITANTS.

Though the writer of this article is a deep student of all branches of science, the subject is so great and his means so limited he is, in a large measure, compelled to rely upon the work of others for his information.

So far as I know there never was but four systems or methods of creation claimed. There has, no doubt, been a higher state of civilization than we now have, and they no doubt taught the theory of world building, evolution and reincarnation. But this was buried in the debris of past ages by the decay of civilization. It is again coming to the front.

After the decay of civilization Methology took the place of science, and the earth was supposed to be hatched from an egg. But just what kind of a criter laid the egg, or where he came from was left a mystery, just like the mysteries in all Bible records, except this egg story was admitted to be a myth, or to have come down from mythology. This story was backed up by other unreasonable stories, such as the earth resting upon a turtle's back, with no explaination of what the turtle rested upon.

The next oldest theory of creation is the mythical Bible story that God created the earth in six days and rested on the seventh. In this there is no more effort to tell us where God came from or what he made the world out of than there was to explain the unreasonable stories about the egg system of creation.

Both of the above stories were so unreasonable and illogical that scientists have atempted to work out a scientific solution of the problem and give a reasonable theory to the world, at least one which they can back up with philosophy, arguments and mathematics.

This theory is that our earth, or rather our whole solar system, was produced by a slow process of development, through what has been termed the nebula theory. To be brief, the sun was a great gaseous body which, in its motion, solidified and threw off rings of gaseous matter which formed its satelites, starting with a planet beyond Neptune and ending with the last nearest the Sun, Mercury, or possibly one still nearer called Vulcon. The size, description and distance of these bodies will be briefly treated of in this article.

Of course the scientist leaves us as much at sea as to the origin of matter, or the Planner, as does mythology or the Bible. But on the other hand, they produce facts and figures together with comparisons which pretty thoroughly establish the fact as to the maner in which the bodies of our solar system was brought into existence.

Before I proceed farther with this system, which we must recognize as the true system until a better one is found, I will say that lately there has been another theory sprung upon the world. This is called the spiral system, using the little whrilwind and water spout as a symbol or sample of the manner in which the spiral system gathers the waste matter in space and forms it into heavenly bodies with their satelites. This, of course, must presuppose the same conditions in space that we have on the Earth. This theory also leaves us in the dark as to where matter came from or the originator of the plan or the force of the Universe.

The spiral idea originated with the Bible called Oaspa. This Bible, like the Christian Bible, the Coran, the Mormon Bible, and in fact all other Bibles, is a child of superstition, begot in mystery and clothed in humbug. Like them all, it is full of hogepoge, of bright things and the drivel of idiots.

There is at present many good and scientific reasons to show that everything is mind, or, in other words, that mind and matter are one and the same thing, that it is an eternal whole whose manifestations are the work of a master mind which controls all lessor organisms, and they a part of the one great organism, that which we call matter is the same thing as mind, a substance which can vibrate. All visible matter is that mind on a lower plain of vibration than our own, thus it becomes visible to us. Therefore world building, evolution and reincarnation must be treated of through comparison and deductions. Having treated of these matters in the "Universe" and "Poetical Drifts of Thought," and to some extent in "What Is Coming." I will not mention it here. But will igve some of the scientific evidences to uphold the claims of scientists and show what they claim.

Scientists admit that our solar system is but a speck in the great sea of larger and smaller systems. Let us draw a few comparisons.

An atom of lead is estimated to be 888 trillionths 490 billionths of a cubic inch in diameter.

An atom of hydrogen is supposed to be several thousand times smaller than that. A carthoid ray is supposed to be 1,000 times smaller than an atom of hydrogin. These figures are incomprehensible to the mind of man. Yet the calculations are made and deductions drawn with such accuracy and such logical reasons given for their existence that no intelligent man doubts their existence. This is largely because chemical analysis and compounds will not admit of rules contradictory to this theory. In establishing a correct rule to work by in any scientific problem a unit of measure must be adopted.

Now, let us take our earth as a unit of measure of the solar system and by that the universe and we may get a faint idea of the vastness of space and the mighty bodies in it and their influence on man.

Our earth is supposed to be a solid ball, whose density is greater than any of the bodies of our solar system, except little Mercury. You may estimate its weight in tons by putting down the figure 6 and then adding 21 ciphers. How many can enumerate it much less grasp its meaning? Or, as one writer puts it, "The earthweighs six thousand million, million, million tons."

The earth is about 8,000 miles in diameter, or 25,000 in circumference. It revolves upon its axis in twenty-four hours, giving us a free ride of 25,000 miles daily, or over 1,000 miles per hour. Only for the atmosphere moving with it we would be swept off its face. It makes its trip around the sun every year, giving us an additional free ride of 600 million miles yearly. It gives us an additional ride of 33 millions of miles per day as it follows the sun in its orbit, supposedly around the star "Alcyone." Making its circuit in about 26,000 years. Alcyone is the central star of the pleiades.

Prof. Eugene Dubois, a French astronomer, figures the earth to be at least forty-five millions of years old and probably much older. His estimate is made from the amount of carbonate of lime annually carried into the sea by rivers.

Should the earth stop in its motion, as the Bible story tells us it did, at Joshua's command, the vast machinery of the universe would be thrown out of order and the effect could not be imagined. Is it possible the maker of the universe would stop the machinery of heaven to please a poor, weak man while he slew a few more poor beings as weak as himself? Let us draw the veil and not cause the poor fool to blush who can believe such nonsense.

We will now consider the sun, which gives all things on earth life, light, heat and all that is necessary to our being. In this we will draw comparisons with other suns and solar systems.

Our article must be brief, as it is almost out of place in a work of this kind.

The sun, or central body of our solar system, as large as it is, is one of untold millions of bodies, thousands of times larger than itself. According to the Nebula theory, the sun once extended out beyond Neptune, which is three billion of miles away, and yet the sun is six hundred times greater than all of its satelites put together. Prof. Simon Newcomb, writing of the stars, which are so distant that they have no measurable parallax, remarks that one of these brilliant stars—Canopus—for instance, can be said, with confidence, to be thousands of times brighter than the sun. Rigel and Spica are at immeasurable distance, and must, in view of their actual brightness, enormously outshine the sun.

Taking our earth as a unit and then giving a description of each satelite of the sun will enable you to more readily grasp the magnitude of our sun and its insignificance in space.

The sun has been calculated to be a burning gas ball, but this is probably erroneous. Let us use a little judgment in this matter. Let us remember that the law governing heat and light is that intensity decreases as the square of the distance from the origin increases.

The sun's heat, our scientists estimate, to be from one hundred to one hundred and fifty degrees on our earth, but if one hundred, then one hundred as to ninety-two millions of miles, the distance from sun to earth, is to forty-four thousand squared, and we get four million three hundred and seventy-one thousand nine hundred degrees, which must be the heat of the sun's surface. Three to four thousand is the greatest heat yet produced by the compound blowpipe or electric arc. Suppose it ten thousand, and that would be less than one thousand four hundred of the heat of the sun. According to this figuring, and if the sun were of the material of our earth, it would be vaporized beyond gas. Now, scientists intimate the volume of the sun to be one million four hundred and seven thousand one hundred and twenty-four times greater than the earth. If the sun was so light a vapor it could not possibly exert so mighty a power on the earth and its satelites. Our earth vaporized to that extent would expand to a greater body than the sun. No, no. The sun is not a burning gas ball, but possibly an inhabited body.

The sun is 1,000,000 miles in diameter, against the 8,000 of our earth. It equals the bulk of 1,260,000 worlds like ours, or 125 globes like our own could rest side by side across its interior. The sun's weight is equal to 330,000 of our earth, though not so dense as the earth. It darts through space at the rate of thirty-three million miles per day; yet there are visible in the heavens a hundred million other suns of greater weight and magnitude, all in as great or greater motion than our sun. Stop one of them for an instant and what must be the result?

The sun's distance from the earth is ninety-five million miles. Light comes to us from the sun in eight minutes. A train running continually at the rate of thirty miles an hour would require three hundred and fifty years to reach it, while it would reach the moon in about eleven months. At one cent per mile your fare would be $930,000.

Our nearest fixed star is "Alpha Centaur," in the constilation Centaur. Its distance from us is 230,000 times greater than the sun.

At the rate of speed of sensation, if you had an arm that you could stretch to the sun and burn your finger there, it would take one hundred and fifty years for the sensation to travel to your brain. Now, if you burn it in "Alpha Centaur," it would require 35,000,000 of years before you could feel the burn.

The sun and all heavenly bodies are animals flashing through space gathering food. They are continually being fed by the meteorites, our earth receiving at least 20,000,000 meteorites every twenty-four hours. Some of these are very small, and there are occasionally one of many tons weight. Where they come from, of course, cannot be known, but they are thought to be remains of decomposing celestial bodies, as it is supposed all bodies are built up by accretion and pass away by erosion; therefore planets or suns are born, have their periods of youth, old age, death and decay.

The satelites of any solar system are called planets, the sun's stars. The planets are parasites of the sun, as we are parasites of our earth, and we must partake of the influences of all of these heavenly bodies in acordance with their power and directions of their rays or vibrations.

Few people have the faintest conception of the vastness of space. Human eyesight varies; yet how far into space the eye can penetrate no one can tell.

You see a distant star in the heavens night after night, possibly so far distant that its light has been thousands of years reaching us, traveling at nearly two hundred thousand miles per second. If you see that light to-night it started possibly three thousand years, or may be as many millions of years ago. So if stars are blotted out of existence by a sudden catastrophe, which is doubtful, that star may have been dead thousands of years ago. Thus, if the story of the crucifixion of Christ must be taken to every one of the untold millions of stars at the speed of thought, the news never has or never can reach the most remote bodies.

Here is a fine comparison. Now, if you look upon a landscape from the top of an ordinary sky scraper or twenty-story building, then stop and think you would have to view 900,000 similar landscapes to get an approximately correct idea of the size of the earth. Now place five hundred earths like our own side by side and Saturn's outermost ring could easily enclose them. Three hundred thousand earths could be stored in the sun. Now, consider the size of our sun in comparison to some of the other suns. Sirius, for instance, called the Dog Star in the constilation Scorpio. One authority says it is 2,668 times larger than our sun, and is distant 82,000,000,000,000.

The Pole Star is distant 292,000,000,000,000.

Capella is distant 425,000,000,000,000, or 425 trillion of miles distant.

The Milky way, says another authority, is composed of 100,000,000 stars, and distant 50,000,000,000,000,000 of miles. Yet there are other nebula or milky ways so far distant it has taken five million years for their light to reach us. It is said the telescope reveals over three hundred nebula or milky ways resembling ours, and each bright spot a sun, which is like our sun or greater, and each carrying with it satelites. Thus the planitary bodies would run into figures like this 6,000,000,000,000,000,000,000,000,000,000,000,000,000,000,000,000,000,000,000.

Now, who can grasp this? Yet the astronomer's figures are likely to double this number.

Let us put down our system of enumeration. Units, tens, hundreds, thousands, or a unit and three ciphers; millions, a unit and six ciphers; a billion, a unit and nine ciphers; trillion, a unit with eighteen ciphers annexed; quadrillion, a unit with twenty-four ciphers; a quintrillion, a unit and thirty ciphers; a sextillion, a unit and thirty-six ciphers; a septillion, a unit and forty-two ciphers; octillion, a unit with forty-eight ciphers annexed; nonillion, a unit and fifty-four ciphers; decillion, a unit and sixty ciphers. This is mere play figures. There are rare occasions where a billion comes in play with the general work of a mathematition; yet these play figures are used many times above the decillion. But what good has ever been accomplished by all of this mass of figures and wonderful knowledge? Aside from its use in navigation and something of that sort, what benefit has this knowledge been to man, gained, as it has, by the cost of hundreds of millions of dollars? Has the astronomer aided the farmer to add to his production? Has it helped the business man or mechanic? Has it helped the individual to become a better man or woman? Is it even correct? Do astronomers agree? How do they arrive at their conclusions?

The astronomer to get the distance of a planet formerly did so in the same way as an engineer measures the distance across a river, namely, by selecting a base line and drawing an angle and measuring a portion of one side of the angle he is able to calculate the distance to the point fixed without going there. But since the invention of the spectroscope they are not only able to measure distance by light waves, but to know what substance must be found there to cause such light. And yet mathematics is the greatest instrument of the astronomer or the astrologer. The position of Uranus was first figured out because of the observance of the erratic motion of Saturn. Finally Le Verrier, of Paris, noticing the erratic motions of Uranus, he told Galle, of Berlin, where to point his glass and he would find Neptune, which he did September 23rd, 1846.

The eclipse and the return of comets have been figured out to the second, and they were on time. But again I ask what good has it been to man, more than to gratify his curiosity?

The astrologer uses the same means to reach his purpose that the astronomer does. He tries to make a practical use of the astronomer's knowledge. He tells the farmer when to set a hen to get the best results, when to plant his trees, when to trim them, when to cut his timber, when is the best time to destroy noxious weeds, and other things too numerous to mention. He helps the physician, the judge, the business man, tells the parents how best to understand their children and how to bring them up. He tells the individual when to push and when to lie quiet, where and how marriages should take place to avoid unhappiness and divorce. And yet for all of these efforts he is looked upon with disgust by the clergy, with contempt by the press, and sneered at even by the astronomer.

Not long ago the Detroit Evening News contained an editorial on a seemingly suicidal epidemic, and asked if anyone could tell whether or not the moon had anything to do with it. I wrote a well prepared article and sent it in. Did they publish it? No, but the editor sneeringly remarked that it was too bad that a man could not speak of such a matter in a pickwicking sense without being taken in earnest. The News had a half column article for three days on this grave subject, and yet talking in a pickwicking sense. What in this world do they give their readers in earnest that will benefit them? If the people will read more books and less newspapers they will be better off. The stuff published in the press is so often contradicted that one never knows whether he is getting truth or a lie. But why all of this opposition to astrology?

The answer is plain. Because for so long it has been tabooed by a hypocritical church.

Let us hope that both the church and the press will soon get their eyes open and be willing to let some men benefit humanity, if they are not willing to do so.

THE OBJECT OF GIVING THE DESCRIPTION OF PLANETS

Is that the student can get a better understanding of their meaning and influences of the planets.

Mythology mixed the affairs of the gods with the rulers of earth. It was simply to show the nature of those rulers was produced by planitary influence. The reason we only go so far as Saturn is the vibrations produced by the influence of the planets run in octaves. Thus the sun, moon, Mercury, Mars, Jupiter and Saturn represent the octaves of harmony ruling while the sun in the great Zodiac was passing through Pisces. He has now entered Aquarius, and we are just beginning to learn the influence of the higher octave, bringing into action Uranus and Neptune, and after 1953 Celestia, a planet not yet discovered.

DESCRIPTION OF OUR SUN'S SATELITES.

VULCON.—The symbol is the anvil and hammer. The name is from mythology. The Roman God of Fire and patron of all metalic handicraft. The son of Jupiter and Juno, on account of being very ugly in appearance and deformed, his mother was ashamed to own such a child and she threw him out of heaven. When nine years of age he was restored to his father. Jupiter and Juno quarreled, when Vulcon took sides with the mother, and for his pains the father, in his anger, again threw him from heaven. In falling to earth he sprained his ankle. This time he erected forges and became the master of metal work, finally becoming reconciled to the father he forged thunder bolts for Jupiter to hurl from heaven. He was finally given Venus, the Goddess of Love and Beauty, for a wife.

We may add here that ever since it has become that "Beauty and the Beast" should come together; or, in other words, it is seldom that two beautiful people marry. One may be comely and the other the reverse. One of the reasons for giving these sketches of mythology is as an evidence that mythology must have been based upon astrology, because the influence of each planet gives to the person born under his influence much of the character, and nature attributes to the mythological person of that name.

ASTRONOMY.—Vulcon was supposed to be discovered in 1859, but most astronomers express doubts of the existence of such a planet.

The Rev. Irl R. Hicks, of St. Louis, claims to figure many of his storm periods through supposed movements of Vulcon, or at least calls certain storm periods Vulcon periods, as he names other periods after the various planets. And what is more, he seems to strike it more times than he misses. And any person interested at all in such things will find Hick's "Word and Works" magazine of value many times above its price, which is but $1 per year.

ASTROLOGY.—If Vulcon does exist he must be very small and revolves around the sun about every twenty-four days. What effect he could have on earth it is impossible at present to calculate.

MERCURY.—In mythology was the son of Jupiter called the Messenger of the Gods. It was given to him to conduct the souls of the dead to hades, and he presided over orators, declaimers and merchants. He is also said to be the god of thieves, pickpockets and all dishonest people. He was called MERCIBUS, the God of Merchandise. On the day of his birth he gave proof of his craftiness by stealing the oxen of Admetus. (*Oxen was the basis of all money of ancient Greece.*—Stowe) while Apollo attended them. He increased his fame by robbing Neptune of his trident and Venus of her girdle, Mars of his sword and Jupiter of his ceptre and Vulcon of his tools of trade. (*Jupiter, probably acting on the business principle that a sharp scoundrel well watched, is a better employee than a slow coach or fool*), took him for his messenger, interpreter and cup bearer. Though a thief and a scoundrel he delivered Mars from long confinement which he suffered from the superior powers of Aloides. He also purified the Daniades of the murder of their husbands. He bound Ixion to his wheel in hades. He destroyed the hundred-eyed Argus, and sold Hercules to Omphale, the Queen of Lida, and did many other wonderful things.

ASTRONOMY.—Mercury, unless Vulcan exists, is the next planet to the sun, being about thirty-seven millions of miles from the sun. Its diameter, 3,082 miles or a little over a third the size of the earth, revolving upon his axis in about twenty-three hours. His real motion around the sun is about eighty-eight days. Or, to be exact, two months twenty-seven days twenty-three hours fifteen minutes and forty-seven seconds and fifty-two one hundredths of a second. His apparent motion, Geocentrically, is about a year, as he never gets more than thirty degrees from the sun. In his real motion he travels about 110,000 miles per hour. Or, in other words, thirty miles per second; two hundred times faster than a canon ball. Compared to the earth, his density is that of lead. He probably shows but one side to the sun, the same as our moon does to earth. Therefore, if we judge of the heat of the sun on Mercury, as we judge of heat, scientifically, it must be 333 degrees or 127 degrees greater than that of boiling water to that side toward the sun, and intently cold on the side away from the sun. If inhabited the sun would appear seven times larger to its inhabitants than to us. But it could not be inhabited by people like ourselves. Yet conditions may be entirely different from what our system of science would prove and as the new thought proclaim all to be mind. Every planet must be a body of great organic intelligence and all inhabited by beings fitted to each peculiar sphere. Let this be remembered for all planets.

Swedenburg, who possessed such wonderful power that he, while in London, England, saw his native city in Stockholm, Sweden, burning up and described the progress of the fire. It was noted down, and months after, when the news came by the slow methods of those days, his description was found to be exact. He claimed in the same way to visit the planets and described their inhabitants. Those of Jupiter, he said, were of a large body, tall, but stooping, as if just arising from walking on all fours.

ASTROLOGY.—The Influence of Mercury, when with a god planet is for good, or with an evil planet for evil. He governs the intellect, causes fluency of speech, making an orotor or a chattesbox, according to how favorably aspected.

Tricky lawyers will be found to have Mercury in a position to influence such a nature, according to the strength of his position at the birth they will exhibit his influence. It is his influence largely that makes thieves, robbers, pickpockets and so forth. He also influences journeys, letters and literary matters. Makes sharp traders and periods of his rule are excellent for rapid business. When people are born strictly under his influence he produces slim people with sharp features and thin hair on face or head. These influences are lessoned as his influence decreases. Note this for all planets. Mercury rules Gemini and Virgo.

VENUS.—In mythology Venus was the Roman Goddess of Beauty, the Mother of love and Queen of Laughter. She arose from the sea near the Island of Cyprus. She was carried to Olympus, where all of the Gods admired her beauty. Jupiter tried to gain her affections, but she refused him. To punish her Jupiter gave her in marriage to his homely son Vulcon. (See Vulcon). The worship of Venus was universally established in statues and temples erected to her in every kingdom. The rose, the myrtle and the apple were sacred to her.

ASTRONOMY.—Venus is next to Mercury and the nearest planet to the earth, being sixty-eight million of miles from the sun, 7,621 miles in diameter; nearly the size of our earth. She revolves upon her axis in a very peculiar manner. Her artic region must be much greater than ours, while her blazing day of a half a year must be succeeded by a night of tremendous cold of the same length of the day. Even her tropical and temperate zones must be subject to sudden and severe changes. She revolves on her axis in twenty-three hours and twenty-one minutes.

It travels around the sun in two hundred and twenty-four days, or to be exact, in seven months fourteen days sixten hours forty-nine minutes nine seconds and twelve one hundredths of a second. Thus its year is much shorter than ours.

Venus was no doubt the Star of Bethlehem. I have shown this very clearly in my spiritual side of astrology, also that the story of the Son of God and the Sun God are one and the some, or that the sun and stars enact the story of the Christian religion every year. It is a marvelous parallel.

Venus travels at the rate of 83,000 miles per hour and is of about the density of our earth. Like Mercury, she has no moons. The earth would appear to inhabitants to Venus nearly twice the size that Venus does to us.

ASTROLOGY.—Venus to astrologers is called the Goddess of Love, and by her we judge of love, marriage, courtship and friendship. If a person married one born in the sign Venus was in at date of birth married life will no doubt be a happy one in that case, as she causes marriage through natural attraction. Well aspected or placed, Venus lends her tendencies to produce a grand and noble nature, but evilly placed to produce a lazy, licentious and dissipating nature. Evilly aspected Venus effects disease of a venerial nature, also of a urinary nature, and weakens the sex functions. While well aspected she leads to music and fine arts. When the leading ruling planet to those born under her, they will havo beautiful forms, round, full face, dimpled cheeks or chin, large, full eyes and an abundance of fine, silky hair. Venus rules Taurus and Libra.

EARTH OR ZENDAH.—This name is not taken from mythology, but from the works of Zoraster (*vend-Avesta*) Persion, meaning living word; reviled by ORMUZD, the good spirit or spirit guide of Zoraster. These works consisted of five volumns, treating on creation and telling man how to master the influence of the planets, putting it in words, "I will be what I will to be."

Our earth is the third planet from the sun, distant astronomically, being 92,000,000 of miles from the sun. Diameter, 8,000 miles. Revolves on its axis in twenty-four hours. Revolves around the sun in 365¼ days. (See remarks on Earth in article of Sun.)

ASTROLOGY.—The earth is our mother, represented by the moon, the sun our Father. We judge of the influence of the earth by the time of year of birth, which gives signs of the Zodiac, also the degree a person was born in, also the degree on the ascendent at birth. One born with weak planitary influence will be of the earth earthy, caring little for anything else but stomach, passion and pleasure. The earth has but one satelite or moon, which will be treated of under the name of Moon.

MARS IN MYTHOLOGY.—The son of Jupiter, then the lover of Venus. Though Mars was the God of War he was seized by Otus and imprisoned until freed by Mercury. During the Trogan war he took sides with the Trogans and defeated the favorites of Venus, for which he received unbounded hours.

ASTRONOMY.—Mars is the first planet beyond the earth or away from the sun. Distant from the sun 141,000,000 miles his diameter is a little more than half of that of the earth, or 3,976 miles. He has two moons, makes his trip around the sun in one year ten months twenty-one days seventeen hours twenty-one minutes thirty-three seconds and twelve one hundredths of a second; revolves upon its axis in about twenty-four hours, and thus her day's length is about like ours, but her year nearly two of ours.

While about seventy-two of every one hundred square miles of our planet is water and twenty-eight land, Mars has but very little water and her air is very light and thin. One of our inhabitants would quickly perish for want of air and water if suddenly landed on Mars.

ASTROLOGY.—Mrs rules Aries and Scorpio. He is called the God of War and his influences tend to make warriors, to promote contentions and strife; leads to thievery, robbery and licentiousness if evilly aspected, yet if well aspected he gives us energy, strength, parental love.

He is called the lesser evil because if evilly aspected he brings evil, though not so great as Saturn, the greater evil.

Where Mars' influences predominate he produces the finest of metal workers, also physicians, soldiers, butchers; and if evilly aspected thieves, burglars and prize fighters.

He tends to produce people of medium stature, large bones, florid complexion, sandy or red hair; generally very coarse.

ASTEROIDS are a large number of small bodies between Mars and Jupiter. As they play no part in mythology or astrology they will receive no farther mention here.

JUPITER.—Mythology—Jupiter, because of the benefits he conferred upon the world, was considered the supreme God, but Saturn, his father, usurped the power. Saturn tried to devour every male child. But Juno saved Jupiter by giving a stone to Saturn, which Saturn devoured without knowing the difference. Jupiter was sent to earth at Creet and brought up on goats' milk while consealed in a cave. After growing strong enough he deposed his father, Saturn, and became the God of thunder, but he shared his kingdom (the world) with his brother, Neptune, to whom he gave the sovereignty of the seas, and to

Pluto, the other brother, he gave the infernal regions. But Jupiter fell into bad habits, into quarrels, lust and licentiousness.

As a God Jupiter was worshiped in nearly every country. In choosing Jupiter to represent the God of wealth, they chose a fitting emblem. The world still worships wealth, who stands for woes, wars, lust and licentiousness.

ASTRONOMICALLY Jupiter is next to the sun in size in this solar system. He is distant from the sun 494 millions of miles.

He travels 30,000 miles per hour and is eleven years ten months fourteen days eighteen hours two minutes forty-four seconds and sixteen one hundredths seconds making his trip around the sun. His diameter is 90,750 miles. Circumference over 250,000 miles, revolves upon his axis in ten hours twenty-nine minutes and seventeen seconds. Thus its day is shorter than ours and its year nearly twelve times as long.. He is 300 times larger than the earth, bulk nearly one thousand times larger, density not near so great. Jupiter has five moons.

ASTROLOGY.—Jupiter rules Sagittarius and Pisces. He is called the God of Wealth. A very fortunate planet, especially if well posted at birth. His periods, years, days or hours are fortunate. But if evilly aspected his tendencies are hypocritical and selfish in every way. He produces people of dark and rudy complexion, high forehead, roundish features, rather plentiful coarse hair, large lips, large stature, large stomach, sanguine temperament.

SATURN IN MYTHOLOGY.—Saturn was the son of Cocelus and Terra and the father of Jupiter. He was called the God of Agriculture. He rebelled against his father and attacked him with a prunning hook and cut him badly. He liberated his brothers, whom the father had imprisoned in the bowels of the earth. He married Reah and ascended the throne of heaven, but knowing he must suffer the same fate of his father, should he have a son he determined never to let one live, so devoured each one at birth, or thought he did, but Reah tricked him and gave him a stone instead, which he devoured. She hid her children away and thus saved them. These were Jupiter, Pluto and Neptune. Jupiter, upon finding he was rightful heir to the throne, asserted his right and drove Saturn, his father, from it and seated himself.

ASTRONOMY.—Saturn is next beyond Jupiter, 890 million of miles from the sun, has eight moons and two beautiful rings. His diameter is 79,000 miles. Bulk nearly 100 times larger than the earth. Revolves upon his axis in ten hours twenty-nine minutes and seventeen seconds. Makes his revolutions around the sun in twenty-nine years five months sixteen days fourteen hours one minute fourteen seconds and eighty-eight one hundredths of a second. This makes a very short day and a year of the length of nearly thirty of our years. If the seasons were like ours it would make a winter of seven years. How would you like that? It is worse than Michigan winters.

ASTROLOGY.—Saturn rules Capricornus and is called the greater evil. Yet he is a wonderful spiritual planet, tempting us to cause us to develop a better nature. Makes one unsettled in married life and a person who has him in Libra or Scorpio at birth is sure to loose a married partner by divorce or death; if in Pisces he causes sadness and melancholy, and sometimes suicide. Yet his periods in years, days or hours are ofttimes beneficial for certain purposes. If well posted at birth he often brings good fortune, but if evil he is very evil.

Saturn tends to produce homely people, small eyes, ungainly forms, sickly complexion, but long lived people, often great travelers.

URANIA IN MYTHOLOGY or the MUSES. was the daughter of Jupiter and Mumosine. She presided over astronomy. She is represented as a virgin with a crown of stars. She is draped in garments spangled with stars and holds in her left hand a celestial globe.

GAEA, ZENDAH OR EARTH. THE WIFE OF URANUS, NOW RULES FOR 1,000 YEARS.

Astrologers often make the mistake of refering to Urania, when they mean Uranus the husband of Gaea or earth. There is no doubt as to which Dr. Hershel ment when he named the great planet "Uranus." He ment the male, the husband of Gaea who hated his children, and hid them in the crevices of earth. [He, probaly, hated mankind for his general selfishness and stupidity.) and not the female Urania. The planets rule alternately, as the Sun occupies the sign they rule. Uranus commences his rule in 1914 and rules for 1,000 years, he is the son af the sun god. See Bible Astrology. There being no statury of Uranus I concived the acompanying cut of Uranus fondling the earth.

ASTRONOMY.—Uranus is the next planet beyond Saturn, one billion eight hundred million miles from the sun; makes her trip around the sun in eighty-four years five day six hours forty-six minutes thirty-eight seconds and thirty-six one hundredths part of a second.

His diameter is 35,000 miles, revolves upon his axis in three and one-half hours. According to our planitary conditions his day would be but 3 and one-half hours and his year over eighty-four of our years. That means pretty long years. But his revolutions are very eccentric. He seems to be standing up and spinning like a top. So far as known, he has but two moons. In bulk he is eighty times as large as our earth. He was discovered by Sir William Hershel March 13th, 1781.

ASTROLOGY.—Uranus belongs to a higher octave, and rules the occults. He tears down to build up better. He rules Aquarius, the polar of the sun, and is truly the son of the sun. The people's planet ruling the people's sign. His nature is more like the sun than any other of the sun's satelites. Jupiter has ruled for the past two thousand years. Uranus is about to take the rule for a thousand years, when "The stars of the heavens shall fall to the earth, like a tree casting its untimely fruit, shaken by a mighty wind." This means kings, princes and money hords or trusts, and the people will rule.

This great story appears in Bible Astrology, and is the most startling story of the age.

The tendencies of Uranus is to produce very eccentric people and conditions, causing long journeys, sudden changes, sudden gains and losses. He rules no periods except as a great ruler for one thousand years; that every twenty-six thousand years.

NEPTUNE IN MYTHOLOGY.—Neptune is the God of the Sea. In Grecian mythology he was the son of Saturn and Opes, brother of Jupiter and Pluto. He was devoured by his father on the day of his birth, but again retsored to life by Metis, who gave

Saturn a certain potion.

Neptune shared with his brother the empire of Saturn and received as his part the sea. This did not seem equivalent to the empire of heaven, which Jupiter had claimed, therefore he conspired to dethrone Jupiter. The conspiracy was discovered and Jupiter condemned Neptune to build the walls of Troy, but increased his power, and his domains were not only the sea, but lakes, rivers and fountains, and he was given power to create earthquakes at pleasure and to sink or raise islands with a blow of his trident. The worship of Neptune was established in almost every part of the earth. He was generally represented sitting in a chariot, made of a sea shell and drawn by dolphins, or horses, or sometimes by winged horses. He stands up and holds a trident in his hand as his chariot flies over the surface of the sea.

Homer represents him coming from the sea and crossing the whole horizon in three steps. The ancients generally sacrificed a bull or a horse on his altar.

ASTRONOMY.—Neptune was discovered first by M. Le Verrier, of Paris, who had noticed the irregular movements of Uranus. Mathematically figured out his position and he told Gallie, of Berlin, where to point his glass to find Neptune, which he did and found Le Verrier was right within a degree. This shows how accurate astronomers and Astrologers can be in their calculations. The discovery was made September 23rd, 1846.

The diameter of Neptune is 35,000 miles, makes his revolutions on his axis in twenty-one hours eight minutes, and is distant from the sun 2,862,000,000 miles. He makes his trip in one hundred and sixty-four years seven months fourteen days sixteen hours twenty-three minutes. Thus his day is a little less than ours, while his year one hundred and sixty-four of ours. So far as known, he has but one satelite, but at that great distance it is impossible to say. The sun cannot appear to Neptune's inhabitants to be larger than a day star, judging by our system of calculations.

ASTROLOGY.—So little is known of Neptune that his influence cannot be calculated closely. His nature seems to be both good and evil. He is given no house or sign, but seems to be extremely strong in Cancer, as he is a water planet and Cancer is the first of the water triplicity. We found in mythology he was given power to produce earthquakes, to raise and sink islands; so, by looking back over history, we find when Neptune has been in Cancer an increase of scismic disturbances take place. Earthquakes and so forth. When the great earthquake destroyed the city of Lisbon, in Portigal, Neptune was in Cancer. He is about fourteen years in a sign, and he entered Cancer August 8th, 1901. Now let your memory tell you of the great destruction by earthquakes, volcanoes and sea troubles since that and you will hardly doubt this power in Cancer.

CELESTIA is a planet beyond Neptune not yet discovered, but from an astrological standpoint I predict his discovery in 1953. His influence will be entirely of a spiritual nature.

PROF. LYMAN E. STOWE.

The above paragraph was put in type, by the Record Printing Co in Dec. 1904 and published in other works ten years ago and in the hands of the press, yet Jan. 24th 1909 the press gives credit to Harvard. Is there a studied plan to steal the honors from the common people and give them to the great? It certianly appears so, see preface.

THE SUN, MOON AND EARTH ARE the chief bodies, in a horoscope, to consider, and here are their symbols. ⊙ Sun. ◐ Moon. ⊕ Earth, and from these three symbols all other, astrological and religoous symbols are made. The circle, eternal life. The half circle, or star and crescent, as above, spirit. The circle with cross is the symbol of body or life on earth, for experience.

THE MOON

Has been called Phœbe, Dianà, Prosperina, Luña, and by other names. But Luna is the only name that has any bearing whatever of the influence of the Moon, on vegetable and animal life on our earth. But that the Moon does have a great effect on animal and plant life any person who investigates the matter under the rules given in this book will quickly find out it does.

The word lunacy is derived from Luna, the Moon. Webster says, "Lunacy is a species of insanity or madness; probably the kind of insanity which is broken by intervals of reason, formerly supposed to be influenced by the changes of the Moon; madness, insanity, or any unsoundness of mind."

A little investigation will prove to any man that the Moon does affect the mind of man at times. Who has not heard of Moon blindness? We old soldiers certainly have seen men so affected.

A person who sleeps under the rays of the full Moon, on the coast of Madagascar, will find his face painfully drawn out of shape, which will require days, and possibly medical treatment, before it assumes its normal condition.

"Lunacy, or a lunatic," says Blackstone, the great law-giver, "is one that hath understanding, but by disease, or grief, hath lost his reason, sometimes injuring his senses, and sometimes, not frequently, depending upon the changes of the Moon."

With all of this testimony, there is a large number of people who will scoff at the idea that the Moon has any effect on mundain matters and still they will not investigate for themselves.

In Australia the kangaroos go totally blind, every full Moon. This makes it easy for the natives, who live on kangaroo flesh, to capture a supply of meat every full Moon; hence they are Moon worshipers.

With all of these and many more facts, there are educated asses and wise noodles who sneer at the idea that the Moon has any effect on animal or vegetable life, and some would-be witty farmer says: "I don't do my planting in the Moon; I put my seed in the ground, when the ground is ready." Well, we have many men who think they know it all and will not be benefited, but grumble because someone is more prosperous than themselves.

THE MOON'S MOTION.

It is supposed by many that the Moon revolves around our Earth in loops as she advances; this, however, is not the case. Instead, the Moon travels slower toward the old of the Moon, dropping below and behind the Earth. At the new she moves faster and rises above and goes ahead of the Earth, thus passing around the Earth. The accompanying cut, showing apparent positions of the Sun, Earth and Moon, will aid in grasping the idea of the Moon's transits through the signs of the Zodiac.

APPARENT RELATIVE POSITION OF THE EARTH, THE SUN, THE MOON, AND THE CONSTELLATIONS OF THE ZODIAC.

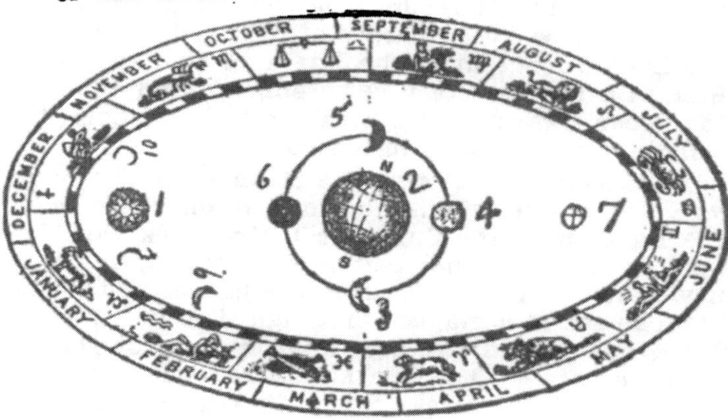

On the 22nd day of December of any year the Earth will be just entering Cancer at figure 7, but the Earth will seem to be at figure 2, in the center of the Zodiac, while the Sun (figure 1) will seem to be just entering Capricornus. Now, as the Earth moves about a degree a day, the Sun will seem to be moving through the signs a degree per day. This is called the Geo-Centric System.

As the Earth rapidly changes its relations to the positions of other planets which are really traveling around the Sun, their positions are taken for the Geo-Centric System of Astrology from where they seem to be rather than from where they really are, while the Helio-Centric System places the planets where they really are, placing the Sun in the center, but calling the opposite degree from the Earth the degree of birth. Both systems as figured from their respective standpoints are right, though subject to many errors, as any matter of so many complications must be.

The Moon must stay with the Earth as she passes through a sign, being the whole 30 days in a sign. Thus it puzzles the ordinary student, for if the Earth is in one sign 30 days how can the Moon pass through the whole 12 signs in 28 days? Would she not have to pass around the Sun 95,000,000 of miles away to do it? No; because the rays of the fixed stars forming the Zodiac focus upon the Earth as well as upon the Sun. So as the Moon is passing around the Earth, the Moon passes through all of the 12 signs, being a little over two days in a sign.

To ascertain what sign the Moon is in at any time, you will notice when the Moon is on the side with the Earth next the Sun it is in the dark (see figure 6). As soon as it passes the Sun (see figure 8), it is new Moon. Thus, by getting the phases of the Moon, you can see at a glance what sign it is in. When the Moon has passed the first quarter it is one-half the distance between the Sun and Earth. The cut shows it passing into Aries; when it reaches the Earth opposite from the Sun (figure 4), it is full Moon and passing through Cancer. Now, as it wanes by the time it reaches three-quarters, it has passed through Leo and Virgo and entered Libra. It is now going toward the dark as it reaches the Sun, which has now reached Aquarius, so the February new Moon comes in Aquarius and her full Moon would come in Leo, and so will each change progress through each month of the year, and by always noting the age of the Moon and placing the Sun and Earth in their apparent positions you can readily see what sign of the Zodiac she is in, and determine closely the degree.

The Moon being so very close to the Earth—only 240,000 miles—it has more effect on vegetable and animal life than any other body of our Solar System except the Sun.

We know to blot out the Sun, the Earth would immediately become so cold that life on the Earth, as we understand life, would be impossible. Just what effect it would have on animal and vegetable life on Earth, if the Moon were blotted out, we cannot imagine. But that the Moon does affect all vegetable and animal life strongly, has been manifestly proved in many instances, though some supposedly wise people pooh, pooh the idea; yet no person thinks of denying Prof. Willis F. Moore, chief of the United States Weather Bureau, when he admits that the Moon, at times, causes the tides of the ocean to rise to a height of 70 feet in the Bay of Fundy.

I ask the reader, if the Moon exerts such a tremendous influence on so vast a body of water, is it unreasonable to suppose it would affect vegetable and animal life, including man, when they are from 70 to 90 per cent water, or that she might raise vegetable matter a few inches?

How unreasonable it is for the rich to give thousands and hundreds of thousands of dollars to fit out astronomical observatories for Astronomers to find some heretofore undiscovered heavenly body, and then sneer at or throw stumbling-blocks in the way of the Astrologer because he wishes to make a practical use of the knowledge the Astronomer has gained, and can never make use of himself.

The ancients thoroughly understood the benefits derived from watching for the best time of the Moon for doing any work of importance. Astrology became one of the lost arts, or rather, a lost science, and yet the whole Christian world, while sneering at Astrology are ignorant of the fact that Sunday is held as a day of rest and religious observance at the instigation of an Astrologer.

The Jewish people's day of rest and worship was on Saturday, presided over by the evil planet Saturn —in Chaldea pronounced Sheetan; in Greek, Teetan, which meant power; but in Babylonian and Babolonic Hebrew was Satan, sometimes called a spiritual devil, because Saturn is a great spiritual planet.

The Jews, then, were the worshipers of Saturn—Satan, the devil. So that was what Christ meant when he said, "Ye are the children of the devil, but I am not of this earth earthy." So Christians worship on Sunday, which is ruled by the Sun. Because Constantine believed in Astrology, the following is

CONSTANTINE'S EDICT.

"Constantine, Emperor Augustus, to Helfidius: On the venerable day of the Sun let the magistrates and people residing in the cities rest, and let all workshops be closed. In the country, however, persons engaged in agriculture may freely and lawfully continue their pursuits; because it often happens that another day is not so suitable for grain sowing, or for vine planting; lest by neglecting the proper moment for such operations, the bounty of Heaven be lost. (Given the 7th day of March, Crispus and Constantine being Consuls each of them for the second time.)"

March 7th, A. D. 321, Constantine issued this famous Sunday edict, which has made Sunday a day of religious observance ever since.

Religious fanatics and some Astronomers today charge the Chaldeans and Romans with being superstitious because they believed in and practiced Astrology, but we must remember that after a great retrograde in civilization, it was Julius Cæsar, with the assistance of a celebrated Chaldean Astronomer from Egypt, called Sosigenes, ascertained the winter Solstice to take place on the 25th day of December at 30 minutes past 1 o'clock in the morning. The religious fanatics of today affect to sneer at the Astrologers of that time, as they do at us today, as mere fortune-tellers, but it is plain that these so-called fortune-tellers were the only persons who had brains enough, or knowledge of Astronomy, to correct the calendar, which had fallen into such confusion that the Israelites counted their year from the first new Moon after the Spring Equinox, and other nations varied their time according to religious whims. These Chaldeans did not figure from mere round numbers, but were so accurate that they figured to the minute, or 30 minutes past 1 in the morning. Thus they had to understand that it was necessary to intercalculate one day and a part of a day every 600 years, as was evident in the regulations of their secret—Magic or Masonic—festivals.

No doubt the priests who wrote the four great books of the New Testament were Astrologers and that Astrology was then falling into disrepute and they were compelled to hide the story under a fable or mythology, but they also knew it would come to the front and yet be known as the rejected corner-stone that is to be the chief corner-stone of the whole structure of science, of creation and religious Christendom.

It is plain that what was meant by observing the proper moment for vine planting and so forth had special reference to the effects of the Moon on vegetation. Most people who are ready to admit the ancients were wise in many things, declare they were superstitious in regard to observing the influence of the Moon. But ask them why the Compus plant always turns to the Pole Star, or what awakens the beautiful Four O'Clock at 4 o'clock, or why the Egyptian Lotus opens its leaves at sunrise and closes them at sunset and the night shade obeys its instincts to the Moon, and they will stare at you with open-mouthed wonder as if they never heard of these facts before. But these are the same class of people that imprisoned Gillieo for declaring the Earth revolves upon its axis instead of the Sun moving around it.

In discussing the effects of the Moon in this work it is desirable to refrain from going into Astrology far enough to confuse the reader, but to give effects of the Moon in the different signs at birth.

To a person who has the Moon high in the heavens, or well posted at birth, denotes one who loves knowledge, fond of science, art, music; in short, loves everything of a refining nature. They are kind, charitable, honest, ingenious, but rather timid, easily frightened, love harmony and peace, but inclined to lack stability, likely to move around and shirk responsibility. Ill-posted or aspected it tends to produce those given to idleness, drink, licentiousness and bad habits.

If in the sign Aries at birth, it increases the temper, fear and liability to mental disturbances, nervousness and so forth.

If in Taurus at birth, it being the strongest place for the Moon, it causes the person to be much of a pleasure-seeker, also a person of large resources, can take hold of almost anything and make a success of it; causes weakness of the throat or throat troubles.

In Gemini, it tends to produce travelers, powerful letter writers, authors.

In Cancer, it adds to good fortune—this is her own sign; causes love of home and domestic life, but like Aries, causes nervousness and timidity; often causes love of drink.

In Leo, causes restlessness, fearlessness, gives self-esteem, increases contrariness, but is quite fortunate.

In Virgo gives original ideas, but causes lack of confidence, gives fondness for children and a love of science, increases weakness of the stomach and bowels.

In Libra, it increases the reasoning powers and causes more frequent spells of despondency, gives many talents and love of music, art and science, and much weakness in back and rines.

In Scorpio, it increases the temper, causes nervous weakness, fondness of the opposite sex, indulgence of habits, and causes weak stomach; indicates thoughtfulness, but also deceitfulness.

In Sagittarius, causes one to be pleasant, jolly, makes him fond of horses, hunting, and out-door sports; makes good medical students.

In Capricornus, gives a stubborn, capricious, deep, materialistic mind, sometimes gloomy, cunning, restless and secretive.

In Aquarius, gives a generous, benevolent, kindly disposition, imaginary, and loving the occults.

In Pisces, gives a nervous, restless disposition, yet slow to act, yet fickle in a way, loving knowledge and very curious.

Says Prof. MacDonald, of Binghamton, N. Y.: "The transit of the Moon through any sign of the Zodiac will accelerate any disease which may afflict the part of the body in which the Moon is in at the time. Accidents are more liable to happen to that part of the body the Moon is in at the time." Let me add, especially if it were in the same sign at birth.

Astrologers, in general, have not given enough attention to the effects of the Moon's changes or to its effects from day to day of its age, from new to dark of the Moon.

Says Prof. Ormsby, of Chicago: "The Moon governs physical expression. When a person is born at the new of the Moon, they talk easily; if at the first quarter, they swing their arms and extend the hand to explain what they mean. At full Moon they swing the whole frame in the same way. At the last quarter they walk and move around much or desire to."

Now let us consider the age of the Moon from new to old, on the day which a person was born, though this will be modified by the effects of the sign the Moon was in at birth.

To ascertain the age of the Moon at birth or the sign it was in, see instructions to Moon's tables and index to Moon's tables.

In this I have carefully looked up all authorities and find Prof. McDonald, of New York, is most brief and most accurate in his "Astrology Revealed." Of course it is not always supposed to be absolutely correct, as there are many complications to take into consideration.

Here is given the effects of the Moon on a person born at any date of the Moon's age, also what the day is best adapted to, if anything in particular:

1st Day of the New Moon.—Insures long life and good fortune or more than usual luck. It is a good day to start on long journeys.

2nd Day.—Causes great love of the opposite sex, denotes large families and good luck in finding lost or hidden treasure. It is a good day for surgical operations if the Moon is in the right sign, especially not in the sign covering that part of the body that is to be operated upon.

3rd Day.—Denotes a fortunate but not a very long-lived person, also a bright mind. A bad day on which to be taken sick or to start a new enterprise.

4th Day.—Denotes a good reputation, prosperity and honor, and to own much real estate. A good day to start new enterprises and to buy and sell.

5th Day.—Those born on the fifth day of the month as well as on the fifth day of the Moon are generally unfortunate, especially those born on the fifth day of the Moon are generally subject to ill health and are short lived, and it is always an unfortunate day for any person whom the Moon strongly influences.

6th.—A person born on the sixth day of the Moon's age is generally fortunate, but restless and always in search of something, which no sooner found than they search for something else—that is, it is the tendency. If a man hath opportunities he will become a good hunter, or thief catcher, or tracer of stolen goods or minerals; generally sickly when young, but long lived and fortunate, and are always slow to recover from illness. It is an excellent day to buy and sell.

7th Day.—This day is almost identical with the sixth day, except better to buy goods to sell again, not so good for hunting, and the person born on this day will be very changeable, and if ill the disease will change sharply every seventh day.

8th day of the Moon's age is generally a fortunate day to be born on, other things being equal. It is an unfortunate day for surgical operations on man or beast, or to get into quarrels or lawsuits.

9th Day.—A person born on this day is subject to sudden attacks of illness and to accidents, also to sudden losses. Far more fortunate in love affairs than in money matters. It is not a good day to start anything.

10th day of age of the Moon produces great travelers and long life. Causes frequent changes in abode or business places. But it is an unfortunate day for buying and selling and for the sick.

11th day of age of the Moon produces a love of knowledge and often a love of religious and scientific studies. It is a good day for travel or love affairs.

12th day of the Moon's age is an unfortunate day to be born on, in all things. It is rarely one born on this day succeeds in any enterprise and it is a bad day to be taken sick or to start a new enterprise.

13th day of the Moon's age causes one born this day to be very nervous, dissatisfied and short lived; but it is a good day for marriage, especially for a woman, and is a good day for business.

14th day of the Moon's age causes one born that day to be too impulsive, cannot keep a secret, and if they become known as informers they fall into contempt. It is generally an unfortunate day to attempt to carry out designs or business enterprises.

15th day of the Moon's age denotes one born with some mark, blemish or weakness; a nervous, sickly person, and is subject to frequent small accidents. It is also an unfortunate day to start new enterprises.

16th day of the Moon's age tends to make a person born that day rather unfortunate in money matters and in health and subject to many accidents, but long lived. It is a bad day for sickness, but generally good for business. Prof. McDonald says if a person is taken sick on this day they should remove at once or they are liable to die in the present locality.

17th day of the Moon's age is likely to cause a person born this day to be afflicted with some mental trouble, and in danger of losing the mind. It is an unfortunate day for business or making exchanges.

18th day of the Moon's age causes the person born this day to be fortunate, but too free with their money. It is a good day for business, especially to make investments.

19th day of the Moon's age causes to those born that day, accidents, frequent spells of ill health, and high temper; unless they strive to overcome they will become disagreeable. It is an evil day for business.

20th day of the Moon's age is little better than the nineteenth, and the person born on this day should guard the nervous condition and temper closely, lest they fall into bad habits and contempt of others. The latter part of life will be the most fortunate in all things. It is somewhat better for business, yet demands great caution, to avoid sudden breaks.

21st Day of the Moon's Age.—This is rather a bad day to be born on. Don't be born this day if you can help it. But if you are, then have no truck with games of chance or speculation. You will have bad luck and become dishonest if you do.

22nd day of the Moon's age is a good day to be born on. Those born on this day will be fortunate and loved by everybody for their large hopes and cheerfulness, yet they will be quite flighty and changeable. This is not a very good day for business, especially for ladies.

23rd Day of the Moon's Age.—Those born this day are hardly ever happy in marriage; generally fortunate otherwise, but high tempered or petulant. It is a good day to draw up and sign papers, or settle matters of law.

24th day of the Moon's age causes honor and preferment to those born on this day; very likely to hold positions of honor and good pay, and to be steadfast and trustworthy. This is a good day to travel or make changes.

25th day of the Moon's age is not a good day to be born on or to send letters or dispatches. If born on this day you will meet with many disappointments and much illness through life. Be very careful of all your acts or you may not be able to avoid imprisonment. It is a very bad day for all business.

26th day of the Moon's age is a mixed, or good and evil day, often causing early death, but if you live long you will be admired for your good looks and become wealthy in old age. Never start a journey on this day.

27th day of the Moon's age is very unfortunate to those born on that day as it causes accidents and dangerous illness, though it gives a lovely disposition and many friends. Wait until the new moon for all important business matters.

28th day of the Moon's age is the worst day of all, as the twenty-eighth year is always an evil year. Persons born on this day have generally weak constitutions and see much sickness, also trouble in love affairs or domestic matters; though they often make money they are subject to sudden losses. It is a good day to hunt, fish, look up old matters or make real estate deals.

It should be remembered that these matters are all subject to other favorable or unfavorable planitary positions; thus a fortunate person will notice the evils less and the good more, and an unfortunate person will feel the evil more and the good less.

Suppose a person born on an unfortunate day of the Moon has a very fortunate position of Jupiter and other planets, he would hardly notice the Moon's effect only as it chances to exert them when the other planets are at bad aspects. This is why a horoscope becomes necessary. Besides it often happens that the position of a fixed star at birth may be the real cause of all of the good or evil in a person's lifetime, though it is not general.

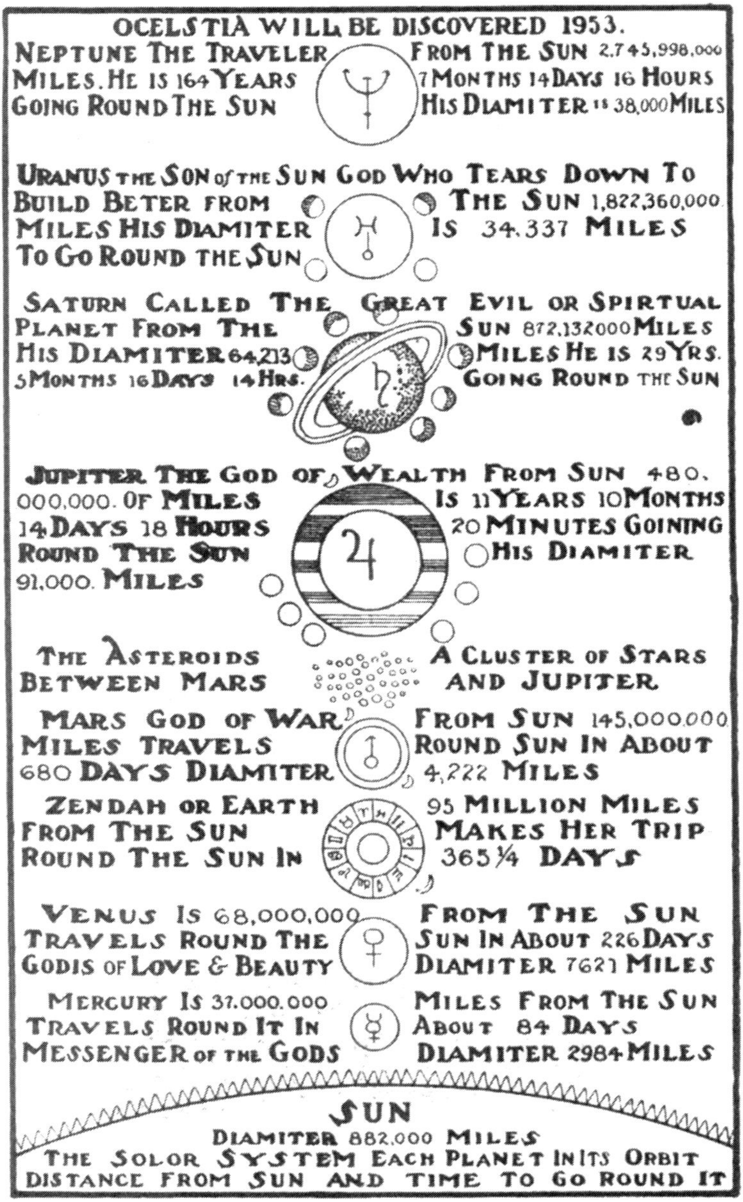
OCELSTIA WILL BE DISCOVERED 1953.
NEPTUNE THE TRAVELER FROM THE SUN 2,745,998,000
MILES. HE IS 164 YEARS 7 MONTHS 14 DAYS 16 HOURS
GOING ROUND THE SUN
HIS DIAMITER IS 38,000 MILES
URANUS THE SON OF THE SUN GOD WHO TEARS DOWN TO
BUILD BETER FROM THE SUN 1,822,360,000
MILES HIS DIAMITER IS 34.337 MILES
TO GO ROUND THE SUN
SATURN CALLED THE GREAT EVIL OR SPIRTUAL
PLANET FROM THE SUN 872,132000 MILES
HIS DIAMITER 64,213 MILES HE IS 29 YRS.
5 MONTHS 16 DAYS 14 HRS. GOING ROUND THE SUN
JUPITER THE GOD OF WEALTH FROM SUN 480.
000,000. OF MILES IS 11 YEARS 10 MONTHS
14 DAYS 18 HOURS 20 MINUTES GOINING
ROUND THE SUN HIS DIAMITER
91,000. MILES
THE ASTEROIDS A CLUSTER OF STARS
BETWEEN MARS AND JUPITER
MARS GOD OF WAR FROM SUN 145,000,000
MILES TRAVELS ROUND SUN IN ABOUT
680 DAYS DIAMITER 4,222 MILES
ZENDAH OR EARTH 95 MILLION MILES
FROM THE SUN MAKES HER TRIP
ROUND THE SUN IN 365 1/4 DAYS
VENUS IS 68,000,000 FROM THE SUN
TRAVELS ROUND THE SUN IN ABOUT 226 DAYS
GODIS OF LOVE & BEAUTY DIAMITER 7621 MILES
MERCURY IS 37.000.000 MILES FROM THE SUN
TRAVELS ROUND IT IN ABOUT 84 DAYS
MESSENGER OF THE GODS DIAMITER 2984 MILES
SUN
DIAMITER 882,000 MILES
THE SOLOR SYSTEM EACH PLANET IN ITS ORBIT
DISTANCE FROM SUN AND TIME TO GO ROUND IT

MIND, MATTER AND PLAN OF GOD.

It has always troubled man, to know where God got the material to make the world of. Genesis, says "In the beginning God created the heaven and the earth." But, does not tell us what he made it out of.

It is the purpose of this article to show that mind and matter are one and the same thing, an eternal whole, God. The purpose of creation, that there may be something for an active mind to do. God and man must learn by experience.

Emerson said, "Matter exists, to us, only in accord with our conception of it." Thus agreeing with other authority I have, elsewhere quoted. The reader will, nodoubt, feel amply repaid in the perusal of this article, whether he agrees with it or not.

First, let us understand th eeternal universe is a great whole, yet divided into organic bodies called suns, with their solar systems. All of these bodies are in motion, directed by a mighty driving will force; they obey through the laws of centripetal and sentrifugal forces. Each sun and its satellites are divided into bodies of organic substance such as our own bodies, and other smaller and more crude organisms. Every organism has its divisable portions in molecules and atoms. An atom is the smallest indivisable portion of anything, and a molecule is the smallest indivisable portion of an organic body. Every atom is in motion, and so is every molecule. When the atoms are joined in molecules they do not touch each other, but each revolve around a central atom and then the whole molecule takes on another motion of its own. So that if you could look into a pail of water with a glass strong enough, it would not look like a continuous mass as it appears to the naked eye, but would look like a pail of shot; each one in motion and no two touching each other. Now, if you can use a larger glass, it would appear like a pail of large shot with two smaller ones revolving

around each large one. The human body or any other body would appear the same. This is proven by the fact that there is room for atoms composing the X-rays to pass between the atoms composing the body, that a photograph may be taken on the other side. Thus the universe is composed of these atoms: forming molecules, bodies, worlds, suns, systems. Now, it is a well-known fact that all bodies attract or repel other bodies according to weight, bulk and size. As all bodies are in motion, the vibrations of that motion becomes harmonious, bringing health and happiness; or inharmonious, bringing sickness, sorrow, bad luck, quarrels, divorces.

"The fool says, in his heart, there is no God." Fools say, How can the planets, millions of miles away, affect us?

The sun is 95,000,000 of miles away, yet it sends us light and heat, through vibrations of the ultimate atoms. An eclipse by the moon shuts off some of the life-giving light and heat. Just so some planets give us harmonious vibrations, while others break up the harmony. Just as the harmonious sound comes to our ear, from the piano chord, bringing harmonious vibrations to the ear. Drop a loose wire on the chord and it breaks up the harmony, and the sound grates upon the ear; the closing of a door, or mingling of discordant sounds will have the same effect. Then you move to get out of it.

We should remember thoughts are things; we never made a thought, we can let them in or keep them out, but we cannot create thought.

Newton, the Astronomer, said: "There is nothing in the universe but mathematical points."

Foraday said: "There is nothing in the universe but mathematical points of force."

Sir Humphry Davy said: "There is nothing in the universe but thought.'

Earnest Loomis says: "Every atom is a thinker."

Edison says: "Any man's intelligence is but the aggregate intelligence of his constituent atoms."

Dahoma Pada says: "We are the result of what our thoughts have been."

If the above be true, we should be careful what thoughts we let in, lest we have to fight against their inharmony in a future life.

It was left for Stowe to prove, by analogous reasoning, that, not only the above is true, but that matter and mind are one and the same thing, on various plains of vibration. That man has both a physical and spiritual body, composed of these souls and governed by a trinity, as man is made in the likeness and image of his creator. If this be true, then man is a universe in miniature and his ruling soul atom a God, hence the Scriptures say, "Ye ARE GODS." But, if a man is a trinity, where are these ruling atoms located?

Some have claimed the stomach, or at least the solar plexus is the seat of the soul; others say the seat of the soul is in the cerebellum; still others claim it is in the pineal gland.

Let us first consider why all organic bodies from a molecule of water to a sun or God himself have an entity or directing soul atom, then we may find the seat of the soul. Just how much free moral agency the minor organism may have is qutie another question.

The solar Plexus is situated in the epigastric region, just back of the "pit of the stomach" on either side of the spinal column. It is composed of white and gray brain matter, similar to that composing the other brains of man. Some writers call it the "Abdominal Brain."

The cerebellum is at the base of the brain in the back of the head, and is the balancing power in man. When this is at rest, or the throne impaired, it produces dreams or insanity, and vagaries of all kinds.

The pineal gland is in the top of the head above the eyes; it is the real seat of the perceptions. It is this faculty that gives way to hypnotic influence, because it being the immediate director of the system, when it gives up to another mind, the soul in the solar plexus and that in the cerebellum act together and obey the directing power. Therefore Hudson has called this in the pineal gland the objective mind, and the others the subjective mind.

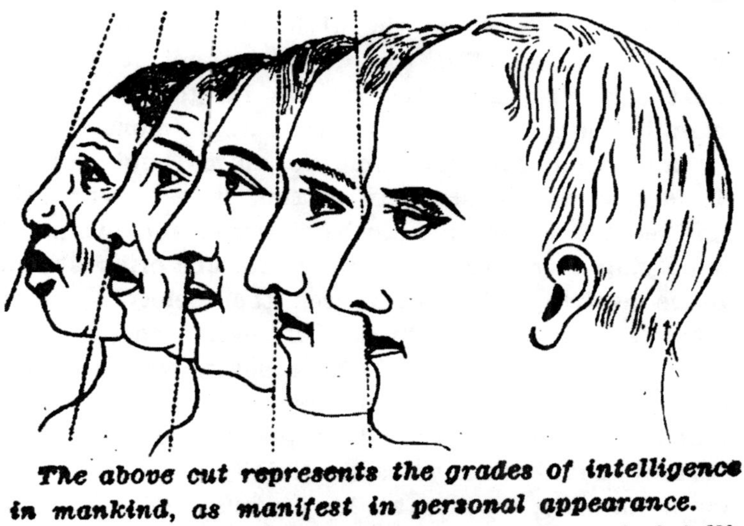

The above cut represents the grades of intelligence in mankind, as manifest in personal appearance.

Now, how do we judge of the rate of man's intelligence? Is it not by his wants and his means of supplying his wants? It is true we cannot take a single individual for this, but must take the average of a community or government. Thus a wise nation's wants are many and their means of supplying those wants intricate. The people of one of the foremost nations want beautiful grounds, palaces, railroads, steamboats, churches, libraries, schools, art, music and thousands of articles of utility which the people of the degraded nations could never understand the use of, much less the means of producing them.

Take the first head on the cut, as representing the most intelligent of men, and run down the scale to the savage, whose wants are so few he can sleep under a stone or tree. He wants no clotihng in a warm climate, and for food he can eat his fellowman.

Now tell me where the dividing line for the immortal soul is. Has the wise man got it and the next less wise man not, or has he got it and the cannibal not, or has this man-eating monster got it, and your faithful domestic animal not got it? It is a very unobservieng person, indeed, who cannot see the lower animals have wants and means of supplying these wants. Their wants are often shown to be aspiring when they seek the society of their masters in preference to that of their kind.

If the domestic animals have souls, we could not draw the line among them any more than we could that of mankind, as their intelligence is also graded. If they have souls we cannot deny it to the still lower animals, as they all have wants and means of supplying their wants, until we reach the earth worm, which is said to show the least intelligence of all animated life; yet he shows he has wants and means of supplying his wants, when he seeks the companionship of his kind or crawls out of the ground because he wants to. If we cannot yet find the dividing line for the immortal soul, let us go further. The tree sends its roots in the rights direction for water, never in the wrong direction, makes no mistakes,

It will also wrap its roots around a stone to hold itself against the wind, when it cannot get them deep enough in the ground.

Could you or I do more in such emergencies than to hang on, to save ourselves from being blown away, or to go for what we want?

To be sure, we have more complicated means to supply our wants, but that I have shown is the case all through animated life, we also see a display of intelligence through all other vegetable life; and this can be dwelt upon at great length or the manifestation multiplied many fold. Nor can we stop here, for when combustion takes place two atoms of hydrogen fly to one of oxygen because they love it, thus forming a molecule of water, and the atom of oxygen is the soul of the molecule. Two atoms of oxygen fly to one of carbon because they love it, thus forming a molecule of carbonic acid gas. This shows wants and means of supplying the wants, or like and dislike, as four-fifths of the atmosphere is nitrogen and it does not love the carbon, oxygen or hydrogen, and will not unite with them. Now who gave any one authority to call this wisdom in man, instinct in the lower animals, nature in vegetable life, and cause and effect in the uniting of the atoms, when it is one and the same law through the whole manifestation?

MAN KNOW THY SELF.

"The proper study of mankind is man."—Pope.

If man is to know himself he must analyze man from a chemical standpoint, as chemistry is the basis of all knowledge of mind or matter.

Ques. How can you analyze man?

Ans. By first understanding that there are 73 elementary substances in the form of gases, carbons, earth salts, minerals, etc., etc., etc.

Second, to understand that these elementary substances are in small particles, called ions, electrons, or atoms, which are continually forming molecules.

We must now understand that matter and mind are one and the same thing, or, in other words, that every atom is a thinker, an entity, and that every molecule is an independent thinking body, a kingdom, a god; that inanimate, apparent dead substances are experiencing worlds of their own. As every atom is a thinker, there is nothing but thought; thus, we eat thought, we drink thought, we breathe thought.

If every atom is an entity to itself, and all is thought, then all is mind, all is God, is it not?

Certainly everything is God, and every atom is life, an entity that either strives to become the head of a kingdom or willingly unites with others to enlarge, increase or build greater the kingdom it becomes a member of.

Ques.—How large is one of these atoms?

An atom of lead is estimated to be eight hundred and eighty-eight trillions, four hundred and ninety billions of a cubic inch in size, while an atom of hydrogen is many times smaller. Yet an electron or particle of cathoid rays is a thousandth part of the size of an atom of hydrogen. Every one of these is an entity, a thinker, capable of joining others to form organic bodies. Just as man is always seeking a higher position or seeking companionship from the higher order, or as a dog will leave its kind to follow its master, so are these atoms continually seeking to get nearer to the God-head or powers above them, always striving to please the master, which in the organism is the soul. Hence every molecule has a soul, and that soul is the commander or leading atom of the structor.

I wish you to understand that mind and matter are one and the same thing: Mind could not express itself without something to express on. As all matter is divisible into atoms, on various planes of vibration, and each individual atom a thinker, mind is always the higher vibration expressing themselves on the atoms who are on a lower plain of vibration.

Slow but sure, through the law of vibration, these atoms have been obeying the laws of the great Creator, through the soul atom, or God within, forming more perfect bodies. Thus, the more harmonious and perfect we become the higher rank we take in the great God-head; for, remember, we have organisms within organisms, or worlds within worlds, and while we are apparently an individual entity, we ourselves are each a part of a higher organism as much or more than we were when in our mother's womb, and there we were experiencing a world, and that world was made for us by her. Thus, we are making worlds for other organisms within ourselves.

By this it may be seen every planet or every lump of apparent inert matter is an inhabited world, fitted to the condition under which they exist.

Ques. How can we prove man is composed of atoms, in molecules of matter which are thoughts, which are things?

Ans. We know there are laws governing all bodies, from an electron, or ion, or atom, to a sun or solar system; which are the laws of attraction and cohesion, and of expansion and repulsion, which are simply the laws of centripetal and centrifugal forces.

Where two or more particles unite because of their attraction to each other, and are held together by that magnetic force which binds them in one body until a greater force disbands them, shows that one or more small particles are held in the orbit of a larger one, just as the moon is held in its orbit around the earth, or the sun's satellites are held in their respective orbits revolving around the sun; just as the cut below shows a pail of water to appear, under a powerful glass, like a pail of shot each revolving upon its axis and no two touching each other. Now, if we take a stronger glass, the water would look like a pail of large shot with two smaller ones revolving around the large ones, held in their places just as the satellites are held in the orbit of the sun.

These molecules are composed of one atom of oxygen as the ruler holding the two atoms of hydrogen attracted to it because of their affinity for each other. The conditions had to be produced just the same as it is with a man and a woman who are attracted to each other, through affinity or like for each other, but they could not marry until the conditions were right for their acquaintance.

Ques. But how are you going to show that man's body is a structor of separate atoms; in other words, like a sieve or like a cloud of floating dust?

Ans. Since the discovery of the carthoid ray it has been made possible to photograph the bones through the flesh, or even to photograph an object through the whole human body.

This shows the rays of light must have found their way between the atoms and molecules.

Ques. If an atom of matter is so infinitessimally small, and yet is an entity of itself, a thought, what is the size of the human soul, and how do you prove that thoughts are things?

Ans. That thoughts are things is evident from the fact that you had thoughts you never invited or desired; in fact, you tried to get rid of them, while you labored to bring the thoughts you desired. If you did not create these thoughts in one case, you did not create them in the other.

Again, as an evidence that thoughts are things, it has been proven that thoughts can be photographed. By placing the hand on a sensitive plate and fixing the mind very positively on a certain object, that object will, after a proper time, appear on the sensitive plate. This may explain the phenomena of spirit pictures.

That we are made up of a bundle of thoughts has beeen proved to me several times by a clairvoyant telling me of things that I would do, and which I did do, but only in thought, ten years afterward.

That the reader may understand this, I will relate the circumstance:

In August, 1893, I called on Albert Stanley, a clairvoyant, in Detroit, Mich. Among many things that he told me, which came as predicted, he told me I would build a stoop to my house, and that I would build it out of brick I would make of cement, ashes and sand, ornamented with broken glass. Further, that it would be so odd, beautiful and attractive that people would come by my house to see it; they would come on foot, on bicycles, in carriages drawn by horses and in carriages not drawn by horses. This was before the automobile was in use.

Being a very busy man, prosperous, and no brickmaker, I could not see how such a thing could take place. But misfortune came upon me; my property needed repairing, and I had men at work with me repairing the property. We were using sand and cement. I thought I must rebuild the front stoop of my house. Now, this was ten years after the prediction, or in 1903.

Now, let us see whether his suggestion had anything to do with the matter.

He could not have known that I would have to rebuild such a stoop; besides, why should he think that I would have such a thought as pressing my own brick?

But the stoop did fall into decay; I must do something.

My attention was called to some beautiful brick made of cement, ashes and sand. So I conceived of the idea of making the molds and using up material I had on hand.

A little way from my house was a bottling works, where I saw a lot of broken glass of various colors. The thought struck me I could quickly and easily make these brick and ornament them with this glass. I then began to speculate as to how the thing would look.

It became an airy castle, so beautiful that I saw the citizens coming from every direction and in every sort of a vehicle, including the automobile, which was not in existence ten years before, when the prediction was made.

I laid the matter before my workmen, and we figured the stoop could be built for seventy-five or a hundred dollars. This was a larger sum of money than I cared to expend at that time, so I looked the stoop over and found the upper portion needed but little repairing; that by putting a new foundation under it and repairing the whole thing would make it as good as new at an expense of ten dollars. So the beautiful brick stoop was never built except in my mind, and Stanley's suggestion ten years before could have had nothing to do with the circumstances which caused me to design the stoop in my mind. This shows that we are a bundle of thought, and it is this thought that enables a clairvoyant to read the future. But he cannot tell whether it will only be presented in thought or will be expressed in act. It also shows that we should be very careful what kind of thoughts we attract to us. If we frequently brood over troubles and contemplate suicide, or even in a joke threaten it, we are encouraging thoughts of that kind to come to us which may express themselves afterward. If we desire prosperity and happiness.

we must continually think and believe we have it.

As Christ said, "Whatsoever ye desire, pray for it, believing that ye have it, and ye have it."

That is, it will come to you in due time. Of course, the more determination, force and energy you put into it the quicker you will get what you desire. But no matter how hard you labor, if you have no faith in your work, you are attracting more of the unfortunate atoms to you than of the fortunate thus bringing to yourself misfortune.

You may ask, Can I make myself believe what is not so?

I answer yes; many a man has told a lie until he believed it himself. But he is dealing with things of the past; what you want to do is to attract to you things that are to come, and they will come in some manner as you have all things within.

We often hear it said, "History repeats itself." In a way this is so, yet in another sense neither history or anything in nature repeats itself exactly. No two things can ever be just alike, because the vibrations of the ultimate atoms when forming organic bodies can never be in just the same position relative to other bodies.

The masses of the people have no conception of why our earth and all upon it, including man, can be affected by stars and planets billions of miles away. Even a majority of astrologers could not give a logical reason for the effect of the stars and planets on us.

That this may be more comprehensible to the casual reader, I will explain some of the laws of matter and vibration as understood by the world's best thinkers:

From the preceding pages we understand mind and

matter are one and the same thing. Then reason teaches us that if there is a universal intelligence we call God, he is everywhere; there cannot be an atom ever so small but what he is in it. If not, he would be circumscribed just in proportion to that space where he is not. Then, as before stated, there is no room for anything but God—no room for a devil.

We can only judge intelligence by the expressions of desire or want, and the methods of supplying those wants, and this must not be judged by the individual, but by the aggregate of a class or community.

Just as a wise nation expresses great wants and complicated methods of supplying the wants or the atoms of hydrogen and oxygen come together to supply their wants or likes, one shows the same desire that the other does; it is the same law acting in both cases.

This recognition of universal life answers the question so often put to the teachers of the evolution theory, "Where did the first life principle come from?"

If all is thought and thoughts are things, then it is plain the great thinking principle we call God must have something to do and something on which to express himself. That something we call matter; therefore, mind and matter are one and the same thing. It is always the higher thought expressing itself on the lower thought and endeavoring to draw the lower thought upward. The lower thought, like the barnacles on a vessel's bottom, is forever hitching on and dragging the higher thought down to its level. Hence the Christian's devil is not so far out of the way. If we make it harmonious for the lower thought by enjoying the pleasures of a moment which drag us down, we are inviting the barnacles which impede our progress, and we may as well call it devil as anything else.

While we cannot see or comprehend the plans of one on a plane of vibration above us, any more than those on a lower plane can comprehend us, yet when we encourage a lower thought we make it easier for them to come in and harder for us to entertain the higher thought.

THOUGHTS ON VIBRATION.

Now, let us show that if we could master a knowledge of vibration we have the key to the mysteries of the universe.

We must remember that the blows that break an arm or a leg, or that knock the foundation from under a building, are no less vibrations than that which brings the harmony of the sweetest musical tone to the ear. The ponderous shell is driven twenty miles from the gun by vibration; rocks and mountains split asunder, amid terrible uproar, by vibration; while the mellow sunlight is brought from the sun, ninety-five millions of miles away, or the star light from so far distant that it has taken thousands of years to reach us traveling at the rate of nearly two hundred thousand miles per second, all of vibration. Thus, we know that light, sound, color are all made manifest to us through vibration. In fact, all phenomena of life is the expression of vibration. The knot on a tree, or the crook of a limb, is the result of vibration of the atoms at a particular time in the growth of the tree.

It is claimed that thirty vibrations per second is the lowest vibration the human ear is cable of hearing, and the highest 32,768.

It was once supposed the ant could neither hear or see, but an experimenter found, on straining a very fine wire to a high pitch, he could produce sound that seemed to fill the ant with horror. This shows the ant can see and hear in a world on a different plane oi vibration from ours. Then what worlds and worlds may not be surrounding us.

It is so well known that light or color and sound are one and the same thing or vibration of the ultimate atoms that colors have been made manifest in octaves by striking the keys of a piano the strings of which were attached to a proper mechanism for the purpose. Quoting from Camille Flammarion:

"That sound waves or vibrations run in octaves is made manifest by letting a number of people hold each a tuning fork all tuned to a certain pitch in unison; cause one to vibrate, and all of the others will vibrate in unison with it.

"Now let them hold as many more forks tuned to another pitch, and they will not vibrate. It is the same if you sing close to a piano; the string tuned to the pitch of your voice will vibrate, the others will not."

Having shown that the vibrations producing sound are on a plane from 24 to 32,768 per second, we then come to a plain of vibrations unknown. From 1,073 to 741,824 we have electricity manifest. Now we have another vast plane unknown. But from 281,474,976,716,656 to 1,125,890,906,842,624 gives us light or colors. These vibrations produce the sensation of light, or 400 trillions produce red light and 768 trillions produce violet light; above this we enter the realm of darkness.

As music is time, and sound, color, light, electricity all depend upon vibration of the ultimate atoms, and we find wireless telegraphy depends upon certain waves of vibration, we may well assume these vibrations are as certainly affected by the planets as they are when you strike the piano keys and the sound becomes harmonious or inharmonious according to the manner of use. The reader should then easily understand that if the sun and stars are sending us light by vibration, some of the other unknown planes of vibration are producing the different effects upon us.

Supposing, if you please, Jupiter is sending his harmonious strains of vibration, which tunes the vibrations of the atoms of your system for life, insuring to you harmony and happiness, health and wealth. But just in the wrong time Mars comes in at an angle creating cross vibrations; he upsets the whole thing, and you are born unfortunate instead of fortunate. As you were born under the vibrations of the stars effecting the sign and degree of the sign you were born under, every human being born under that degree should be one just like the other if other influences were not at work. What are these influences?

First as every one of the heavenly bodies is continually in motion, continually changing their relative positions, the vibrations are continually changing, and yet retaining something of the motions of first cause.

Second, every degree and minute of longitude and

latitude is presenting different positions of the earth's surface to these changing rays of vibration.

This is again affected by vibrations influenced by environments and races. This is called heredity. This shows us that nature never exactly repeats itself. No two of any type of organism are exactly alike, and yet there is enough similarity in all animal life to see certain characteristics in those born under the same sign and degree of the Zodiac. Then, in this sense nature repeats herself.

The sun makes its circuit in the great Zodiac in about 26,000 years, or a little more than 2,000 years in a sign. Thus we transit the same positions every 26,000 years; and yet as the fixed stars, so called because of their great distance, their relative motion is hardly perceptible, yet is always changing, so we never return to just the same position.

The earth revolves around the sun annually, bringing the four seasons of the year; yet there are never two of these seasons just alike, yet you may count on them regularly.

Each one of the planets or satellites of the sun has its periods of returning to its original position relative to us or our date of birth. Yet, as a whole, it never exerts just the same influence on you that it did at your birth. For all of this, the effect of these returning periods can be calculated, in a general way, to give the good and evil periods of any person's life, and that is the object of getting a horoscope, also to know the locality best suited to you, where you would be most fortunate, what business best adapted to, and many other things too numerous to mention.

Flammarion publishes a table giving the vibrations in trillions per second:

Bright red	460	trillions.
Limit of red and orange	490	"
Limit of orange and yellow	558	"
Limit of yellow and green	590	"
Limit of green and blue	596	"
Limit of blue and indigo	675	"
Limit of indigo and violet	760	"
Bright violet	756	"

He also gives the length of light waves, but space forbids my quoting further.

Many philosophers have held that matter is a condition of mind. This would imply that mind and matter is one and the same thing, and that it is a ponderable something, as we cannot understand how something can be made from nothing, or an expression perceived without a substance on which to make an impression, or as an expressor.

Emerson said, "Matter only exists for us because mind can perceive it."

Pope evidently believed mind and matter one eternal whole of intelligence, as he expressed it:

"All are but parts of one stupendous whole,
Whose body Nature is, and God the Soul."

As we understand vibrations to be the machinery of the universe, there must be something to vibrate, consequently we have to admit of matter, though it have the attribute of mind. Therefore, as we use mind on a different plane of vibration, why should we not also be used by those on another plane of vibration? So, as we shovel coal into the stove, we are using unseen worlds to supply our physical comforts.

while we in turn are being used, possibly in the same manner, without inconvenience to us.

Our comprehension of time, space and matter is limited to our knowledge of our condition of mind.

We cannot conceive of the size of an atom of lead which is estimated to be eight hundred and eighty trillions, four hundred and ninety billionths of a cubic inch in size. Yet this is very large compared to an atom of hydrogen, and an electron. A carthoid ray is said to be one thousandth part of the size of an atom of hydrogen.

There is insect life so small that we can only perceive it is life when thousands of them are in a mass, yet this life exists in organisms possibly as perfect in form as our own bodies. This shows us we have no conception of time, space or size beyond our condition of life. Then, why may there not be unseen worlds around us. Take one of these microbic bugs and place him on your hand, and what conception could he have of the giant that holds him and could crush him instantly? Then may not our earth be an animal on which we are a parasite, and its atmosphere its spirit body. I think it is so. The earth turns over, pulsates, breathes, and is everlastingly being fed by dropping aerolites.

That we may build up or tear down through knowledge of handling vibrations is quite clear, since a bridge which will not show a tremor of vibrations under the uneven tread of an elephant has been known to vibrate and sway under the uniform trot of a dog. A violinist proved he could produce vibrations with his violin sufficient to destroy a mighty structure of masonry, and we know how quickly the orchestra of any theater will change the air if the audience begins to beat time, because they have such instructions. This will call to mind the Bible story of the throwing down of the walls of Jericho by the seven blasts blown on rams' horns.

Undoubtedly the mighty stones in the pyramids of Egypt were transported there by the power of vibration, as the only instrument ever found around the pyramids was a flute containing more holes than any musician of our times is able to manipulate.

VIBRATION THE POWER OF THE UNIVERSE AND THE HAND OF GOD.

God is the intelligent whole, his plan enforced by vibration. We say thoughts are things, but thoughts are the vibrations of the ultimate atoms which flow in currents. As before stated, man never created a thought; he merely lets them in or keeps them out. Thus, thoughts are the vibrations of the brain.

We must prove that man has but very little free moral agency, but that he is the instrument being played upon by the hand of God, or, as Brother White and Brother Maddock, of the Adept, put it, the Great Dinamus, which is merely a name for a bigger, broader God than the orthodox churches speak of.

We will now proceed to show how the plan of the universe is ruled by vibrations.

All bodies, from the smallet atom to the largest sun, express an influence on other bodies through the law of attraction and repulsion, or like and dislike; every atom is a center to itself. This will be more readily understood when we understand the meaning of A ZODIAC. I say a Zodiac, but I will describe the sun, earth and moon's Zodiac, and then you will be able to gather the whole meaning.

Imagine our solar system on the inside of a vast hollow sphere whose sides are studded with brilliant lights, small and great, sending their rays of light to the sun and to each one of its satellites. Here you will see each body is a center of the sphere so far as receiving the rays of light is concerned. But as the sun and its satellites are continually moving, the vibrations of light are intercepted and somewhat changed by rays of light cast from each of the sun's satellites. It is these changing vibrations that give us the variations in all created things, so that nature never repeats itself, as there are no two things exactly alike, from two blades of grass to two of the largest heavenly bodies.

That you may get a faint idea of the magnitude of the universe, I will state the planet Jupiter is thirteen hundred times larger than our earth, yet the sun is larger than all of its satellites put together, and, if a hollow ball, would hold three hundred thousand globes like our earth, and yet there are suns many times larger than our sun is in proportion to our earth. These suns we call fixed stars, because they are so far away their motion is not perceptible in comparison to our earth, yet they are flying through space at a prodigious speed. These suns or fixed stars, which are the lights spoken of and which form the Zodiac of 12 signs, each sign influenced by a cluster of these stars, gives a different meaning or influence to each one of the signs, as follows:

The heavens are divided into the eastern and western hemispheres. They are divided by the Zodiac, a band running zigzag through the heavens, from 8 to 9 degrees each side of the ecliptic. All circles consist of 360 degrees. As before stated, the Zodiac is divided into 12 signs of 30 degrees each, and the degrees are divided into minutes and seconds; and, as stated, these signs are influenced by the fixed stars, so that each sign has a definite influence on everything set in motion under its rays. It is through the vibrations of the fixed stars and the planets which chance to be in a sign at a given time that produces the effects whereby an astrologer can read the fate of a man or things on this mundane sphere.

Every atom is as much the center of the Universe as is a sun, and has a Zodiac of its own, which focuses on some other body just as the moon has a Zodiac which focuses on the earth, and the earth has a Zodiac which focuses on the sun, and the sun a Zodiac which focuses on a point somewhere between Polarious and Vega. See further description of the sun's and earth's Zodiac further on. The following is a description of the moon's Zodiac:

The moon does not revolve around the earth as it seems to, but as the earth advances the moon travels faster at one period than another. It drops below and behind the earth and then catches up and rises above the earth, thus seeming to revolve around the earth. The earth being ninety-five millions of miles from the sun, and the moon only a hundred and forty thousand miles from the earth, of course the moon cannot travel around the sun except as the earth travels around the sun, or it would sometimes be twice ninety-five millions of miles from the sun. The moon, however, transits through all of the signs of the Zodiac in 27½ days as it focuses on the earth. Thus in that 27½ days the moon will cast her vibrations from each of the signs, alternately as she passes through them, while they focus on the earth, and the earth remains in one of the signs just as the earth and planets transit all of the signs while all of the time in one of them, with the sun. Therefore, we have 12 polarities in each month, and as the earth revolves upon its axis every 24 hours, no part of the earth receives the same vibrations, but for a few moments at a time; hence every minute of time, and every spot or locality is receiving different vibrations; this is why twins often differ so much in nature and no two men or any two things of growth are exactly alike.

Many have argued that the period of conception is the proper time from which to figure a nativity. But that is wrong, as at that period the child is not an independent being. But the moment a child is born into this world and breathes its air, it feels the shock of the changed conditions and sets up a cry; this is the proper moment to figure from, as it is now an independent being, receiving the vibrations sent to it at the moment it breathes, and that controls its whole life. This is why an astrologer can diagnose disease, often better than a physician, and why Hypocrates, the Father of Materia Medica, said:

"A man is better fitted to be called a fool than a physician who does not underdstand Astrology."

That a man's life and his organism are subject to these vibrations is manifest by the expression upon his five senses.

If sound is brought to the ear by vibration, and light to the eye, of course the sense of smell and touch and taste are expressed by vibration. Take, for instance, the taste of sweet. Sugar is compposed of 24 parts of carbon to 22 parts of hydrogen and 22 parts of oxygen. The tendency of oxygen is to fly from heat, and as each atom of oxygen is supposed to possess two polar forces, thus: —O—. When we take the lump of sugar upon the tongue and it dissolves, there is sufficient heat in the mouth to give a quickened action to the atoms of oxygen which causes the sharp corners or polar forces to rapidly revolve upon the tongue which cuts through the coating; this cutting, in a mild form, we call sweet, but if we eat too much sugar the tongue becomes sore and the sensation is no longer delightful; this shows us that taste in its various forms is the result of vibration. The scent of the rose is lovely because the vibrations are pleasing, but the scent of decaying carron are nauseating because it is another plain of vibration; just as Flameron shows the different colors are produced by differing plains of vibration.

Now let us show that the sensation of touch is vibration.

Who has not noticed the touch of one person is pleasant and soothing, while that of another is disgusting and almost painful. If you have not observed it I would advise you to be more thoughtful, and you may profit by it, for there is a safe guard in the sense of touch.

Everything in nature has its own peculiar magnetism or vibration. We come in contact with certain vibrations which shock our systems, not understanding it we pass it by without notice, soon we are sick and we say we caught this disease or that disease because our systems were unsettled by a change of vibration.

This sometimes settles in one locality and then we call it inflammation. Heat, burning is inflammation. Doctors used to resort to bleeding to reduce this exhilarated vibration, finally they discovered bleeding weakened the patient and then they resorted to ice and found that was a safer method. A magnetic healer, whose vibrations are harmonious to us, will be beneficial, but one whose magnetism is inharmonious will be injurious, just as a medicine may be one man's salvation and another man's death.

Doctor's should give heed to these things instead of scoffing at them.

Doctors have noticed often that they thoroughly understand the case in hand and yet the patient grows worse, another doctor is called in, the patient immediately begins to recover and the new doctor gets great credit for understanding the case, while the first doctor is censured. He may have understood the case better than the second one, but his magnetism or vibrations were injurious to the patient while the second doctor's vibrations were more harmonious.

If doctors will study the Zodiac and its influences and work in harmony with each other and with patients they will be doing themselves and humanity great good.

The question will naturally be asked. If we are destined by planetary influences to receive certain vibrations which shape our lives, is it possible to get out of the evil influence. In answer, let me give you an illustration.

Imagine a beautiful miniature lake, containing a few fish. You throw a stone to the center of the lake and the water begins to vibrate from the center in circles. This may be very pleasant to the fish and they swim with the vibrations. But you cast another stone near the outer circle of vibration and this sets up counter vibrations, very unpleasant to the fish. They try to get out of it and find by certain movements they can leap over an inharmonious vibration, or suddenly turn and swim to the other side of the lake where the cross vibrations have not reached, thus they avoid the unpleasant effects of the inharmonious vibrations. So there are ways of overcoming, in a measure, planetary influences by exercising our will force, this sometimes is aided through the assistance of another who is not laboring under an evil period or aspect.

This shows the necessity of a horoscope, showing good and evil periods. Of course a wise noodle and a contemptible fool will scoff at these things, but the truly wise will profit by them.

Of course everybody has a right to his opinion, and we may honestly differ one from another, but when we do we should be able to give a logical reason therefore, and not merely say, "Well, I don't believe it and that is all there is to it." Any fool can dispose of the strongest philosophy in that silly manner.

As Astrology is based upon the vibrations of the ultimate atoms set in motion by the influence of the great bodies, and is proven to be an exact science, it holds to reason, man should seek to control nature, by controlling these vibrations. This is why scientists are turning to electricity for the cure of disease, where medicine fails, because electricity is nothing more or less than accelerated vibrations of the ultimate atoms. While disease of body or mind is the result of irregular or inharmonious vibrations.

Therefore we believe the medical battery is the most essential article of utility for every household. It not only changes vibrations and so enables the patient to reach an equilibrium and health, but it rekindles the fires of vitality and renews life. Heat is motion, accelerated vibrations. Decay is the result of inflammation or uneven vibrations. Death is loss of vitality, motion, dying vibrations. Many people are pronounced dead when a spark of life remains which might, by the use of the medical battery, be fanned into a flame and the patient saved from being buried alive.

Vibration is the mainspring of life; when it is run down we die.

Strike a piano chord and it reflects the life that struck it until the vibration ceases; then the expression of life ceases. The vibration may be stopped suddenly by an accident or cutting the string. It is so with man. He is wound up and set in motion with vibrations tuned to harmonize with the planet casting its most direct rays upon him; his life may be cut short by accident or violence, otherwise he grows old, his blood circulates slowly, the vibrations are slowly dying out. He may accelerate them, artificially, for a time, but at length they die out and he dies. He may learn by the use of an electric battery to renew the vibrations possibly to an indefinite period.

The moment a patient seems to be dying the battery should be applied, together with restoratives. Dear reader, you or your family are not safe without a medical battery in your house. Just look at the list of diseases that have been successfully treated with a medical battery:

Abscesses,
Ague in the breast,
Amaurosia (see diseases of the eye),
Anus, Prolapsus or Falling of
Anus, Induration of
Apparent Death,
Appetite, Loss of
Aphonia (see loss of voice),
Apoplexy,
Asthma,
Back, Weak
Bruises and Sprains,
Bowels, Constipation of
Bowels, Inflammation of
Bowels, Looseness of
Bladder, Paralysis of
Bladder, Inflammation of
Brain,
Bronchitis,
Burns and Scalds.
Cancer,
Canker,
Catarrh, Acute
Change of Life,
Kidneys, Bright's Disease of the
Leucorrhœa,
Liver, Inflammation of
Liver, Torpid
Liver, Enlargement of
Lockjaw,
Eyes, Opacity of Film,
Eyes, Amaurosis,
Faceache,
Felons,
Fevers,
Fever, Typhoid,
Fevers, Eruptive,
Fever and Ague,
Fever Chills,
Flooding or Menorrhagia,
Falling of the Womb (see Prolapsus of the Uterus),
General Treatment,
Goitre,
Gravel,
Hoarseness,
Heart,
Headache,
Headache, Sick
Hernia,
Hip Disease,
Hysteria,
Inflammation,
Insanity,
Indigestion,
Indurations,
Kidneys, Inflammation of
Circulation of the Blood,
Corns,
Chilblains,
Crick in the neck,
Crick in the back,
Consumption,

Colds,
Cold Feet,
Cold in the Head,
Contracted Muscles,
Croup,
Cramp,
Cholera, Infantum,
Cholera, Morbus,
Cholera, Asiatic
Cutaneous Diseases (see Scrofula),
Deafness,
Debility,
Dyspepsia,
Diphtheria,
Diarrhœa (see Bowels),
Diabetes,
Dropsy,
Earache,
Ears, Running of
Ears, Swelling of
Enlarged Glands,
Enlarged Tonsils (see Quinsy),
Epilepsy,
Eyes,
Eyes, Inflammation of
Eyes, Granulated and Thickened Lids,
Eyes, Ulceration,
Eyes, Obstruction of the lachrymal duct,
Eyes, Cataract,
Uterus, Inflammation of
Uterus, Ulceration of
Uterus, Enlargement of Irritation of
Spleen, Inflammation or Enlargement of
Sprains,
Stammering,
Lungs, Inflammation of
Loss of Voice, or Aphonia,
Measles,
Menses, Suppression of
Menses, Painful,
Menses, Retarded
Menses, Too Copious,
Miscarriage (see Flooding),
Mouth (see Sore Mouth),
Neuralgia,
Nose-Bleed,
Nose, Swelling,
Ozœna,
Ovaries, Inflammation of
Ovarian Tumor,
Obstructions,
Palsy, or Paralysis,
Piles,
Pleurisy,
Polypus,
Pregnancy,
Quinsy and Sore Throat,
Rheumatism, Acute,
Rheumatism, Chronic,
Scrofula,
Sore Mouth,
Sore Nipples,
Sore Throat (see Quinsy, Diphtheria and Colds),
Sleeplessness,
Spasms,
Spine, Curvature of
Spine, Inflammation or and Induration of
Vagina, Inflammation of
Vomiting,
Whites (see Leucorrhœa),
Womb (see Uterus),
Waterbrash,

St. Vitus' Dance,
Sunstroke,
Tonic Treatment,
Toothache,
Tumors,
Urine, Retention of
Uterus, Prolapsus of
Stomach, Inflammation of
Whitlows,
White Swelling,
Wounds,
Weak Sight,
Weak Stomach,
Weak Lungs,
Worms,

and nearly every other kind of illness has been successfully cured with the use of an electric battery.

The following and similar items may be frequently seen in the papers:

MEDICINE OF THE FUTURE.

DR. D'ARSONVAL SAYS ELECTRICITY WILL REVOLUTIONIZE THERAPEUTICS.

PARIS, July 4.—The famous electro-therapeutic specialist, Dr. d'Arsonval, lecturing this week on the effect of electricity on living beings, expressed the belief that the world was on the eve of a therapeutical revolution, electricity being the medicine of the future.

He said also that a strong, continuous current through a patient could produce local anasthesia, permitting, slight surgical operations without narcotics.

Dr. d'Arsonval demonstrated the utility of electricity in skin diseases.

I have found, during my investigation, in the application of electricty, that I got the best results when passing the current throu my own body and applying it as magnetic force rather than electric energy. Those who have never noticed the difference in the two forms of applicaton could hardly imagine the more favorable results with the magnetic treatment. I used a small metal band, with the chord attached, one I put on the patients wrist the other I attach to my own wrist. This leaves the hands free and the application is made throu the hands magneticly applied throu gentle strokes or. throu the more vigorous massage. Hypnotic suggestion should be made at the same time, reciting the benefites that is to be derived throu this application.

The public in general are continually asking: "If there is any good in Astrology, why do educated people, astronomers and scientists, make so light of it?"

I answer, because there is no prejudice so great as that produced by false teachings, no ass so great an ass as an educated ass. By a bigoted fool religious prejudice was raised against Astrology and has been kept up ever since. Let us show up some of the work of this class.

Opposition and ridicule of truth does not originate with the ignorant, but with educated bigots.

Nor are the great majority of the inventions and discoveries made by college-bred people, but on the contrary by people of limited education, yet there is an apparent conspiracy to throttle the latter class and push the over-fed, college-bred, brain-stuffed class to the front. Even in our business houses and workshops, so the true thinker and natural student has a double obstacle to overcome.

This is so manifest in your literature that your newspapers and magazines may be classical in machine work, but they are trash in comparison to the papers and magazines of 30 to 40 years ago. The sons of money-bags must have an honorable business position: they can show a knowledge of grammar and perfect orthography, but their stories are barren of beauty, logic or thought, and a dearth of reason.

To be sure, when some bigot, fool or educated monkey declares a thing to be true or untrue, of course every other educated ape must chatter in unison. Understand me, I am not speaking against education, but against the public holding up the image of an educated ass as a guide to the people, or a stumbling block in the way of the man who has given his time to deep study and thought, and left the details of machine work to brains fitted only for stuffing with the rudimentary elements necessary to present a thought to the public in a polished manner.

A beautiful carriage is not made for heavy hauling, or a truck for a carriage, so the deepest thinker is seldom a polished scholar, and it is often those who are great in one direction of thought are weaklings in another.

It has become popular to brand all thought of foretelling the future as superstition and ignorance, the earnest investigator, as a fool, crank or a knave.

Yet I will dare to give the results of my investigations of different metods of

FORETELLING THE FUTURE.

Cup reading is one of the oldest methods of clairvoyancy. It is older than any written history, because the Bible, supposed to be one of the oldest histories we have, speaks of cup reading. As in Genesis xliv.:2-15; Numbers xxiii.:23.

I need not go further to show the use of the cup by ancients was a well-established method of foretelling the future. But still older histories than the Bible prove their use. In Chaldea, Babylon and Egypt, for we not only find the cups engraven on the pyramids and obelisks, but we find the cups themselves in the tombs and in buried cities. These cups bear inscriptions showing they were used for such purposes, not alone by the lower class, but by the great men. Genesis xliv.:15, Joseph said, "What deed is this that ye have done? Wot ye not that such a man as I can certainly divine" Remember Joseph not only interpreted the dreams for the King's Butler and his Baker, but for Pharaoh himself. The Bible is full of this matter, not only speaking of Cup Reading, Palmistry and Astrology, but of Spirit Manifestation, or talking with the dead.

For instance, the woman of Endor, 1 Samuel xxviii. This woman is commonly called the Witch of Endor by the bigoted people of our times, but the Bible does not speak of her in that way.

All of these methods of foretelling the future were called divining. So this is the root of the word "Divine"—one who can divine, foretell the future. This was supposed to be a gift of God that few possessed. Hence a Divine Oracle, these became priests and teachers, because they were gifted with these sublime powers. These things have been practiced in the far East in all ages. "Norden's Travels," published in 1856, says when he and his party were at Derri, on the confines between Egypt and Nubia, and in circumstances of great danger, they sent a threatening message to a malicious and powerful Arab. He replied: "I know what sort of people you are. I have consulted my cup and have found by it that you are the people of whom one of our prophets has said the Franks should come in disguise and spy out the land that they would afterward bring a great number of their countrymen, conquer the land and exterminate all."

How true this is because this chief could see into the future and try to save his people from being exterminated, he was called a malicious person. But we know it too true that under the guise of advancing Christianity our supposed civilization carry the Bible with loaded cotton, shoddy and rum, to dazzle the eyes of the people while they establish false systems they call laws, which bind the people in bonded slavery, backed by the sword and the machine gun.

What has the boasted Christian civilization done for the world? It has carried with it hypocrisy, rum, fire and sword.

Ancient pagan Greece was a nation of scholars, artists, poets, thinkers; to-day she is a Christian nation of nobodies.

Under the pretense of Christianizing and civilizing old Peru, Pizarro invaded the country, where he found thirty-seven millions of happy people. A land without a prison or a criminal, a poorhouse or a pauper. To-day it is a Christian nation of seven millions of miserable people.

The once powerful and enlightened, though pagan nation, Rome, whose power and statesmanship was felt the world over, is to-day Christian Italy. Classed among the degraded nations.

Spain, whose colonies were unnumbered, and whose white sails of commerce dotted every body of water of note, and who became the right hand of the Catholic church and slew her thousands by the dictates of the inquisition, supposedly for the benefits of Christianity, has lost her colonies and is to-day a degraded nation.

At the beginning of her last war she was blessed by a Christian pope, but for all of that, in three months she was humbled by a power who has no God in her constitution.

Great, overgrown, Christian Russia, of whose population but 25 per cent can read, but whose forces are marched into a church and blessed, are being defeated and cut to pieces by heathen Japan, whose people fully 75 per cent can read and write. So much for your Christian civilization.

In all ages, where the people have used this God-given power for self-protection, it has been tabooed by the dishonest politician and Priesthood. It is true it is prohibited in some places in the Scriptures. But by whom was it prohibited? By Saul, a reprobate King that afterward took advantage of it himself, and was reprimanded by the spirit of Samuel for breaking his own laws. Thus proving Spiritualism a truth, if the Bible is true.

Many honest preachers oppose these things because they do not understand them and because they know they are honest and yet have not these powers. They do not stop to put this and that together, or try to get the real truth from the Bible, because they are creed-bound they cannot progress. Why do they not reason upon the XII. chapter of 1st Corinthians, 1 to 11:

1. Now concerning spiritual gifts, brethren, I would not have you ignorant.

2. Ye know that ye were Gentiles, carried away unto these dumb idols, even as ye were led.

3. Wherefore I give you to understand, that no man speaking by the Spirit of God calleth Jesus accursed; and that no man can say that Jesus is the Lord, but by the Holy Ghost.

4. Now there are diversities of gifts, by the same Spirit.

5. And there are differences of administrations, by the same Lord.

6. And there are diversities of operations, but it is the same God which worketh all in all.

7. But the manifestation of the Spirit is given to every man to profit withal.

8. For to one is given by the Spirit the word of wisdom; to another the word of knoweldge by the same Spirit;

9. To another faith by the same Spirit; to another the gifts of healing by the same Spirit;

10. To another the working of miracles; to another prophecy; to another discerning of spirits; to another divers kinds of tongues; to another the interpretation of tongues.

11. But all these worketh that one and the selfsame Spirit, dividing to every man severally as he will.

Now look at 1 John iv.:1: "Beloved, believe not every Spirit, but try whether they are of God." Third verse: "Every Spirit that confesseth not that Jesus Christ is come in the flesh is not of God."

If the Bible is true, is this not evidenec of the truth of Spiritualism?

I once attended a Spiritual meeting. It was a dark seance. A heavy musical voice with French accent rolled out over my head. He said his name was Dr. Lamont, and that he had been in the Spirit life for 250 years. Being a ventriloquist, I knew it could not be that kind of imposition, so I put the above test and asked the spirit if he believed that Christ came in the flesh. "Certainly," was the reply.

The voice then went on with a 20-minute eulogy of the character of Christ. It was the most beautiful talk I ever heard. It closed with the story of the woman brought before Christ, who was caught in the act of adultery, where Christ stooped and wrote in the sand, and then said: "Neither do I accuse thee, go sin no more."—John viii.:3-12.

The voice then asked: "Mr. Stowe, do you know what Christ wrote in the sand?"

"I do not. It is not in the Bible," I replied.

"Would you like to know?" was then asked.

"I would," said I, and the following was given me:

"Write the errors of your fellow-man and sister-woman in the dust, where the slightest breeze will sweep them forever away:

"But their virtues engrave upon tablets of enduring memory, and learn to cherish and imitate them."

"Well," said I, "whether that sentiment comes from God, Spirit, Man, or Devil, I never heard anything finer from any pulpit, and if this is what I hear at Spiritual meetings, I shall not be afraid of them."

But why should the investigation of these things be so bitterly opposed? The answer is plain. The corrupt politicians and preachers fear their corruption will be exposed.

Have not the priesthood opposed every step of progress? Not only the priesthood, but many supposed intellectual people, college-bred asses, have opposed progress in every direction. The worshipers of idols contended with each other as to whose idols were the best, until paganism arose above the lesser of their kind and contended with Catholicy, which arose above them, and Catholicy contended with Protestantism, and both have fought every step of progress of science; and selfish, ignorant, educated asses, calling themselves scientists, oppose progression in all branches of science they are not familiar with.

Camille Flammarion, in "The Unknown," in showing the weaknesses and superstitions of the supposedly wise men, says: "The School of Pythagoras, having discarded the common ideas of the age concerning nature. rose to the belief in the diurnal movement of our planet, found the public arrayed against him, even the wise Plato and Archimedes, the two giant intellects of the time, ridiculed the idea. Even such astronomers as Hipparchus and Potolomy laughed heartily at the supposed absurdity, saying: 'The movement of the earth is simply ridiculous.' "

"Socrates drank hemlock to escape the persecutions of the superstitious of his time."

"Euclid, the great mathematician, whose work was so perfect that no mathematician since has been able to take from or add to one proposition; taught that mathematics is the basis of all things, and his gifted daughter, the beautiful Hypatiea, foretold the future by the use of numbers, and was rewarded for her gift by being torn limb from limb, at the instigation of the superstitious priesthood of her times."

"Anaxagoras was persecuted for having dared to teach that the sun is larger than the Peloponnesus. Two thousand years later Gallileo was persecuted for affirming the vastness of the solar system and the comparative insignificance of our planet."

"When Lavasier analyzed the air and discovered that is was composed principally of two gases, oxygen and hydrogen, his discovery aroused the indignation of the old school of thought, and they berated him; and Baum, the great chemist, who invented the Arrometer, firmly believing in the four elements, earth, air, fire and water, wrote a learned dissertation upon the subject, saying: 'It is not to be imagined that these elements, regarded as such for two thousand years, are now to be placed among compound substances. Or that the results, by experiments to decompose air and water, can be looked upon as certain truth, or that reasoning upon that subject, to say the least, can be anything but absurd.'"

"It was the scientists themselves that denied that ariolites could come from anywhere but from the earth itself. They claimed they were thrown from the earth by volcanic action.

"When Galvani discovered animal magnetism he was scoffed at and his life made miserable by the supposed wise; and animal magnetism was condemned by the Academy of the Faculty of Medicine in Paris just as their blundering brothers to-day condemn magnetic healing or hypnotic therapeutics.

"When Mesmer first introduced hypnotism to the world he was hooted at and chased from pillar to post by the same class of educated asses who are tabooing hypnotism to-day.

"Fulton was called a fool and a crazy man for attempting to build a steamboat.

"The discovery of the use of gases was opposed by the great and wise because it was claimed a lamp would not burn without a wick.

"Railroads were opposed by the same class; even M. Thiers, the great French statesman, admitted railroads might furnish some advantages to travelers, provided their uses were limited to a few short lines. But in Bavaria the Royal College of Doctors.

having been consulted, declared if railroads were constructed it would cause the greatest deterioration to health."

Even free schools have been, and are to-day, opposed by some bigoted or weak-minded people.

"So late as March 11th, 1878, DuMond introduced Edison's phonograph to a learned assembly at a scientific institution in France, when a professor of the institute, Monsieur Bovilland, seized the operator by the collar and cried, 'Wretch, we are not to be made dupes of by a ventriloquist.' Six months later Sept. 30th, the same professor declared, after careful examination, he could find nothing in the invention but ventriloquism."

This is the class of people who are enacting laws today, depriving the people of the right to employ whom they please to doctor them. Under the pretense of protecting the dear people, they make war on Christian Science, and the magnetic healing and hypnotic therapeutics, under the pretense that they alone know what will cure the ills of mankind. They know that medical science, so-called, is nothing more than an experimental science, and it is not for the public they get these laws passed, but it is that they may monopolize that line of business, and so they are rapidly forming classes and class legislation and depriving the people of their rights. They are also kindling the fires of revolution, which will, like the blind Sampson, destroy the temple and destroy the persecutors at the same time. "Those whom the Gods wish to destroy they first make mad."

If the church people oppose Spiritualism, Clairvoyancy, Astrology, Palmistry, Cup Reading, etc., because an old Jewish law prohibited it, why do they not insist on the people adopting all other Jewish law, and even nail a servant's ear to the door post, and other such things that would not be tolerated to-day?

If because the Bible, in some cases, prohibits the practice of these things, they insist on frowning on all investigation of these matters, we shall have to ask them to investigate the mistaken Bible.

No one need to fear a truth, it will stand on its own bottom, but a falsehood will sooner or later fall to pieces.

All that can ever be said against the Bible, or in denying the divinity of Christ, will not detract one iota from the golden rule or Christ's command to love one another.

He who would throw a slur at such principles, is beneath contempt.

He is seeking knoweldge who asks for an explanation why Christ should say, "He that hath faith even as a mustard seed can say to yonder mountain move hence and it will move and then he lose his faith, at the supreme moment when he needed faith he cries out, 'My God, My God, why hast thou forsaken me?' "—Matthew xxvii.:46.

We shall have to ask them how it is that Proverbs xvi.:32, tells us that he who overcomes his spirit, temper, is greater than he that takes a city, greater than the mighty; and then Exodus xxxii. tells us the great God of the Universe lost his temper and caused four thousand of his chosen people to be slain, and would have slain all of the rest only he was persuaded to overcome his temper by a poor weak man, one of his subjects and creations.

Is this the kind of a God we are to worship? One who tells us to love our enemies, and then he roasts his forever and ever?

Again Proverbs iv.:7 tells us: "Therefore get wisdom; and with all of thy gettings get understanding."

How are we to get wisdom and understanding if we are not allowed to investigate these things? If God is the author of all things, why were these things placed here if we are not to investigate, and make use of the good we find?

The same class of bigoted men who made war on the various forms of divination then, or have put in the restrictions since, or oppose the investigation of these things to-day, are the same class of selfish men or ignoramuses who say in one place no man shall see God and live, or no man ever saw God, and in another say Moses saw God face to face and walked and talked with him. See:

"Agnostic's Lament," by Lyman E. Stowe.

"The Three Greatest Poems of the Age," 10 cents. For sale at 133 Catherine St., Detroit, Mich.

Also "84 Years in Hell Unless Sooner Discharged for Good Conduct," a satire, 10 cents, same author.

Look at Judges 1-19:

"And the Lord was with Judah; and he drove out the inhabitants of the mountains, but could not drive out the inhabitants of the valley, because they had chariots of iron."

Now look at Matthew, 1-14 and 15, and again at Luke the III., and find for Joseph two distinct lines of genealoegy.

These things need no comment.

If they are mistaken your book is not infallible. If it is left for interpretation, one man has as much right to interpret his way as another has his way.

Do not ask me to go further, or I shall not leave much but the doctrine of Astrology and Spirit Manifestation for any one to stand on.

Now, my Christian friends, doctors, judges and police, stop your making war on all Astrologers, Spiritualists and clairvoyants, because you find some dishonest ones.

Remember the Church is a pretty big cloak of hypocrisy. It is as inconsistent to sneer at all medical practitioners because there are some dishonest ones as it is to sneer at all Spiritualists or Occult professionals because you find some dishonest ones.

Since, much, of this book was put in type there has been quite a change in expressions of the pr-ess, towards the Occults, except as the pope has orderd his followers to make war on all advance thot, of this kind. It is not safe or wise to persecute or imprison the thinkers, to-day as they did the Gilleo's of a few hundred years ago so now they are flooding papers and magazines with trashy ridicule, finding this will fail of its purpose, and that the people are getting tired of a fat well fed priest hood and of building stone temples to, their revengeful god, they will resort to more drastic measures.

Shall we longer support colleges to turn out doctors and lawyers who can't stand on their own merits, but must become a privileged class and have laws passed to prevent all others from coming into their field of action? Just as our churches are setting themselves up to be more holy than thou. None can be right but them.

Let me, as an Astrologer, warn you, like the giant Sampson, the people are slowly awakening up to these wrongs, and your temples will come down about your ears. Away with your class laws, and your political rings and creed superstitions, and attack dishonesty wherever you find it, and the true Occultist will extend the hand of fellowship to you.

My Christian friends, do you want to know why your churches are empty? I will tell you. You are hide-bound by creeds and superstitions. You have become a stumbling block in the way of getting wisdom in God's workshop. You do not follow Christ, who had no place to lay his head, no magnificent temple and a big salary. He had no creed, but he said. "Where two or three are gathered together in my name there am I in the midst." He did not say two or three of this kind or two or three of that kind of thinkers.

Stop and think. Your people have advanced faster than you have; they want explanations for these great truths that are manifesting before them every day, and "When they cry for bread ye are offering them a stone." There is but one of two things for you to do—away with your creeds and your exclusiveness, and advance with the world, or lose your audience and your salaries, and if you lose the latter you would close your church doors yourselves.

If you wish to attack the dishonest and tricksters attack them in every branch of the political and social world, and we will extend to you the hand of fellowship.

Now let me ask you, my Christian friend, do you know that Astrology is the oldest science in the world, and that it is the basis of the Christian religion, also of Free Masonry, and all other organized bodies, and even of your clock dial and of your Bible?

Of course you do not. Well, you are not to blame for what you do not know. But let me tell you. When Egypt was beeing rocked in the cradle of her infancy, Astrology was hoary with age in India, and it has been honored by great thinkers of all ages.

It was the magi or wise men of Chaldea who predicted the birth of Christ. They were philosophers and physicians, healing disease by faith, magnetic healing, hypnotism, and by other occult powers.

Hypocrates, the father of Materia Medica, so-called, said: "A man is better fitted to be called a fool than a physician who does not understand Astrology."

Shame on the doctors of to-day, whose profession must be supported by law. I would not employ a physician who is afraid to risk his reputation without the support of law.

Astrology has been honored in all ages by illustrious men.

Cicero declared that he knew of no country either so polished and learned, or so rude and uncivilized, but always allowed that some particular persons are gifted with an insight into futurity; and are gifted with a talent of prediction.

Anaxagoras predicted the invention of the telescope by Astrology.

Men whose wise sayings, in other matters, are quoted frequently, are also believers in Astrology, such as Aristotle, Anaxagorus, Virgil, Cicero, Hypocrates, Keepler the astronomer, Tycobrah the astronomer, Dryden the poet, and we might give enough names of illustrious men who believed in Astrology to fill a large volume.

Edwin Booth, the great actor, was a very good Astrologer, as are thousands of men of our times.

CREATION, ASTROLOGY AND DESTINY.

If God is everywhere there cannot be one of these atoms without him or he would be circumscribed, but as it is all God he must have something to do. There is nothing he could do but to think, as there is nothing else but him. Even he could never know the difference between bitter and sweet or pain and pleasure if he never thought of the two opposites, therefore experience is necessary to wisdom. There could be no pleasure without experience of pain or sorrow. God being everywhere, there is no room for anything but him, not even for a devil. God represents Good, Evil represents the Devil. Now as everything is material mind on various planes of vibration, that of each plane attracting its kind, yet all reaching for that on a higher plane, with a tendency to drag it down, it gives us the impression of two opposing forces, one we call God and the other we call the Devil. And so far as we are concerned it might as well be called that as anything else, as the result is the same, except in the mistake of the orthodox teaching concerning an everlasting punishment of physical pain for disobedience to certain teachings that no one can bring proof as being the correct teaching, except such proof as very weak men claim to find in a book they cannot understand without understanding Astrology.

These people are so uncertain of their positions that they are divided into many factions and disputing among themselves. But in giving this theory to the world I am giving a logical cause as a basis for an explanation of all phenomena.

In considering this, however, we must admit of the truth of evolution and re-incarnation.

In that we will briefly discuss God's plan, according to this theory, which shows Astrology to be the basis of mythology, religion and Free Masonry, the three leading subjects that ever agitated the minds of civilization, until science comes in to unravel the mysteries of the ages.

The Bible gives us an allegorical story of the Garden of Eden, wherein Adam and Eve were placed, and where grew the tree of knowledge, which was a temptation. There was also a tempter, that man might fall and become wise. People reason that this was terrible for God to place man under such temptations when he knew man's weakness and that he would fall. But I have shown you that there could be no happiness where pain and sorrow were never known. Now, on the other hand, let us imagine ourselves surrounded with all that the heart can desire—grounds, palaces, books, music and everything we can conceive of. It would certainly be a heaven to us but after we have enjoyed it over and over again it becomes our hell. We become so tired of it we are willing to do almost anything to get out of it. We look across the street and see something different we do not understand; curiosity prompts us to go there, but between us and the desired place is storm, hell. This we at first turn from with a shudder, but we look at it again and again, until "familiarity breeds contempt." And we plunge out into that hell, because it is no worse to us than the monotony of that which was once our heaven.

So when we get on the other side we enjoy more because we know more.

JUPITER
480,000,000.
SATURN
URANUS
1,822,360,000.
NEPTUNE
2,745,998,000.

THE PICTURE ON THE OPPOSITE PAGE ILLUSTRATES THIS MATTER. The all-seeing EYE represents God and his system of Zodiacs, the smaller eyes represent the various bodies, parts of him like you or I, yet being an individual entity of ourselves. The picture below the eye represents a crude conception of heaven, where we tired of its enjoyments and willingly partook of the forbidden fruit from the tree of knoweldge, dissolving our kingdoms and going into Chaos or God's workshop. The next picture under represents the formation of the molecules, from the elementaries or soul atoms, which had been a part of our heavenly bodies before dissolution.

The Sun in several ways gives us the story of the Christian religion. In the picture below, forming molecules, represents the sun in a gaseous state when it extended out beyond Neptune and still further beyond Celestia, a planet not yet discovered but which will be discovered within the next 50 years.

The planets in the picture stretch away toward the upper right-hand corner. The celestial city represents the planet Celestia.

No. 1, or first child of the Sun. The Sun here represents Christ, the Son of God or Sun God and his 12 Satellites or disciples; the second is Neptune; 3rd, Uranus; 4th, Saturn; 5th, Jupiter; 6th, a dark planet between the Asteroids and Jupiter; 7th, Asteroids, a planet which was broken to pieces, or Judas Iscariot, who by committing suicide destroyed his kingdom, and every suicide who becomes dissatisfied and destroys his kingdom, must start over again, or his opportunity for a time lost. The 8th planet is Mars, the 9th the Earth; 10th, Venus; the 11th, Mercury; the 12th. Vulcan.

The planet Jupiter is pictured in a state of combustion, surrounded by a carbon cloud, so dense the sunlight cannot penetrate it; this also represents the condition of our earth after throwing off the Moon, which was once a part of Earth, or this was the Earth's condition after forming its crust.

Under Jupiter with a slanting top is a picture of the storm period shown during the process of cooling a crust on the Earth. (*This is beautifully explained in verse and illustrated, in "Poetical Drifts of Thought," by Lyman E. Stowe, and sold by this Company. Price,* $2.50.)

The little square above the planet Saturn represents the volcanic period, or when the internal heat of Earth burst through the crust forming mountains, valleys, seas and rivers.

Under Uranus is seen a fungus growth, or first vegetation, all dark, except that on the right containing the white spots, representing the first color after vegetation has taken up enough of the carbon cloud to let the sunlight through. The picture above it represents the Sun penetrating the cloud. Just to the right of this picture may be seen primitive life, headless fish and saurians of the deep; then follows fur-bearing animals up to man; then men climbing the stairs of intelligent development, with Christ at the head of the stairs assisting him and passing him on to a higher plane in heaven, than whence he left to enjoy more because he knows more. Thus from the time we left heaven to go into God's workship we passed through each phase of this development; we were in the gaseous matter, until our Earth left the Sun and in the firey condition of the Earth, the storm period where pandemnoium reigned, in the crust, in vegetation and then through the various phases of vegetable and animal life. We lived and died many times in the various forms of vegetable life; we even broke away to become moving vegetable life, or the first link to animal life, and many times in the various forms of animal life before we became men of the lower grades, and we have been men and women time and time again. YES, THIS IS EVOLUTION, and evolution and reincarnation are truths.

Believing the reader would like some reason for this I here give some of the evidence of it. But first let me explain the process of evolution. Re-

" MAN MADE IN THE LIKNESS AND IMAGE OF HIS CREATOR."

There can not be an atom in the universo, ever

so small, but God is in it, or else he is circumscribed and is only like one of our selves, on a larger scale. There is no room for anything but God, consequently mind and matter are one and the same thing. A great whole, in man yparts.

If the above paragraph is true, man must be a minature universe, and has millions of sonls, but one ruler, thus, the Bible's assertion, "Ye are gods" has some meaning, admit it and you can easily find an answer to every phenomenon.

"I belive all the matter in the universe can be compressed in-to a globe an inch in diameter, and if to that why not to the size of a cherry, a pea, a grain of sand. There is nothing in the universe but mathamatical points" Sir Isaac Newton.

"There is nothing in the universe but mathematical points of force." Faraday. English chemist.

"There is nothing in the universe but thot, impressions of pains and pleasures." Sir Humphery Davy. English chemist.

"Every atom has its proportion of thot." Cook's n ew chemistry.

"Every atom is a thinker." Loomis,

"I belive any man's intelligence is but the aggregate intelligence of his constituent atoms." Edison.

"It is proof that thots are things, because we have thots come to us we do not want, and we fight them away" Lyman E. Stowe's Universe.

"We are the result of what our thots have been." Dahomapada.

"To the clairvoyant, distance and matter do not exist. Time, space and matter vanish away." Emanuel Swedenborg. Clairvoynt and author.

"Nothing but God, so great a mind must have something to do, something on which to express its self, consequently, to the higher mind, the lower mind becomes matter." Lyman E. Stowe's Bible Astrology.

member the authority I have quoted says every atom is a thinker, then it is natural for birds of a feather to flock together, or kind to seek kind, and that in all such cases a leader soon steps to the front and in all well-organized bodies there are lesser officials who report to the head office. Thus when the first molecule was formed, one atom became the leader or king, and kingdoms grew in size and form, in accordance with the surrounding conditions. As no sunlight could penetrate the carbon cloud the first vegetation was necessarily a black mass of fungus growth, which on account of its soft nature grew rapidly and fell down and covered vast beds of this fungus growth, which could not decay, because there was little oxygen in the atmosphere, besides that the lower strata was shut out from the oxygen by that on top of it.

Perhaps I had better explain the operation of decay.

The greater portion of water, by weight is oxygen and one-fifth of the air we breathe is oxygen, each atom of oxygen is supposed to possess two polar forces, thus —0—. The tendency of oxygen is to fly away from heat, and the atmospheric pressure of 14 pounds to the square inch drives it back again. This creates a motion, and motion is heat, and heat expands and rises into a higher strata of air, causing a vacuum; the heat creates by its tendency to rise. This motion of the atoms of oxygen drives it into the orbit of an atom of carbon and two atoms of oxygen go whirling around an atom of carbon, forming a miniature sun with its two satellites. This is what we call a molecule of carbonic acid gas. In rapid combustion we call this fire. In slow process of oxidation like water upon iron we call rust. In case of putrifying flesh or vegetable matter we call decay. But the process is just the same in either case, so your body burning or rotting is one and the same thing.

The food you take into the stomach and assimilate goes out and builds up one end of a muscle while the oxygen you breathe is driven through the heart and lungs and goes to the other end of a muscle and seizes an atom of carbon, and it comes out of your mouth in carbonic acid gas. So you are being built up and torn down at one and the same time.

The carbonic acid gas floats out in the atmosphere and is taken up by every waving leaf, in the sunshine, and the carbon goes to build up the plant, while the plant exhales the oxygen as we do the carbonic acid gas. Now we eat the plant so that a part of your body may have been a part of my body a year ago, or vice versa. You will now see that decay or burning is oxidation or change of conditions, as nothing is really lost except form, which is continually changing. You close the drafts of the stove, thus shutting out the oxygen, and the fire goes out.

We pour water on a burning building to put the fire out because the oxygen in the water can take no more hydrogen or carbon, so it shuts out the free oxygen in the air and puts the fire out. It is the same when you shut out the oxygen from your lungs or when you keep it from fruit by canning. It was the same with primitive vegetation, which could not decay so fossilized, and became the coal we now burn. But some of the vegetation was continually building new forms because of the changing conditions, so that when the sunlight was able to break through the carbon cloud, hardy vegetation grew rapidly. Because of so much of the carbon having been taken up and covered in beds of fossilized vegetation, the living vegetation took on colors and new forms; some of it broke away from the parent stem and became traveling vegetation, gathering its sustenance from the decaying particles of former vegetation.

Let me here quote from a writer on science of breath:

"A writer has stated that if the air cells of the lungs were spread out over an unbroken surface, they would cover an area of fourteen thousand square feet.

"The air is drawn into the lungs by the action of the diaphragm, a great strong, flat, sheet-like muscle, stretched across the chest, separating the chest-box from the abdomen. The diaphragm's action is almost as automatic as that of the heart, although it may be transformed into a semi-voluntary muscle by an effort of the will. When it expands, it increases the size of the chest and lungs, and the air rushes into the vacuum thus created. When it relaxes the chest and lungs contract and the air is expelled from the lungs."

Now before considering what happens to the air in the lungs, let us look a little into the matter of the circulation of the blood. The blood, as you know, is driven by the heart, through the arteries, into the capillaries, thus reaching every part of the body, which vitalizes, nourishes and strengthens. It then returns by means of the capillaries by another route, the veins, to the heart, from whence it is drawn to the lungs.

The blood starts on its arterial journey, bright, red and rich, laden with life-giving qualities and properties. It returns by the venous route, poor, blue and dull, being laden down with the waste matter of the system. It goes out like a fresh stream from the mountains; it returns as a stream of sewer water. This foul stream goes to the right auricle of the heart. When this auricle becomes filled, it contracts and forces the stream of blood through an opening in the right ventricle of the heart, which in turn sends it on to the lungs, where it is distributed by millions of hair-like blood vessels to the air cells of the lungs, of which we have spoken. Now, let us take up the story of the lungs at this point.

The foul stream of blood is now distributed among the millions of tiny air cells in the lungs. A breath of air is inhaled and the oxygen of the air comes in contact with the impure blood through the thin walls of the hair-like blood vessels of the lungs, which walls are thick enough to hold the blood, but thin enough to admit the oxygen to penetrate them. When the oxygen comes in contact with the blood, a form of combustion takes place, and the blood takes up oxygen and releases carbonic acid gas generated from the waste products and poisonous matter which has been gathered up by the blood from all parts of the system. The blood thus purified and oxygenated is carried back to the heart, again rich, red and bright, and laden with life-giving properties and qualities.

Upon reaching the left auricle of the heart, it is forced into the left ventricle, from whence it is again forced out through the arteries on its mission of life to all parts of the system. It is estimated that in a single day of twenty-four hours, 35,000 pints of blood traverse the capillaries of the lungs, the blood corpuscles in a single file and being exposed to the oxygen of the air on both of their surfaces. When one considers the minute details of the process alluded to, he is lost in wonder and admiration at Nature's infinite care and intelligence. Where intelligence is displayed there is a necessity of a directing power, as I have shown the tree has a directing power, as it always sends its roots in the right direction for water, never in the wrong direction. As the tree was continuously improving it showed a knowledge gained from former experience. Thus a soul becomes a necessity. Therefore the ruling atom always forms a spiritual as well as a physical body, and at each death of vegetable or animal life the spirit rests in the spirit state for a time and then goes into the workshop, forming a new body on a higher plane than the last, thus benefiting by the former experience. So reincarnation becomes a necessity.

After moving vegetation had advanced far enough to shape its own course by moving from place to place it is called animal life.

The first animal life was a mere hollow tube and the soul had his throne in its internals and has had its throne there ever since. It is the directing force, though being directed by the heavenly bodies that put it there at its birth. As the tendency to refinement, the atoms it attracted to it like good soldiers, were ever striving to perfect the kingdom, so as the soul sent word to those out at the mouth of the tube not to let in such coarse matter, the soldiers at the opening drew together and formed the first rudiments of a mouth. Still the soul called for finer material and the best soldiers stepped to the front and made a projection over the mouth, to assist them by smell, in choosing their material. In the same manner and for the same purpose the eyes were formed, and finally to better prepare the food to build up the kingdom the jaws, teeth, glands, intestines, nerves and other necessary organs were formed.

In its endeavors to move about, to find better conditions, the back bone, fins, and finally legs were evolved. To shield the body scales, and afterward hair was produced through the intelligence of the soul atoms of the structure always stepping to the front to obey the wishes or directions of the king and its officers which formed the spirit body at each death, and then through the experiences of former lives built better and better at each succeeding life. So as you build here so will your next life be.

The evidence of the truth of evolution may be found in many forms. We see evolution in our clothing, in our laws, in our churches, in vegetable and animal life.

The shoe is evolved from the sandal and moccasin. Once we had a button shoe for men, then came the elastic, and the buttons remained for appearance for a long time. Our forefathers used to wear a muffler or stock which covered the whole neck. Now the shirt and coat collar is made different, but a little necktie is left for appearance, but that is often left off. The buttons on the back of a frock coat, you would tell me, were placed there for appearance. Not so; our fathers, a hundred years ago, wore swords, and the buttons were put there to keep the sword belt up. The sword is gone, the belt is gone, but the buttons still remain, as in evidence of evolution in costume.

Now look at your agriculturists and see how they are evolving new varieties of potatoes, grain and fruit. Who would recognize in the luscious tomato the love apple of 60 years ago. Wheat was evolved from a species of grass long since become extinct. The horse has the splints in his hoofs showing he was once a five-toed animal.

Man has muscles behind his ears which he used to wag the ears to drive the flies off when he ran on all fours. He has several other organs of the body he has no use for, such as the appendix, the seat of appendicitis, and the coccyx, or stub that was once a tail, but now sometimes troublesome when getting a fall upon that part of the anatomy.

The church once sacrificed human beings to appease the anger of their gods; they evolved out of that to sacrificing the lower animals, and finally to eating a little piece of bread and drinking a sip of wine, which is far more humane. Once they taught eternal damnation or a hell of torment for those who could not believe as they did. This has been modified and most people can now see the inconsistency of an all-powerful being putting on his poor, weak mortals a punishment out of all proportion to the crime committed. Or in telling those poor, weak mortals to forgive their enemies while he roasts his.

Many people will say, "Oh, yes, we can see evolution in all of these things you speak of, but a dog was always a dog, a horse a horse, and where did the first life come from?" I have proved to you that mind and matter is one and the same thing, that matter is merely the expression of mind, that everything is life, and the links between higher and lower animal life have died out as did the grass from which wheat was evolved.

I have shown you that re-incarnation is necessary, as the spirit body which came back to earth, came to rebuild, to increase its size and intellect, to experience more that he may enjoy more because he knows more. A man who has not evolved far enough above an ass to see that the lower animals exercise reason, and possess souls as well as man, may have to die and come back a good many times before he can see the necessity or truth of re-incarnation.

I advise the reader to get my "Poetical Drifts of Thought" that he may see that I have evolved thoughts higher than I once possessed and what a necessity it was for me to go through my former line of thought.

I find our Spiritualist friends dislike the idea of re-incarnation, or as one of them said this morning: "I believe when we die we just begin to live."

"Do you think that periods of rest are necessary?" I asked.

"Why certainly," said he. "It is all rest in the spirit state."

"We have night as a rest after our day's work. The winter is a rest after the summer, and the compound state of the elements is a rest after the struggle of combination. Then it is clear the spirit state is a rest after this life," said I.

"Yes, I admit it," said he.

"I have shown we could never know anything without experience, have I not?" I asked.

"Well, I guess that's true," said he.

"Then we would tire of resting all of the time, would we not? And we all need further development, is certain, is it not?" I asked.

"Well, yes, I guess that is all right."

"Then, sir," said I, "why do you want to take the workshop into your parlor or bedroom?"

"It is clear if experience is necessary to knowledge and knowledge to growth or development, re-incarnation is necessary or you must take your workshop to your place of rest, or you must come back to your workshop, which is the most consistent?" I replied.

"By gosh," said he, "I never saw it in that way before."

To show you that spirits differ in their opinion and that they make no progress, but present their opinions as they are impressed by the medium they speak through, I will quote from Dr. Buchanan in a work entitled "Primitive Christianity." Published 1897. Medium not known, says on page 83, under caption of a "Synopsis of the life of Jesus Christ." Given by the spirit of James, the Less, brother of St. John. He says:

"Jesus was born in the last year of the reign of Herod, on the 12th of January which was observed by the early Christians as the true nativity." This book is well written and is a very interesting work, and as this spirit has been on the spirit side of life for two thousand years, he ought to know what he is talking about. But does he?

Let us see what another spirit says who has been over equally as long.

In a book entitled "Science and Key of Life," Published by the Astro Publishing Co., Detroit, Mich., 1902. Compiled by Mr. Henry Clay Hodges, a gentleman well known for his intelligence, integrity and honesty of purpose, receiving his information through a medium of undoubted honesty, loved for his truthfulness by all who knew him, and by a spirit giving his name as "ALVIDAS." Publishes the horoscope of Jesus of Nazareth, from the date December 25th, Julian year 45.

I do not wish to antagonize any of these people connected with this matter I know and deeply respect them all, and know their earnestness of purpose, and I can highly recommend the books as valuable. But I wish to show these spirits have no advantage over us, because they have made no progress on the other side of life.

The spirit Alvidas claims to have been an astrologer of his times and to have progressed since he passed over yet he makes mistakes that we today can correct him in.

For instance in Vol. 2 of the same work, page 110, under the caption of HELIO-CENTRIC ASTROLOGY, he says Helio-Centric Astrology originated in America. But I have shown the system is older than the Geo-Centric system. Potter's Bible Encyclopedia, edited by the Rev. William Blackwood, D. D. L. L. D., Vol. 3, page 1007, says, "No scholar pretends to know what time of year Christ was born, but that it was probably in the spring."

The books of the Bible, written, God knows when or where or by whom, gives us no information in the matter, except in the first chapter of Luke, which tells us the angel visited Zacharias and Elizabeth to prepare for the coming of John, the Baptist, who was born six months before Christ, and in the 26th verse it says this same angel visited Mary in the sixth month. Counting from June, our 6th month, and allowing nine months for gestation it would bring the birth in February. But when we remember the Jewish year began with the month corresponding to our March, it would bring August, the 6th month, and of course the birth would be in April.

All intelligent Bible students admit none of the books of the new testament were written until a hundred and fifty years after Christ. We would not put much credence in other histories that were written so long after the events. Why should we in this? Especially when we find such blunders as the following: 2 Chronicles XXI. and XXII. gives a chronology so erronous that King Jehoahax would have to be two years old when his father was born to reign at the time given.

In Matthew XVI-13, Christ asked the disciples: "Who do men say that I, the son of Man, am?"

14th verse. "And they said some say thou art John, the Baptist."

This is quite inconsistent as John, the Baptist, was contemporaneous with Christ and baptised him at 30 years of age.

Again Matthew 13 and 14 and Luke III, 23 and 24, gives two distinct lines of genealogy for Joseph, Christ's earthly father, or husband of Mary. Thus, the Bible of our Christian friends can take no precedence over our spiritualist friends. But, dealing with a question of such vital importance one would think a spirit, of such intelligence as either of these, or one who had been in spirit two thousand years, would be able to speak intelligently of such an important a matter.

No the Spirit cannot progress on the other side of life. To think is to burn substance in the machinery of the body which must be fed, and to progress is to think, to live in rest in the spirit state is to enjoy the experiences of the past without effort, which would require consumption of fuel or food. If these experiences have been shameful, the law of progress will cause a desire to forget them and we come back to earth to get rid of old experiences and gain new and better ones. I would advise those who want to rest long in the spirit state, to make the best possible use of their time while here. To court experiences they will not be ashamed of over there. If not they must quickly return to the workshop again.

In my investigations I find some spirits tell me they believe in reincarnation, others say, "No. Neither evolution or reincarnation are true."

Why do spirits differ in regard to all such matters? Answer, because they see things just exactly as they saw them here and no different. I find the spirits contradict each other as much as people in the flesh. I also find when I have apparentely convinced a spirit of the truth of evolution, I have to convince him over again the next time we meet. The spirits simply enjoy what they knew here.

If man makes life a burden here it will be there and he will soon come back for a broader expansion. If a man did many wrongs here remorse may drive him back to atone for the wrongs he did by suffering the same things he caused others to suffer. A man must educate or elevate the soul atoms with which he builds up his system or kingdom, and there is no way of getting them except through attracting them to his kingdom by eating and drinking and raising their vibrations to his standard of thought while in the flesh. When a man tries to advance his physical force, he eats the right kind of food and takes the right kind of exercise to assist him. If he advances in music he studies music and practices teaching his fingers until they seem to act independent of the brain, now he can't buy or coax these attributes from another, he must cultivate them in his organism. Neither will he be able to get them in the spirit state but must come back, and the spirit body is his Karma that rules the next life. If this were not so he would not have been sent here in the first place. Experience being necessary to wisdom, is why one person is naturally wiser than another, he has lived more lives.

Most people are so taken up with speculation of the future world that they have no time to note the experiences of this world and so will have to come back here to learn more about it.

Many ask the question, "Why don't we remember our former lives?"

I will answer there are many of us see faces and places which are familiar to us which cause us to wonder, yet we refuse to believe we saw them in a former life.

Again the answer is because you would go on developing in the same old rut, and develop along the same lines you did when here before. But instead you come back under environments for better developments. Just as an Englishman or German coming to America in childhood develops into an American, forgetting the ways of their countrymen. Once in a while however, memories are brought back which produce a musical prodigy or mathematical prodigy, or some other talent for which we have no better explanation than to call it a gift, but it is the experience of a former life. Tell me why the little chick knows enough to break the shell to let himself out of the prison. Or why he knows enough to pick up the food or run to his mother for aid when he hears the cry of the hawk? Is that not the result which experience has taught him to fear, or on the other hand taught him not to fear and he becomes tame. That is no more instinct than the same acts would be in man.

Many will say I would not believe in reincarnation unless the Bible says it is true. Well, the Bible has not room for everything, but there is plenty of it taught in the Bible. Elijah ascended 880 years before Christ. See II Kings, 2-11. Malachi, 4-5, says: "Behold, I will send you Elijah, the prophet before the coming of the great day of the Lord." The first chapter of Luke will show you with what care God's messenger provided for Elijah's return by selecting Zacharias for an earthly father and Elizabeth for an earthly mother.

Mark, 9:11-13, says: "And they asked him, saying, why say the scribes that Elias must first come? And he answered and told them, Elias, verily cometh first. But I say unto you that Elias is indeed come, and they have done unto him whatsover they listed."

Remember they took his head off.

Elias is the Greek for Elijah.

Again Matthew, 17:10-14, says: "And his deciples asked him, saying why then say the scribes that Elias must first come?" "But I say unto you Elias is come already and they knew him not, but have done unto him what so ever they listed. Then the desciples understood he spake to them of John the Baptist." It is true John did not know that he was Elijah any more than you know who you are. But in the spirit state we see all of the lives we have experienced. Some of our church people try to get out of this by saying John came in the spirit of Elijah, thus laying God in a lie when he said he would send Elijah. He did not say he would send another fellow in the spirit of Elijah. Now look to the ninth chapter of St. John, where Christ healed the man born blind. "And his deciples asked him, saying, Master, who sinned this man or his parents?"

Now how could this man's sins make him blind, when he was born blind, unless he had sinned in a former life? Certainly that is the way they looked at it.

Now look to the eighth chapter of Luke, 10th verse: And he said, "Unto you it is given to know the mysteries of the Kingdom of God, but to others in parables; that seeing they might not see, and hearing they might not understand. Both in this chapter and in John 12, it is cleverly stated certain ones should not be saved. Why? Because they had not advanced far enough to graduate, and so must die and come back again before they could be advanced far enough to graduate.

I hope I have made this matter of perpetual life, evolution and reincarnation clear enough to be well understood, although this subject is more fully discussed in my Poetical Drifts of Thought, $2.50, or in my Universe, 50c.

A COMRADE'S EXPERIENCE.

An old comrade of the War of '61 to '63 just came in and said: "Comrade, if I was ever in heaven I am sure I would have never left it to come into this world of misery."

I first drew the comrade's attention to his war experience and the hell we passed through. He waxed eloquent in reciting his experience and said he never tired of telling of his narrow escape and his hardships. Said I, "No money would buy your experience?" "No, siree," he vehemently exclaimed."

"Your father was well off; you had a pleasant home," I replied.

"Indeed I did," said he.

Said I, "Comrade what made you exchange that happy home for a rough soldier's life?"

"Well," he drawled, "I got tired plodding around on the old farm; I wanted to see something of the world, and I was patriotic, and thought there was a good opportunity to see the world and help to save my country."

"And you took pride in being a good soldier?"

"Indeed I did," he replied.

"Well," said I, "That is just why you left heaven; you got tired of the same old thing and you became patriotic; you wanted to go into God's workshop and you enlisted, so now be a good soldier and you will rejoice over your past experiences when you reach heaven, a thousand fold more than you now rejoice over your soldier's experience."

"Where is heaven?" he cried.

I explained that heaven is a condition of mind, as the dream is a condition of mind, the hypnotic state a condition of mind, and Christ said, "The Kingdom of God is within you," which, of course, is a condition of mind. Then also is this life a condition of mind because God would not make this life more tangible than he would make His kingdom.

"Very well," says my comrade, "How am I to reach that condition of mind?" I replied.

The drift of this article is to show that everything is mind that every atom is a thinker seeking a home in a higher organism.

(In these days when every man is trying to outsrtip every other man in finding something new to hang his name on, some scientists have claimed to divide the atom into electrons, which is merely discovering that the supposed atoms of some substances can be divided, and so they try to prove the falsity of the atomic theory by calling the divisable portions of the supposed atom electrons, which in reality is a distinction without a difference, as an atom is the smallcst indivisible portion of anything?"

I wish to show we are the result of what our thoughts have been, that what we are today was our thoughts of a former life. That what our next lives will be is what we attract to us now, that is what we allow to remain with us now. If we prefer to be in the saloon and brothel now that will be the bent of our next life. That is why the musical prodigy was born into the world; his whole mind and desire was upon that thought at the close of his life and he brought it into life to complete his experiences.

"Hold on," cried my comrade; can't we be bettered in this life by the same rule?"

"Certainly," I replied. "Disease is largely a condition of mind. I might say entirely so. Something has caused us to attract thoughts of the disease and we either did not expell them or could not expell them until, like a colony of foreigners, the numbers grew until those atoms in our bodies were brought to the same vibrations as themselves, so the whole structure became sick, and we now set up a fight to master or drive out the foreign elements. It is sometimes done by faith, with will power; sometimes medicine aids faith or will power. Sometimes the Divine healer aids faith, and often the magnetic healer will do more than either because he sends in his healthy atoms and expells those of the diseased, as Christ did with His will force in driving the seven devils out of Mary Magdalene or the legion out of the insane man at Gardarenes. These were simply diseased soul atoms, or what we term elementaries—souls who have not yet arisen high enough to be fit companions to man and yet aspire to be so as we aspire to be with greater than ourselves. This proves to us that not only disease of the body is disease of the mind and that there are various remedies which after all are but the changing of vibrations. Therefore any force which will change the vibrations will be a benefit or an injury, but when the body is diseased the magnetic healer may use an electric battery to assist him in changing the vibrations, or this may be used by the patient himself, but if so used the patient should keep the mind positive in the direction of the good he wishes done. It is claimed by many of the new thought that poverty is a disease, and a number of our society claim to have been greatly benefited, and we trust that all who purchase this book may become prosperous through its teachings.

In this discussion we must remember that there are unseen worlds all around us, as each world is a condition of mind. We use the bodies of the people of unseen worlds as material comforts, without in any way disturbing the conditions of their worlds. In this way we may have been enjoying heavenly bliss while we were a part of the seathing mass of fire during the early stages of our earth's history. If all is mind, as I have brought evidence to show, then that burning world was mind also, and heat we know to be a condition that may be made quite tolerable, for we find some men who can stand to work at great depths in the earth where the heat is so intense that other men can hardly endure it. We also find living fish thrown from the hot springs where the water is too hot for man to thrust his hand in without producing great pain.

We also find life manifest to our conditions of mind in degrees of cold and heat in which we once thought it was impossible for life to exist.

Much light is thrown upon this subject in Prof. Stowe's "Poetical Drifts of thought." "The Universe" "What is Coming.,, and "Bible Astrology." Also in his articles in the Adept. This magazine should be read by every student. It is published by Judge Fredrick. White. Crystal Bay, Minn.
Editor.

A STRANGE EXPERIENCE.

I once had a strange experience. In investigating along these lines I had two very good hypnotic subjects. These were two unusually bright young men, and, by the way, to disprove the foolish theory that it is only the weak-minded who can be hypnotized, I found the brighter the mind the better the subject.

There seemed to be a great difference in the form of manifestation of these subjects. Harry N. proved to be a fine clairvoyant, much better than Otis O. They could readily hypnotize each other and Otis could hypnotize himself and lie in a trance asleep for a given length of time and always awake at the moment given, whether he or I suggested it. I once asked him how he did it and he said, "I always see a watch before my face." Then that watch he saw must have been a condition of mind, yet it corresponded exactly with a watch dial of our condition of mind.

On one occasion Otis misunderstood my command and dropped to the floor before I was ready, and, as he was standing up, he fell heavily and his head struck on the corner of an open safe, and it cracked like a pistol shot. I was terribly frightened, as I feared he had fractured his skull. But, of course, I could not expect him to awaken until the seven minutes were up, the length of time I had given him to sleep. I felt of his head, but could find no scar or mark, and I waited as patiently as I could for his awakening. At the expiration of the seven minutes he awoke as bright as a dollar. I asked, "Otis, is there a sore spot on your head?" "No," said he; "why do you ask?" And I told him of the fall and what I feared. He laughed and said, "When I am in that state I think you might strike me with an ax and not hurt me."

At another time there were eighteen of our society sitting around a small but very heavy table. We were all investigators, and there was no selfish motive or money transaction in it. We had tried to get spirit manifestations and failed, as we had no mediums with us. At length I thought I would try an experiment, so I put Harry and Otis in the clairvoyant state and asked them to describe the spirits they saw, but both declared there was none present. At length I told Harry to think of his cousin, whom I knew had died a year or two before. Finally he said, "Here she is," and began to talk to some (to us unseen) person, and he began to cry. Said I, "Harry, why do you cry?" He replied, "Clarrie is blaming me for not attending her funeral when I could not help being away."

I then addressed the spirit and said: "Clarrie, you should not make Harry cry. Now say something to him to make him laugh." I did not suggest to Harry, according to hypnotic law or rules, that she would make him laugh, but let the spirit, if there was one, do that. At any rate he burst out laughing and seemed very much amused. When I asked him what he was laughing about he replied, "Oh, at what Clarrie is telling me."

Finally I told him to ask Clarrie to call other spirits. After a few moments he said, "Well, there are a lot of people and there is a man here who says he wants to talk."

Said I, "Describe him." He did so, but none of us recognized him. Finally I asked his name. Harry replied, "He says his name is James Fisher."

I asked if there was anyone in the hall who knew a person of that name who had died, and no one did. I then asked Harry who the man wished to talk to and he replied, "Mr. Stowe."

I now asked if that was the James Fisher who was a schoolmate of my older brother, when he replied, through Harry, that it was. Said I, "If that is so, let him rap on the table the number of years since he died." Ten heavy raps came upon the table, and not a soul was touching the table. I know not another living soul in the room knew anything about Mr. Fisher, and he was far from my mind when Harry announced him. Besides I had to stop and count up how long it really was since Mr. Fisher died, and I found it was ten years, as announced. But the strange part is yet to come.

The circle now drew nearer the table and began discussing the phenomena, when I wished to ask Mr. Fisher a question. I had paid no attention to Otis except to tell him he could see spirits. Otis began talking to someone, but we were all so engrossed with our own part of the investigation that no one paid any attention to Otis's conversation. But I asked Harry to tell Mr. Fisher I wished to speak to him.

"No," Harry replied. "He is talking to someone and I do not want to interrupt him." I insisted on it, but in no way, either by persuasion or command, could I get him to interrupt Mr. Fisher, until I became vexed and finally said, "Otis, who are you talking to?" He replied, "Mr. Fisher."

Said I, "Harry, Mr. Fisher is talking to Otis."

He replied: "Where is Otis? I don't see him."

I then asked, "Otis, do you see Harry here?"

"No," he replied. Then he asked, "Where is Harry?"

Said I, "Harry, here is Otis; Otis, here is Harry," and both seemed very much surprised, but exclaimed together: "Why, hello, Otis; when did you come here?" "Hello, Harry; I did not know you were here."

Now here was a strange condition. Neither could see each other, nor did they see those present except myself, yet both saw a spirit I had not suggested that they should see and one whom I was not thinking of. Certainly neither had any former knowledge of Mr. Fisher. If they read it from my mind, it was at the time a blank to me. But here was at least three worlds within touch of each other and neither could look into the condition of the mind of the other until they were brought to the same condition of mind.

I now asked Harry where Mr. Fisher stood.

Said he, "In the middle of the room."

"But," I replied, "Harry, all of these people are here and the table sets in the circle. Now where is there room for Mr. Fisher to stand "

He replied, "I know what you say is so, but he is there all the same."

At another time Harry could at first see no spirits until I told him to call them together by asking his cousin to get them to come. At length he cried:

"Oh! There they come. Oh! what a lot of them. There are millions of them."

"Oh! Harry," I exclaimed, somewhat vexed and puzzled, "my little hall won't hold a hundred people; now how can there be millions here?"

In a worried manner he replied, "Oh, Mr. Stowe, I know it, but they are here, for I see them." He described a number of persons some of the members recognized as friends and people he or others knew nothing about.

Now where did he get this knowledge or is everything merely a condition of mind?

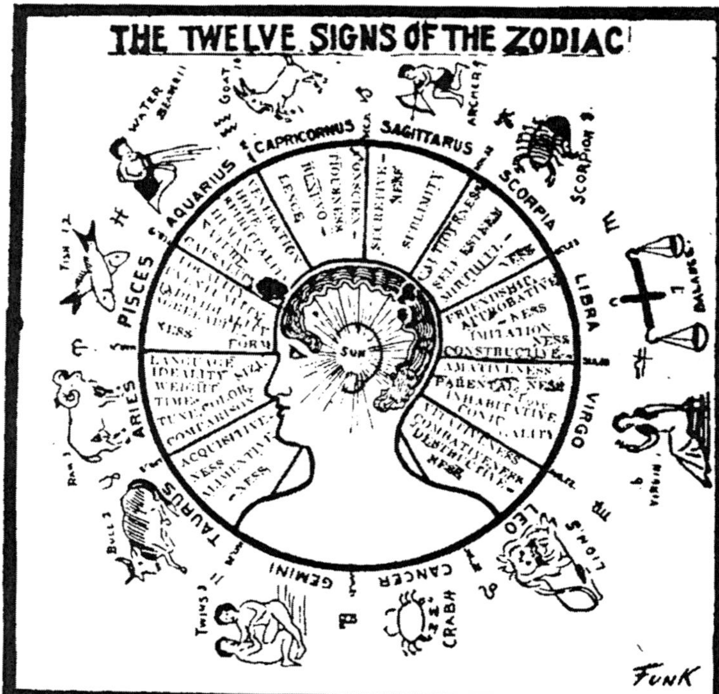

THE CELESTIAL HEAD.

The Bible says "Man is made in the likeness and im age of his creator." The above cut shows us the Zodiac or Celestial head, and Bible Astrology gives us a clearer understanding of the Bible's meaning of creation. The Phrenologest points out the various functions, and where they lie but the astrologer, not only, does all of that but much more, he points out what puts them there, and how to take advantage of them, including good and evil periods of life, and how to take advantage of them.

NO. 1

INFLUENCE OF THE TWELVE SIGNS OF THE ZODIAC.

THE TWELVE SIGNS OF THE ZODIAC.

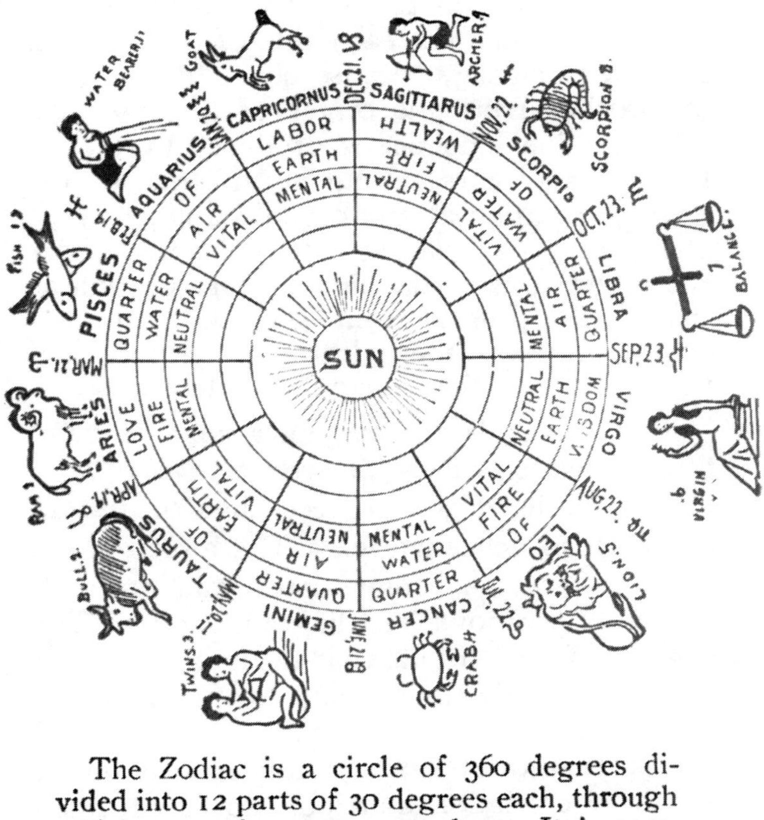

The Zodiac is a circle of 360 degrees divided into 12 parts of 30 degrees each, through which our solar system revolves. It is com-

NO 2.

INFLUENCE OF THE TWELV SIGNS OF THE ZODIAC.

posed of stars in constellations named the same as the signs of the Zodiac which once corresponded with them. This band extends from 8 to 9 degrees each side of the Ecliptic. somewhat zigzag, because some of the stars lay farther from the center of the line than others. The influence is produced by the vibrations the stars set up at the time of the birth or creation of any organized body which chances to be brought into existence under the direct rays of the sign or constellation as the earth passes from one sign to another during the different periods of the year. See diagram above.

The Zodiac is an imaginary zone or band through which our solar system revolves. It is a circle of 360 degrees, divided into 12 signs of 30 degrees each. The affect of the signs differ at different dates and through planetary positions (see diagram above). The quarter of love means that those born in that quarter are affectionate and lovers of home and domestic life. The quarter of wisdom means that those born in this quarter make much of education and look up to educated people and strive to educate their children. The quarter of wealth means that those born in this quarter make much of wealth and are

NO. 3.

INFLUENCE OF THE TWELVE SIGNS OF THE ZODIAC.

generally dickerers or traders. The quarter of labor means that these people are active, must be on their feet, and are best adapted to business where great activity is requisite.

The domains are Fire, Earth, Air and Water, and they rule the temper. Those born in the fire signs are of high temper, even dangerous when fully aroused, but easily satisfied, and not revengeful. People of the Earth signs sulk a little, even when outspoken, but do not generally hold revenge. People of the Air signs are quick of temper, flashy, and quick over it, and easily overcome their temper, and are seldom rash. People of the Water signs vary in temper and nearly always hold a grudge until they get even. If they forgive even, the memory of the injury will never down.

The quality of domains run alternately from Aries to the left—mental, vital, neutral. The mental signs mean that the mind is too strong for the body, and where two mentals marry, the child must be physically trained, or the body will be too weak to sustain it. The vital signs show stronger physical power, and quick to recuperate from any form of ill health. The neutral signs show a balance in mental and

NO.4.

INFLUENCE OF THE TWELVE SIGNS OF THE ZODIAC.

physical forces and a reservation in expression of feelings of like and dislike. The tables below give the effect of the signs on the general health and character. Those born on the cusp or line between two signs are changeable in likes and dislikes, and partake of both signs

People generally agree best together who are born in the same sign, or in polars, opposite signs, or in the same domains, which are trion to each other.

Thus Aries and Sagitarius are trion fire signs. So the fire signs are trion and the water signs are trion and the earth signs are trion. Thus fire and water make steam, and an explosion. Earth and water makes mud, the air lashes the water to foam. Fire scorches the earth, and air blows up the fire more fierce; while the air drys up the earth. Sometimes people of opposing domains get along well together, because they have the same rising sign, or the same ruling planet, and sometimes they may seem to get along when the inner life is h—l. But it is best to marry in trions or polars.

The time of day or houses and planitory positions are what makes the greatest difference between people born of the same sign.

NO. 5.

INFLUENCE OF THE TWELVE SIGNS OF THE ZODIAC.

More people marry their polars or trions than anywhere else.

To find the sign you were born in, look for dates at the lines dividing signs, and whichever date your birth comes between is your sign, then the corresponding figure at the head of descriptive matter of each sign is your fortune of Zodiacle horoscope.

GENERAL INSTRUCTIONS FOR CARE OF CHILDREN.

A person's stomach is the best moderator as to kind of food that is best for him. If possible let a child have what its stomach craves for, but limit the quantity, never letting a child over-feed.

Give children plenty of sleep, but get them up as soon as awake, and it is better that they sleep alone. You cannot guard a child too closely against the development of abnormal sex passions and self-abuse.

It is an old saying, "You spare the rod and spoil the child," but the father of that saying had no soul, and was only fit to keep wild beasts. It is a well-known fact you cannot train even domestic animals by the use of a whip, but kindness will conquer everything. If you must punish a child, do it by keeping from it some desired pleasure and teach it to sub-

NO.6.

INFLUENCE OF THE TWELVE SIGNS OF TEH ZODIAC.

mit to reason, and above all, reason yourself, and see that you do not exact unreasonable things. But don't show anger, don't strike, don't whip.

THE COSMIC MAN.

The above cut showes, without further comment, the part of the body is effected by each sign of the Zodiac. No surgical operation should be permitted when tne Moon is in the sign represnting that part of the body wherein the disease is located.

It should also be rembered that the patient will be worse the days the Moon transits the sign of the body in which the disease is located.

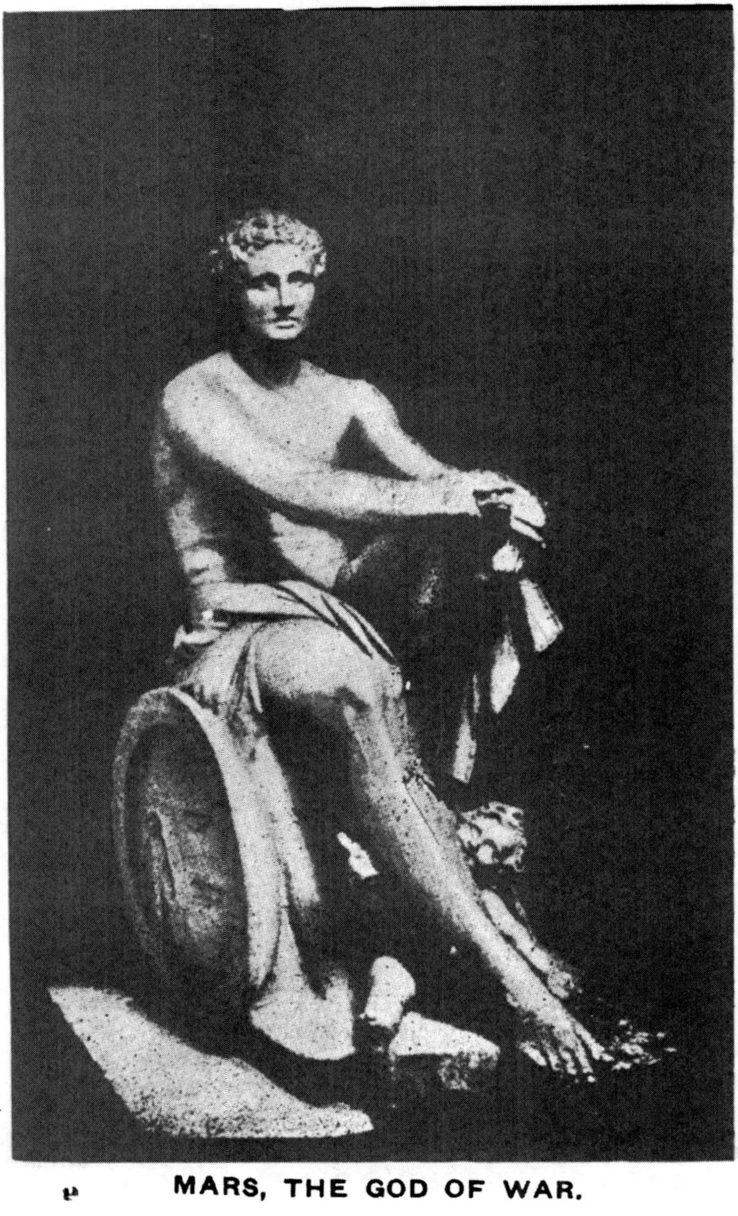

MARS, THE GOD OF WAR.

ATTRIBUTES OF THE SIGNS Page 7.

ARIES.

ARIES- ♈ - March 21 to April 19th is the first sign in the zodiac, from where all astronomical and astrological calculations start. It is at the head of the quarter of love, the first of the mental triplicity, and first of the fire triplicity.

Is 140,000,000 miles from the sun and is 4,230 miles in diameter.

MARS, the GOD of WAR rules Aries

Mars is 1 year 10 months 21 days 17 hours 21 minuts and 33 seconds going around the Sun. He is 57 days in a sign or he travels about a half a degree a day, or to be exact here is the speed each planet makes in the signe.

Mercury in Aries,	5° 18′	per day.
Venus in Aries,	1° 36′	per day.
Mars in Aries,	35′	per day.
Jupiter in Aries,	5′ 24″	per day.
Saturn in Aries,	2′ 9″	per day.
Uranus in Aries,	4° 6′	per year.
Neptune in Aries,	2° 11′	per year.

In this sign we judge character, dress, appearance and nature of any thing.

There is 30 days in this sign, some have more when 2 days are covered by 1 degree.

ATTRIBUTES, OF THE SIGNS. Page 8

When looking for the effects of any sign of the zodiac we should not loose sight of the fact that no person is likely to prove an exact type cf any one sign, as the rising sign will show its effects as strongly as the sign one is born in, and the sign the Moon is in will also be strongly manifest. as will any other sign which chances to hold the Moon or a number of planets, especially if one be the lord of the sign of birth This is why, on looking for the rising sign we first note the effects of the sign of birth, and then of the other effects, and so decide on the rising sign, and then by using the revolving disk of the Solar Bioscope we quickly determine the hour of birth. Any student should have that instrument also our "Secrets of Palmistry."

ARIES the ram March 21st to Apr. 19th, incl.

Discription. This is a mental fire sign. Colors, black, white and red or mixed. Gems, diamonds, opals white stones. Places most likely to drift to or for concealment, England, Germany, Denmark, Poland, Syria, Palestine, the antipodes, Western part of U. S. A. PLACES, mountins, mansions, sandy places, small out buildings, and all unfrequented places. He will seek theaters and all kinds of places of amuesment, and if he be depraved he will seek houses of prostitution. gamboling dens and is likely to make a confident of the opposit sex. The female is more reticent and likely to seek flashy dress and flashy society. Either are dangerous chareaters in a show down. Business men will find Aries people best adapted to head work, they are natural leaders and tho somewhat independent and rebilious, controle them by reason and they are most profitable help. They will not be bossed. The ATTRIBUTES are as follows, the male is generally of a spare, but compact build, rather long, pointed features. resembeling the face of a ram. heavy eye lids, generally, gray or brown eyes tho very sharp. He is spirited, independent, fond of music but rarely a performer, if one a good one. He is springy of step, graceful, generally, neat in dress, often sandy or red eurling hair, and long neck; he is fierce but forgiving, he can nearly always show scars on head or face. When taken ill it is first manifest in the eyes, face. head and stomach, with a feeling of dizziness. Almost invariably he will have the square and usefnl type of hand and the head line runs into the life line. which showes a lack of self confidence, early in life. and if born between midnight and noon he will loose his father before ten years of age and if between noon and midnight his friends are sure to use influence to get him a good position. He will be ambitious to ascend to high altitudes or to fame.

Physical temperment is, if born in a northern latitude, it is bilious-sangu ne, if born in a southern clime it is a nervous bilious temperment.

VENUS, THE GODDESS OF BEAUTY.

TAURUS.

TAURUS- ♉ - April 19th May 20th.

The 2nd sign is a Beastly, cold, Northern, Fixed, Dry, Earthy, Nocturnal, Stubborn, Succeedent, Feminine, Intellectual, Sympathetic, Vital, sign: at the head of the Earth triplicate.

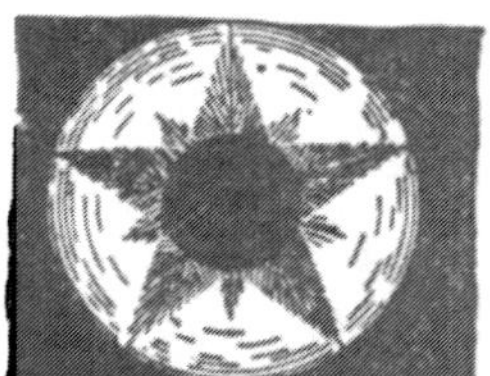

VENUS—LOVE

Is 67,000,000 miles from sun and 7,700 miles in diameter.

Venus, Goddess of beauty is the lordof Taurus. Venus makes her trip around the Sun in 7 months 14 days 16 hours 49 minutes, or she travels a half a degree per day, or is 18 days in a sign, or to be exact here is the speed each planet makes in the sign Taurus

Mercury in Tau.,	5° 37′	per day.
Venus in Tau.,	1° 36′	per day.
Mars in Tau.,	35′	per day.
Jupiter in Tau.,	5′ 24″	per day.
Saturn in Tau.,	2′ 8″	per day.
Uranus in Tau.,	4° 36′ 7″	per year.
Neptune in Tau.,	2° 11′ 7″	per year.

There are 31 days in the sign the 19th and 20th of May being ruled by the 30th degree of the sign and by the 60th of the Zodiac, and we use this sign to judge of wealth and what comes of it.

ATTRIBUTES OF THE SIGNS. Page 11

TAURUS, the Bull, April 19 to May 20th. inc.

TAURUS

This is a vital earth sign. Its colors white mixed with lemon and green. Gemes, emerald and moss agate. Places most likely to drift to, or for concealment, Ireland, Persia, Asia Minor, the Archipelligoes, the southern part of Russia, the Islands of Cyprus, and Samoa. Places, stables, low houses, low rooms, cellers, barnes, pastures, fallow lands and grain fields.

TEMPER, pleasant, easily coaxed but stubborn, cannot be driven, generally slow to anger but unconquorable when aroused, yet very sympathetic.

OCCUPATIONS, geniouses, mechanics, teachers, preacher , lawyers, clerks and literary persuits.

DISCRIPTION, general apperance well built, middle stature, full plump neck, broad forehead, broad between the eyes and rather flat featurs, dull complexion, large eyes, a ploasent apperance. The hand is generally short, plump and the first finger is short, a little above the fiirst joint of the second finger but does not reach the root of the nail. Geneeally a scar, mark or mole on throat orneck.

DISEASES- invaribly troubled with weakness of the throat and sooner or later obeseance or drosycical effections.

Characterestics, generally slow of movement, easly influenced when they think they have their own way, most successful in middle and latter part of life. These people are at home almost any place, they are often victems of theft but seldom recover stolen goods. They commit to memory very easily, they generally enjoy good food and drink and nearly always overcome bad habits sooner or later. While likely to acquire a considerable wealth in middle and latter part of life, will often be assisted by friends and yet subject to loss throu intregues out of wedlock or other unlooked for sources.

If born between midnight and noon the father was a man of some importance, above the average. Brothers and sisters will cause some trouble and many journeys may be expected; if born between midnight and noon one of these journeys will prove dangerous, if from nothing more than an attack from some large animal or a disease of the spine or liver. The children are likely to distinguish themselves in industrial persuits tho there is danger of accident or loss, by death of the first born, especially if it be a male.

The physical temperment of a Taurus person is of a bilious-sanguine in a southern latitude and a lymphatic-nervous in northern clime.

People born in any sign will show the effects of the sign in proportion to the influence the sign has an opportunity to exert upon them, uninfluenced by other signs. The division of the earth at the horizen, or rising sign at birth, as it is called, will sometimes be as manifest as the sign of birth, also the sign the Moon is in exerts a great influence.

MERCURY—MESSENGER OF THE GODS.

ATTRIBUTES OF THE SIGNS Page 13

GEMINI.

GEMINI II the 3d sign, May 21 to June 20th inclusive. It rules shoulders, armes, hands. It is at the head of the air triplicate, and is a common or, cadent, neutral, moist, hot, barren, masculine, intellectual, medium, fortunate, northern sign.

Is 37,000,000 of miles from the sun and is 3,000 miles in diameter.

It is ruled by Mercury, the messenger of the gods. He makes his trip in 2 months, 27 days, 23 hours, 15 minutes. He is very erratic in his moovements.

Here is the speed of the planets in Gemini.

Mercury in Gem.,	6°	per day.
Venus in Gem.,	1° 36′	per day.
Mars in Gem.,	30′ 30″	per day.
Jupiter in Gem.,	5′ 20″	per day.
Saturn in Gem.,	2′ 9″	per day.
Uranus in Gem.,	4° 17′	per year.
Neptune in Gem.,	2° 11′ 7″	per year.

Mercury rules the intellect, and he is a two faced planet, acting with the planet he is most strongly influenced by, so in Gemini we judge of letters, short journeys and father's family.

Gemini has 31 days. June 19 and 20th are covered by the 30te degree of Gemini or 90th degree of the zndiac,

ATTRIBUTES OF THE SIGNS. Page 14

GEMINI the Twins, May 20 to June 21st inclu. This is a Neutral Air sign. Its colors are white mixed with red. Its gems are Chalcedony, variegated stones, some times called Agate Countries most likely to drift to, North America, Lower Egypt, Lombardy, Sardinia, Belgium and West of England. Places; mountains, hills and all high places, theaters, public halls, chests, plastering and walls of houses.

GEMINI

TEMPER, quick and flashy, quick over it and sorry for giving offence.

OCCUPATPON, Excellent teachers, musicians, literary people, clerks, builders, architects, public offi als, or anything where head work is required. One peculiarity of these people is they can easily carry a load on both shoulders, and are often found combining business and travel.

Those running mail order business will find it to their advantage to employ Gemini people to do their mailing, as they are fortunate in this line.

DISCRIPTION, the ladies flesh up very young while the men are slim or raw bone, yet there seems to be two distinct classes or rather types of men, one of which is very small and dapper, and very neat and dressey, and the men are usualy more particular with their dress than the ladies. Both sex are well built except that the hands and armes seem long for the body. They are restless, make many changes, travel much. Often engage in two kinds of business at onetime ,or con template doing so. Can adapt themselves to, most any thing they try to. They are great readers, if they think they can spare the time. Are great lovers of beauty and art.

DISEASES. If tired or ill they feel it first in the armes and shoulders, to a marked degree, and the illness is manifest in fevers, malaria, liver or bladder troubles, and in inguries from animals, reptiles and from secret enemies.

They can nearly always show marks or scars on the hands or evidence of broken or dislocated bones in hands and arms. This sign gives a bilious-nervous temperment in a northern clime and a bilious-sanguine temperment a southern clime.

CHARACTERESTICS. Passionately fond of knowledge, especially scientific, tho intellectualy they are inconsistent, very skeptical, going to extremes,, either dogmatic or extremely fickle.

These people have many friends of all sorts and conditions in life, some of whom will become bitter enemies. These people are easy to get aquanted with because they are, genrally, intellectual, great readers and great talkers, love to be admired an complimented but slow to return it, are destined to a changeable [but, in the end fortunate life.

Aries, Taurus, and Gemini constitute the quarter of love, which means the affectional and emtional nature receives their strongest influence from this quarter; it is also called the intelectual quarter.

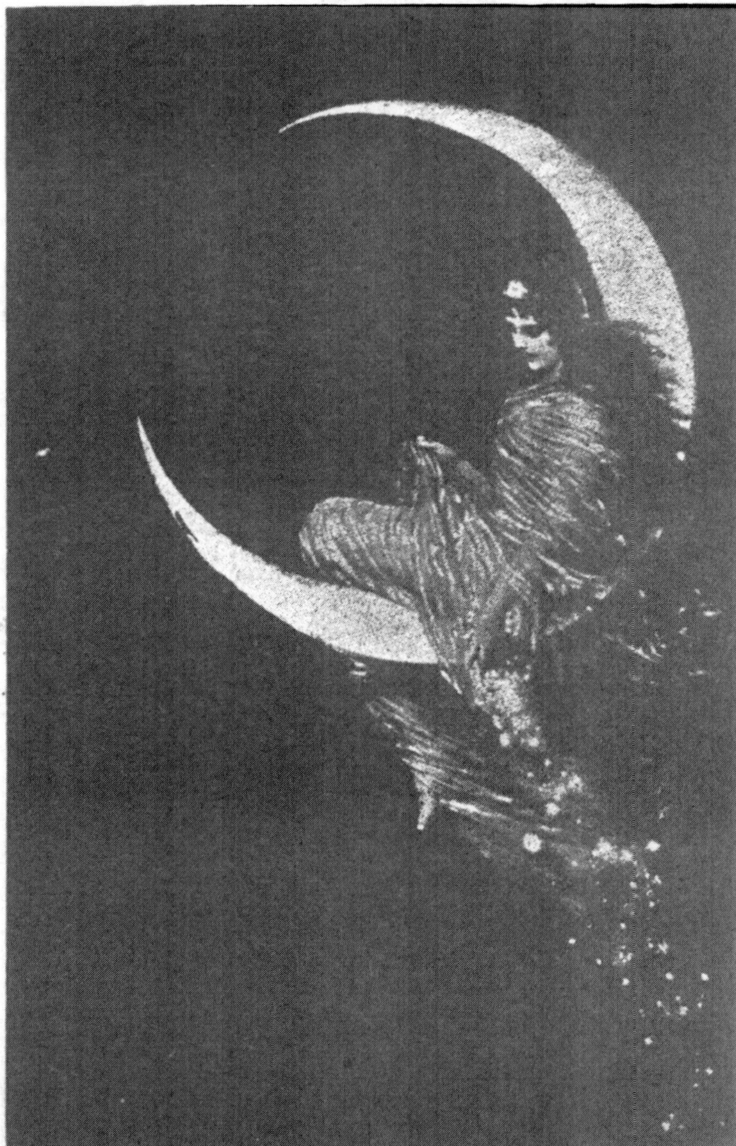

MOON, DIANA—GODDESS OF POETRY.

ATTRIBUTES OF THE SIGNS Page 16

CANCER.

CANCER-♋- the 4th sign June 21st to July 22nd inclusive, is at the head of the water triplicate. It has 32 days, June 21st and 22nd is covered by the 1st degree of Cancer, 91st of zodiac. July 21 and 22nd by the 30th degree of Cancer 120 of zodiac. It heads the quarter of wisdom or north angle, called lower mid heaven it is a cardinal, northern, movable, fruitful, mental, feminine, cold, water sign. It is ruled by the Moon who stands for the mother and we judge of matters concerning the mother by this sign.

MOON-FRIENDS

Is 240,000 miles from earth and is one-third the size of the earth. The earth is 8,000 miles in diameter.

The Moon is 2 days 6 hours, 38 minutes and 36 seconds in a sign, or it requires 27 days 7 hours 4 minutes and 19 seconds to make her changes.

Here is the speed of the planets in the sign Cancer.

Mercury in Can.,	5° 37′	per day.
Venus in Can.,	1° 36′	per day.
Mars in Can.,	28′ 36″	per day.
Jupiter in Can.,	4′ 37″	per day.
Saturn in Can.,	2′ 16″	per day.
Uranus in Can.,	4° 26′ 26″	per year.
Neptune in Can.,	2° 11′ 7″	per year.

Cancer rules the chest and breast.

ATTRIBUTES OF THE SIGNS. Page 17

CANCER– the Crab, June 21 July 22nd incluc.

This is a mental water sign. Its colors are green and russet.

Gems, ruby, cat's eye, and emerald.

Countries most likely to drift to, Holland, Scotland, New Zealand and all of Africa. Places- near large bodies of water, sequesterd nooks and shaded streams, marshes, ditches, springs, washouses and cellars.

TEMPER. Like all water signs, the native is rather slow to anger but when aroused it is fierce and oft times revengeful, at least never forgeting.

OCCUPATION. These peo le are best adapted to commercial life or manufacturing, they make good mechanics or business men in any walk in life yet would appear to best advantage at the commerc al end of the business.

DISCRIPTION. Cancer people are of two, extremes either very fleshy or very thin, and more often light complexioned than dark as this is one of the three signs that produce most blonds. Th y, generally, cannot stand a hard pressure against the chest. The flesh is soft and fla by even if thin; the lips are soft and, generally, full and the hand flaby and the heart line frayed and forked. The features are, generally small and delicately formed or the other extreme, quite angular; the upper part of the body is larger, in proportion, than the the lower.

DISEASES are of the breast, stomach, paps, lungs, nerves, dropsical humors, tumors and cancers.

ATTRIBUTES, OF THE SIGNS. Page 18

CHARACTERISTICS are of timid, thotful and agreeable, with a sensative, affectionate nature, cheif quolities are reflective, sensitive hence excelant mediums and psychics; restless, always contemplating some business scheme, and worrying for fear they wont have enough for old age, or that theives will break in and steal, and so are very careful to see that all is secure, hence make good watchmen. They can generally show a mole or scar on the brest or shoulder. Both sex, generally have a sort of negligee appearence, yet the ladies had rather not go on the street unless they can appear, about, as they want to, yet they are not over dressy, but are excelant mothers and house keepers, never leave dirt in the corners. Ladies in this sign who are led astray may lay it to necessity or the desire for dress or for sympathy, they should, but do not get at home. A lack of confidence and sympathy, on the part of an employer will often caus a Cancer person to suddenly leave a good business, with no apparent cause therefore seldom attain to high aims. They do best near large bodies of water. If a business sceaces to pay they should not remain to try to make it pay. Discreet, generally sympathetic and kind to a fault, they are determined in what thy under take yet are easeily discouraged. Have many aquaintences but few confidental friends. Should never gambol. Will succeed best after 34th year. **Will have trouble with children but end right.**

SUN, APOLLO—GOD OF BEAUTY.

ATTRIBUTES OF THE SIGNS page 19.

LEO ♌

LEO the 5th sign July 23d to Aug. 22d inclusive, is the 2 nd of the fire triplicate and rules the heart and lungs, blood and nerves. It is a northern, fixed, diurnal, hot dry, succeedent, barren, commanding, fortunate, fire sign. Leo has 31 days. July 23d and 24th is covered by the 1st degree of Leo or the 121st degree of the zodiac.

Is 95,000,000 miles from earth, 1,300,000 times greater than earth and is 882,000 miles in diameter.

Leo is ruled by the the Sun who stands for the father and by it we judge of the father, children and pleasures.

Here is the speed of the planets in the sign Leo.

Mercury in Leo,	5° 37′	per day.
Venus in Leo,	1° 36′	per day.
Mars in Leo,	28′ 6″	per day.
Jupiter in Leo,	4′ 45″	per day.
Saturn in Leo,	2′ 2″	per day.
Uranus in Leo,	4° 30′	per year.
Neptune in Leo,	2° 11′ 7″	per year.

The Sun is the ruler of our Solar system and is spoken of as standing still, but nothing in the universe remains still. The Sun with his whole system revolves throu the great zodiac once in 26, 000 years, He entered Aquarius about 1840. See Bible Astrology, price one dollar,

ATTRIBUTES, OF THE SIGNS. Page 20

LEO. The lion, July 23 to Aug. 22rd incluisve.

This is a vital Fire sign.

I ts COLORS are red and green.

GEMS. Ruby and Sardonyx.

TEMPER, Like all fire signs the temper is hot and dangerous when aroused, quick to forgive, not revengeful and the temper is generally well under control.

COUNTRIES most likely to drift to- France, Italy and Bohemia, Places steep, rockey and inacco si le places, castles, forts, parks, pasturs, deserts and woods ana home of wile beasts.

OCCUPATION. These people are natural geniuses and often inventors; can choose any occupation they please, for they can adapt themselves to almost any position in life, so should be left to choose what ever line of work strikes their fancy.

DISCRIPTION. Leo people are of a plump build and ruddy complexion, unless strongly influenced by Urauus and then they are quite slim. are generally full faced and even features The hand is plump even if long; mount of Venus high, They are very secretive and often quite contrary, like the cat nature their sign represents. Ladies of this sign are as ingenius as the men, ask a Leo woman if she wants carpenter work done around the house, if she had not rather do it her self than to wait for a man to do it and she will laugh and say "yess." They are good conversationalst, also witty, and good reasoners.

DISEASES. Being a vital sign they recuperate quickly, from any illness; the discases are of the heart, lungs, blood nerves and bowels, often pains in the ribs and sides and palpitation of the heart and nearly always gray hair before 25 years of age.

ATTRIBUTES OF THE SIGNS. Page 21

CHARACTERISTICS are- the love nature is their chief failing. When ladies of this sign are led astray, it is throu their affeetions. Of a nervous sanguin temperment they jump at conclusions to quickly; happy disposition, good mimicks, good story tellers, kind-hearted, cheerful and happy: in the strugle of life they had rather plan than work and generally look out for their own. They live in an ideal world and in great hopes, but generally too quick to appeal to the law and waste good money, yet law abiding themselves. You will find them near a good warm fire in winter discussing every thing but their own affairs, their love and money matters they positively refuse to say anything about, yet they use exellant judgement in general.

As they love to speculate they are most successful dealing in anything of the earth, either vegetable or mineral tho are seldom successful until after the 35th birth day. Tho not apt to seek honors they are apt to recive them.

There is a well defined taste for pleasure, and like the cat, when he gets a thing in his head he followes it to the end. By his own merrit, he will aquire much property tho he is likely to loose it throu quarrels with relatives over property and family secrets. Likely to travel considerable, to loose wealth or to meet with accidents to head or shoulder while traveling. Is likely to loos the first and possibly the only child. His enemies will be open: his friends many but not much help to him. His employes and servents will give him trouble.

VIRGO, or 6th house, the house of sickness and selfishness, ruled by Mercury.

ATTRIBUTES OF THE SIGNS page 22,

VIRGO.

VIRGO the 6th sign Aug, 23 Sept, 23rd inclusive, is the 2nd of the earth triplicate, rules stomach and bowels, is a cold, barren, melancholy, unfortunate, moral, feminine, nocturnal, northern earth sign. Tho ruled by Mercury it is, properly the home of the Earth, because at the first degree of Aries all astrological and astronomical calculations are made, and all time calculations must be made from an earth stand point and when the Sun appears at the first degree of Aries the Earth is just going out of the earth sign, Virgo, which rules the seat of life.

Lunar time 354⅓ days in a year, Solar time 365¼ days days. Astronomical or prophetic time 360 days "time, times and a half a time" 1260 Astronomical years.

Here is the speed of the planets in the sign Virgo,

Mercury in Virgo,	5° 18′	per day.
Venus in Virgo,	1° 36′	per day.
Mars in Virgo,	27′ 18″	per day.
Jupiter in Virgo,	4′ 40″	per day.
Saturn in Virgo,	2′ 15″	per day.
Uranus in Virgo,	4° 6′	per year.
Neptune in Virgo,	2° 11′ 7″	per year.

We judge of sickness and servants by the planets we find in Virgo or 7th house.

Virgo the Virgin Aug. 23 Sept. 22nd inclusive.

VIRGO ♍

This is a neutral earth sign. Its colors are black speckeled with blue.

GEMES-cornellion, sapphire, onyx.

Countries most likely to drift to are Mysopatomia, West indies, Switzerland, Turkey and Asia. PLACES-dairy houses, and where hay, barley, wheat, peas, cheese, butter, and all such things are stored.

TEMPER- Like all the earth signs, the temper is a little sulky, but quicker to anger than Taurus people and stormy when they break out but they are soon over it.

OCCUPATION- generally good mechanics, proofreaders, printers, painters, traveling men, in any line. as they are most fortunate when moving.

DISCRIPTION- these people are, generally, of medium highth, plump of build in upper part of body but lower limbs seem lacking. The men are rather boisterous, loud spoken, a musical voice end a sentence with a laugh or chuckle. Both sex have large eyes, the ladies eyes are, generally a large soulful brown, they are seldom satisfied with their domestic affairs and expect their husbands to lavish love upon them but can never return it by expression, and nearly always appear sad. Both sex are fond of music but the voice cracks and fails at about 27. You may bet on every male child having a narrow escape for his life before his 10th and probbaly before the 6th birth day. They may eat well but are peculiar about their food and if it does not look, just to suit them they want none of it, and if angry or excited they cannot eat. The hand is short and plump, but the life line is not generally strong.

DISEASES- are cheifly of the stomach and bowels, effecting kidneys and head.

CHARACTERISTICS of those born in Virgo are: ingenious, witty, even tempered, superior mental facculties, lovers of music and harmony, and inharmony destroys the appetite and causes them to become sick. They are sharp in business and inclin ed to be selfiish but very just and if you give them their own way; you are not likely to be wronged.

They are quite changeable, their likes and dislikes very decided, and while good company they are rather timied and bashful. They are most successful in middle life, reach honors throu personal merrit. They, generally, put to high an estimate on wealth and its influences, are inclined to be a little to easely discouraged tho stubborn and tenacious in almost everything. Their wealth comes suddenly as throu patents, mines, or sudden rise of property, are also subject to sudden losses, and to sudden violent happenings, such as loss of friends by accident, nearly all marry more than once and the second marriage causes trouble in the family. There is but little harmony between brothers and sisters, friends few and uncertian, secret enemies in art and finance.

LIBRA the 7th house or sign of marriage, hope and dispare. rtled by Venus.

ATTRIBUTES OF THE SIGNS Page 25

LIBRA.

LIBRA ♎ or7th sign Sept 22 to Oct. 21st. inclucive, is at the head of the reproducing quarter or quarter of wealth. It is a mental, cardinal, equinotical, sympathetic, humain, psychic, fortunate, reproducing, west angle sign.

Libra has 30 days and by it we judg of marriage and of business partnership, It is presided over by Venus the goddess ofbeauty, which also rules Taurus The Moon is also strong in Libra and when she or Venus are their at birth it makes good musicans. Where Virgo, Libra or Sagittarius have a strong influence at birth it tends to produce beautiful form.

Here is the speed of each planet in Libra.

Mercury in Lib.,	3° 55′	per day.
Venus in Lib.,	1° 36′	per day.
Mars in Lib.,	27′ 18″	per day.
Jupiter in Lib.,	4′ 39″	per day.
Saturn in Lib.,	1′ 50″	per day.
Uranus in Lib.,	4° 30′	per year.
Neptune in Lib.,	2° 11′ 7″	per year.

The number of Venus is 45, a luckey number. All of the planets are friendly to Venus except Satarn, If Saturn be in the domain of Venus, which is Libra it denotes early death of the married partner.

ATTRIBUTES OF THE SIGNS. Page 26

LIBRA, the balance. Se t. 23 to Oct 22nd. Inc.

This is a Mental Air sign. Its colors are black, dark crimson or tawny, GEMS. Opals, diamonds, white stones. Countries most likely to drift to are Southern states of America, China, Japan, India, Persia, Austria, and vicinity of the Caspian Sea. Places most likely to drift to, or to conceal selves or property, hill and mountain tops, sandy places, gravel beds, wind mills, barns, saw mills, out houses, cooper shops and all places where wood is cut, chambers, garrets, and tops of drawers.

TEMPER, is quick, flashy, quick over it and sorry for giving offence, late in life show little or no temper.

OCCUPATION. While these people are found in all kinds of business, seeming to thrive equally well in all they often excell as mechanics and inventors; they are natural traders, make most excelant judges and especially of horses.

DISCRIPTION. These people are generally handsome people, large eyes, high forehead, open countenance, gentle, straight forward. This sign produces more blonds than all of the rest put together. If dark complexioned the eyes are much smaller than those of light complexioned. They are extremely fond of amusements and always expect to go on the rostrum or stage sooner or later, and generally do some time in life.

The hand is angular, knockles large, what is known as the philosophical hand, there is often a scar mark, or blemish to be found on the hand or arm.

ATTRIBUTES OF THE SIGNS. Page 27

DISEASES, are weaknesses of the back, loins, haunchs, kidneys, bladder and blood, appearing in eruptions on face and hands. the stomach and head are also often effected.

CHARACTERISTICS. These people are more imitative than original hence often found as actors, lecturers and travelers. Chcif characteristcs are spells of melancholy, or the other extreme of buoyancy and are very decided in their likes and dis likes, are demonstrative in their affections, very apt to have a number of enemies, one of which will be a religious fanatic; are likely to have one great law suit which they will, sooner or later win; natural born speculators, make money easly yet seldom rise very high and seldom go very low, because they are of the sign of the balances. They should never resort to gambling as they cannot be successful. Nnotwithstanding, their frequent spells of dispondancy they posess great hopefulness which is apt to lead them to great risks: they are often led to this throu bad advice of supposed friends; the best luck comes in middle life. They should avoid large bodies of water and cultivate their psychic faculties. If born betwcen noon and midnight the early loss of the father is likely, and there will be trouble with the married partner, and likely a second marriage and a second family or step or adoped children and one child will give much trouble.

Will gain wealth throu marriage and loos position throu the mother or some other woman.

SCORPIO the 8th sign or house of reproduction, death and inheritance.

ATTRIBUTES OF THE SIGNS Page28.

SCORPIO.

SCORPIO- ♏ - Oct. 22 to Nov. 20th. Is the 8th sign, It is a fixed, vital, watery, fruitful, feminine, southern, succeedent, unfortunate sign. It is the night house of Mars, from where we judge of deaths, wills, legacies and insurance, what comes of it.

This sign, with Sagittarius was classed in the domain of the horse. These two signs are religious, hot tempered signs, but like Aries, it produces overcomers. Mars rules both Aries and Scorpio gives us vigor, force, energy, in any direction that other influences may indicate. Here is the speed that Mars and other planets make in Scorpi.

Mercury in Scor.,	2° 36′	per day.
Venus in Scor.,	1° 36′	per day.
Mars in Scor.,	29′ 31″	per day.
Jupiter in Scor.,	4′ 40″	per day.
Saturn in Scor.,	1′ 54″	per day.
Uranus in Scor.,	4° 17′	per year.
Neptune in Scor.,	2° 11′ 7″	per year.

Whil this is a hot moist sign Aries is a fiery, hot, dry, cardinal, equinoctial, sign.

ATTRIBUTES OF THE SIGNS. Page 29.

SCORPIO Scorpin Oct. 22 to Nov 20 th inclusive.

SCORPION 8
SCORPIO ♏

This is a vital water sign. Its color is brown. GEMS the Blue Beryl and Yellow Topaz are the stones.

COUNTRIES most likely to drift to for concealment of self or property are Norway, Barbary, Morocco, Bavara. PLACES, gardens, vineyards, orchards, ruins, quag-mires, ditches, old fences and walls, and infact any place where worms and insects make theri homes.

TEMPER, is like those of all water signs, whether quick or slow, they never forget, and when wronged they seldom forgive.

OCCUPATION. these people are born to serve and be served. They do best working for government, or for some large firm, the same as do Libra people except that Scorpio people make the best foremen and superintendents of any in the 12 signs; they also make fine business people and M. D, s.

DISEASES, are weakness in generative organs, stone in bladder, fistulas, piles, diseases of groin, and stomach and for ladies all female complaints.

In cold climates they are of a nervous bilious temperment, and in a warm climate are lymphetic bilious temperment.

DISCRIPTION. These people are generally of a compact build, tho of small stature, and generally very dark complexioned as there is but about 1 in 40 blonds born in the sign, and invariabley these suffer terribly with stomach trouble. Ask a Scorpio man what he dislikes the most in any man and he will tell you it is to be beat by another or to have a man tell him he will do a thing and then break his word. Nearly all that are light complexioned were born in the 1st 10 degrees of the sign, and the eyes are very large. Scor pio people are very witty and can readily turn a joke. They love the water, and a picture of a vessel under full sail facinates them. High temper he never forgets and seldom forgives an injury; they can eat almost any old time, and enjoy the food but must suffer for it, yet are seldom sick in bed and most of them die of heart troubles, and without warning. If they take to the stage they make excelant actors. The hand is generally short, stubby and round.

CHARACTERISTICS. Skilful, patient, love honor, full of magnetic force consequently strong will power, and corresponding strong passions; like to lead and be led, good friends as long as it pays; easily excited to jealousy. They court public opinion, sake honors and drift to politics ;tho active they dislike to work, yet are generally hard workers; they honor people in high positions and love to appear above their station in life. Have many friends and many enemies, one friend will cause much trouble. If any children there will be manny. Little success in early life, latter part of life is best.

Should marry in water signs.

JUPITER—GOD OF WEALTH.

ATTRIBUTES OF THE SIGNS Page 31.

SAGITTARIUS.

Sagittarius, -♐- Nov. 21st to Dec 20th inclusive. It is the 9th sign, and rules thighs and sciatic nerves. It is a cadent, masculine, fire, common, reproductive, religious, moral, warlike, accident producing; yet fortunate, suthern sign. It is ruled over by Jupiter, the god of wealth, who makes his trip in 11 years 10 months 14 days, 18 hours 20 minutes, or he is nearly a year in a sign, about 5 minutes per day, or to be exact here is the speed each planet makes in Sagittarius.

JUPITER.

Is 380,000,000 miles from sun and 91,000 miles in diameter.

Mercury in Sagit,	2° 30′	per day.
Venus in Sagit,	1° 36′	per day.
Mars in Sagit,	35′	per day.
Jupiter in Sagit,	4′ 42″	per day.
Saturn in Sagit,	1′ 53″	per day.
Uranus in Sagit,	4° 8′	per year.
Neptune in Sagit,	2° 11′ 7″	per year.

There are 30 days in this sign, and we judge of religion, morals, accidents and war, by this sign.

Jupiter is a fire planet and also rules Pisces the sign of the fishes.

ATTRIBUTES OF THE SIGNS. Page 32.

SAGITTARIUS Nov. 21st to Dec. 20th inclusive.

ARCHER.S
SAGITTARUS

This is the 9th sign a neutral fire sign its COLORS are yellow and green.

GEMS the torquoise and topaz.

COUNTRIES, most likely to drift to for pleasure or concealment, Arabia, Spain, Hungary and France. PLACES, Houses on high grounds, and upper rooms, over stables for war horses, and houses where great beasts are kept, and highest places they can find.

TEMPER, like all fire signs the temper is very hot, but not revengeful, yet they hold in memory, for a long time a wrong once done them.

OCCUPATION. These people do best when at work for others; they seldom do well for themselves. They are naturally good in figures, especially in mental arithmetic, so make excelant ticket agents, cashiers, clerks, and all simmilar positions; when starting for themselves they do best with new or untried cnteprises.

DISCRIPTION. These people are well built, never angular, well formed bodies, limbs and features; never corpulent or ill shaped. Laughingly ask a Sagittarius person if he will, ever. admit he is in the wrong and he will say "I never like to admit being in the wrong." Sagittarius people seldom loose their presence of mind, for a moment, under the most trying circumstances, unless they loose the temper. The hand is remarkabely well shaped.

DISEASES. They generally suffer with pain in loins, back, kidneys and sciatic nerves, and are liable to fevers and liver troubles and pains in spine, back head, stomach and bowls and to accidents.

This gives a nervous-bilious effect in a Northern clime but simply nervous nature in a southern clime.

CHARACTERISTICS. These people are dignified and reserved, and like people of all neutral signs; they do not like to express their true feelings; they are capable of loving but cannot express it in words. It is natural for them to have many enemies among the opposite sex. They had rather lie than admit they are wrong in anything. They are fond of outdoor exercises and sports and generally very successful in raising cattle and horses. They love money, yet are not overly selfish, but generally die quite wealthy, and that throu the work of others. They are well meaning and true to those they love, but too indifferent in expressing that love, which often turns the truest love from them. Money is their best friend and they are seldom without it.

It may be summed up, they are honest, generous, without thot of reward or gratitude, verastile, gentle, peaceful, good entertainers, showing child like cheerfulness, except when aroused, then high temper, and sensitive nervous, worrying about trifels. As they are naturally eloquent and gifted, loving art, music and science, they often become fine oritors. Their brothers and sisters are not, generally, numerous and one or more dies very young and they are not on the best of terms with those they have, besides they have some treacherous friends and bitter enemies but also true friends and proctors.

SATURN—GOD OF AGRICULTURE.

ATTRIBUTES OF THE SIGNS Page 34.

CAPRICORNUS.

CAPRICORNUS ♑ the 7th sign Dec. 21st to January 16th inclusive, rules the knees; it is a mental, earthy, stubbern, dry, cold, melancholy, feminine, serving. movable, unfortunate, tropical. suthern cardinal sign, from which we judge honor, dishonor and business. Its ruler is Saturn, called the greater evil. Saturn is a great spiritual planet, and he requires, to make his trip, 29 years, 5 months, 16 days, 14 hours, 1 minute and 14 seconds, or about two and a half years in a sign, or a degree per month.

SATURN.

Is 872,132,000 miles from the sun and 64,213 miles in diameter.

Here is the speed of the planets in Capricornus.

Mercury in Cap.,	2° 43′	per day.
Venus in Cap.,	1° 36′	per day.
Mars in Cap.,	35′ 15″	per day.
Jupiter in Cap.,	4′ 59″	per day.
Saturn in Cap.,	1′ 52″	per day.
Uranus in Cap.,	4° 00′ 0″	per day.
Neptune in Cap.,	2° 11′ 7″	per day.

Saturn once ruled Aquarius, also and still exerts a strong influence there, see "Stowe's Bible Astrology," (wonderful.)

ATTRIBUTES OF THE SIGNS. Page 35.

CAPRICORNUS

Capricornus, the goat, Dec. 21st to Jan. 20th inclusive, heads the Quarter of Labor, or Serving Quarter; (see Stowe's Bible Astrology, $1.) This is a Mental Earth sign its colors are black, brown and swarthy russet. Its gems gold stone, and all speckled and green stones.

The countries Capricornus people are most likely to drift to, or for purposes of concealment are Mexico, the Isthmus of Darien, old Saxony, Bulgaria, India and Persia.

PLACES. offices and places of public, affairs and the other extreme. farm and tool houses and places where old wood is found, and where cattle and sheep are kept, fallows, pastures, thorny fields, dung heaps and dark places.

TEMPER, like all earth signs this gives a stubborn nature, may pout some and only express fierce anger when highly aroused.

OCCUPATION. As this is at the head of the quarter of labor, Capricornus people love active employment, but seldom succeed alone. Anyone wishing a good organizer of societies, political or otherwise. he will do well to look for a Capricornus person, yet they can generally, organize business better for others than for themselves; and they are often good in any line of business.

DISCRIPTION, Capricornus men are, generally well built while the women are more angular and it is seldom you find a very large Capricornus person, while it is an admitted fact January produces more small people than any other month of the year. The chief attribute is a strong sense of duty. Ask one of them if he has not often robbed himself for the sake of duty, and then got the wor t of it, and he will say, "you bet." What ever gains comes to a Capricornus person comes to him in jumps and jeirks. He is up to day and down to marrow, and up again the next day, yet they are good business people. The hand is, generally, short and of the angular or philosophical type.

DISEASES or physical weakness is trembling and giving way of the knees, weak eyes, lungs, and often stomach, bowel and kidney troubles, and to frequent falls, cuts and bruises. The temperment, in northern latitudes is lymphetic nervous, in southern climes lynphetic bilious.

CHARACTERISTICS. They contribute to all kinds of educational interests, and are energetic organizers in social, political, and business enterprises. He is, more, the builder of his own fortune than are tho e of any of the 12 signs. He seldom inherits wealth and if he does, has trouble to get possesion of it. His brothers and sirters will be numerous but more harmful than benificial, and his own family, if any will be a sor. e of tribulation, greater than pleasure. His unhappy family relations and his enemies cause much travle, on which he meets with many accidents and narrow escapes and if born between noon and midnight, is more than likely to be one of the sufferes.

Now I Reign for a Thousand Years
URANUS
THE SON
OF THE SUN
GOD

ATTRIBUTES OF THE SIGNS page 37.

AQUARIUS, ♒

AQUARIUS ♒ the 11th sign Jan. 20th to Feb. 18th inclusive, is a vital succeedent, serving, sanguine, humain, fixed, hot, southern, fortunate, masculine, air sign, by which we judge of friends and what comes of them. It is ruled by Uranus, the son of the Sun god, who, requires, to make his trip around the Sun, 84 years, 5 days, 6 hours, 46 minutes and 39 seconds, or he is 7 years in a sign, traveling but 4 degrees 30 minuts per year, 90 minutes per month, to be more exact here is the speed of the planets in the sign Aquarius.

Is 1,822,360,000 miles from the sun; 34,331miles in diameter.

Mercury in Aqua.,	4° 0′ 0″	per day.
Venus in Aqua.,	1° 36′	per day.
Mars in Aqua.,	37′ 7″	per day.
Jupiter in Aqua.,	5′ 21″	per day.
Saturn in Aqua.,	1′ 55″	per day.
Uranus in Aqua.,	4° 8′	per year.
Neptune in Aqua.,	2° 11′ 7″	per year.

Uranus tears down to build better, he will soon enter his own sign and then rule for a thousand years, (the millenium.) See Stowe's "Bible Astrology." $1.

ATTRIBUTES OF THE SIGNS. Page 38.

AQUARIUS, the water bearer, January 20th to February 18th inclusive, is a vital sign, in the Serving Quarter or Quarter of Labor. It rules the calves of the legs.

COLOR sky blue.

GMES are carbunkles and rubies.

COUNTRIES these people will drift to for pleasure or for concealment of themselves or property. Arabia, Russia, Tartary, Poland and Sweden.

PLACES, stone quarries, mining camps and mines, hilly and uneven places, roofs, garrets, and eaves of houses, newly dug cellars, wells, plowed fields, and vineyards near springs.

TEMPER, is that of all air sign, quick and flashy but, generally, quick over it and sorry for giving offence, tho this sign produces a variety of types, the highest and lowest of all of the signs, you will some times see the most depraved characters asking under, a cloak of virtue; while this may be said of all of the signs, to a certian extent, but not so often as of Aquarius.

OCCUPATION, born in the Quarter of Labor, these people are naturally active and so make the best of agriculturists, superentendents of construction of roads, bridges or other public works. They are found in all kinds of professions but are best adapted to light active employment, or as leaders.

DISCRIPTION. This is the highest and lowest of all the signs and hardest to discribe as you have all kinds of types to deal with. Aquarius, next to

Libra, produces most blonds, tho many of these are of the sandy type. The eyes are, generally, larg and bright. Their chief characteristic is a restless active nature, seldom finding fault without cause.

The hand is well formed, but the Heart line, generally, showes many dots, and the life line, or line around the base of the thumb, and many nerve frays, these are fine lines runing downwards toward the wrist.

DISEASES, these people are liable to accidents to lower limbs, and rheumatism, cramps, nerve troubles and blood disorpers, and of sympathetic heart troubles. They are of a nervous sanguine nature in a northern clime, bilious sanguine in a southern,climate, yet they are long livers.

CHARACTERISTICS: As this sign rules happiness, these people are fond of all kinds of amusements, and are, generlly, very intelligent, good in fine arts and literature. As they are prodigious workers and have the, Leo facculty, (their polar.) of adapting themselves to, almost, anything they are well fitted to deal with the many, and as rulers, tho most successful when dealing with the rich. They are subject to sudden gains and losses, and must be ever on the look out for treachery and for relatives, tho they think much of friends and are true to them. If in public life they are in danger of violent death. They have few brothers and sisters, but are likely to be the parents of twins, yet their children are delicate. Their father will die suddenly. They should live on high ground, away from large bodies of water. They seldom succeed in their birth place and are destined to some great change before success.

NEPTUNE—GOD OF THE SEA.

ATTRIBUTES OF THE SIGNS Page 40.

PISCES.

PISCES ♓ the 12th sign Feb. 19th to March 20th inclusive, rules feet and is a feminine, fruitful, unfortunate, watery, movable, neutral, southern, sign. It is, generally, considered the night house of Jupiter, as Pisces and Jupiter have ruled for 2, 000 years, but Jupiter is a fire planet, and since the discovery of Neptune a water planet, some astrologers have assigned Neptune to Pisces, Neptune is an internal disturber or disturber of the home so is strong in Cancer, the sign of the home.

NEPTUNE.

Is 2,745,998,000 miles from sun
Diameter, 38,000 miles.

The speed of the planets in Pisces.

Mercury in Pisc.,	5° 0′	per day.
Venus in Pisc.,	1° 36′	per day.
Mars in Pisc.,	35′	per day.
Jupiter in Pisc.,	5′ 21″	per day.
Saturn in Pisc.,	1′ 55″	per day.
Uranus in Pisc.,	3° 51′	per year.
Neptune in Pisc.,	2° 11′ 7″	per year.

Neptune travels 11 minutes per month, 2 degrees 8 minutes per year, about 14 years in a sign, 164 years, 7 months, 14 days, 16 hours, 5 minutes, 23 seconds on his trip.

ATTRIBUTES OF THE SIGNS. Page 41.

PISCES-the fishes is the last of the water signs, and in the quarter of labor. It is a neutral, feminine, producing sign. Feb. 19th to March 20th inclusive.

PISCES

COLORS are white and green.

GEMS- are amethyst and hyacinth.

COUNTRIES its people are most likely to drift to, for pleasure or concealment of them selves or goods they care to conceal. Portugal, and all great cities near the sea.

PLACES, near large bodies of water, rivers, ponds, wells, cisterns, mills and wherever fish are kept.

TEMPER. Like all water signs, the natives of Pisces are, generally, slow to anger, but never forget and seldom forgive, a real severe, injury.

OCCUPATION: Good in agriculture, especially in the production of fruit and flowers, as these seem to grow for them without effort. They make good politicians, except, that they are given to fair promises, they do not expect to be called on to fullfill. They are often excellent business people, but should deal in liquids or products of the water.

DISCRIPTION; while this sign produces a variety of forms and shapes, the arms and legs of all will seem to be too short for the bodies. The distinct Pisces type is of short thickset build. The hand is short fingers long and boney and the life line has many nerve frays. The eye is generally dull and of gray color. Their cheif oddity is curiosity and love of knowledge, they must know what is going on in the world; they are also very nerveous and restless and if they are not moving about they will change the bed or room about, often.

ATTRIBUTES OF THE SIGNS. Page 42.

The ♑ people are very skeptical yet will cling to early teachings, until a new idea is forced upon them and they will then cling as tenaciously to that and yet they are always looking for knowle·dge in life nature, art and science. They seem to have a duel nature, hard to fathom, melancholy, restless, finding fault with themselves, slow to anger, kind hearted yet witty, cutting and sarcastic, social, eloquent, in writing or speach, good after dinner story tellers.

DISEASES, are of the stomach, heart, nerves, ears, eyes, liver, blood and feet. In northern latitudes he is of a lymphetic nervious temperme-nt, in a southern clime he is lymphetic bilious.

CHARACTERISTIC: No matter how well qual-ified, they lack confidence, and shrink before the public gaze, and often borrowing trouble, and fe-aring that which never comes. They make money but seldom keep it, and often conduct two kinds of business at one time. They generally marry twice and if any children a large family may be looked for. They generally leave the father's home at an early age and if they marry at all they marry twice. They generally, have more sisters than brothers, and loose one in early life; will contest for estate with step mother. Will travel much and change home and business many times; have many enemies and treacherous friends, and yet are confiding and loose thereby, and are often victems of bribery. They are long lived and die worth more than they ever expected to be worth.

ATTRIBUTES OF THE SIGNS. Page 43.

MARKS AND MOLES OF RISING SIGN.

That we may have every, possible, means at our hand to ascertain the time of day of birth, where it is not known, I give here the marks and moles supposed to be found on the human body when a sign or a part of a sign is on the ascendant. So far as my observation goes this does not always prove out, tho it does prove correct often enough to be of some service, at least as a testimony.

A person born when the first ten degrees of Aries is rising will have a small, raised, mole on the head among the hair. If the second decan be rising the wart, mark or mole will be found on the forehead; if the third part be rising it will be found near the chin. If found in these places a mark, mole or wart is likely to be found on the lower part of the body.

Taurus rising at birth, the first part, causes a mark of some sort on the front of the throat. This is supposed to threaten danger of falls and drowning. The second part rising, the mark will be found on the side of the throat. If the third part be rising it will be on the nap of the neck, but more prominent.

Gemini rising causes the marks on the arms, hands and shoulders. If the first part be rising the mark will be on the right arm near the shoulder; if the second part be rising it will be on the left arm above the elbow; if the third part be rising the mark will be on the right arm near the wrist.

ATTRIBUTES OF THE SIGNS. Page 44.

Cancer rising the mark will be found on the upper part of the right breast, of a whitish color, and generally having a hair or two in the center of it.

The second part rising causes the mark to be lower down on the breast; the third part of Cancer rising causes the mark to be nearly under the breast or on the pit of the stomach. A mole on the right breast is said to indicate good fortune, in agriculture, for a man and inheritence for a woman.

A mole under the left breast indicates, malignant high temper in a man, constancy and sorrow in a woman.

If Leo be on the ascendant the mark will be on the left breast, fiirst part ascending the mark will be high up, second part ascending it will be mid-way; if the third part be ascending the mark will be low down on the left breast.

When Virgo is rising the marks are found on the abdomen, if the first part is rising the mark will be found on the upper part of the stomach but if the second part be rising the marks will be near the navel, and if the third part be rising at birth it will be on the lower part of the belly; these moles are flat and of a reddish color.

When Libra is rising the marks are near the groins, generally raised like warts, and are small, soft and hairy; if the first part be rising at birth the mark will be on the right side; if the second part, it will on rhe left side, and if it be the third part rising, it will be more central.

ATTRIBUTES OF THE SIGNS. Page 45.

If Scorpio is rising nearly the same marks will be found but very low down and very dark of color.

Sagittarius rising causes the marks to be on the thighs; first part rising, causes it to be on the right thigh; second part over the left and third part on the back, over the hips.

Capricornus rising causes the marks on the knees; first part on the right knee; second part on the left knee and third part right under the knee.

It is said a mark on the knee denotes much travel and a peculiar marriage.

Aquarius rising causes the marks to be on the side or back of the leg, long in shape and dark in color; if the first part is rising it is on the right leg: second part on the left leg and if the third part is rising you may look for the mark on the ankles,

Pisces rising causes peculiar, reddish or brown spots on the feet: those on the right foot are caused by the first decan those on the left by the second, and the third decan rising causes the mark to be on the side or bottom of the foot.

It is said a mole on the right leg, below the knee denotes, to a man positon, honor, and success, throu his own merrit, if black sorrow caused by a woman, and to a woman it denotes a happy marriage.

The preceeding 3 pages are given that it may assist in getting the hour of birth, where it is not known, but the Solor Bioscope is an indispensable aid to any real astrologer, and the price, $5, is no comparison to its real valne, for casting a horoscope.

A TABLE

SHEWING WHAT PARTS OF MAN'S BODY EVERY PLANET SIGNIFIES IN THE TWELVE SIGNS.

SIGNS.	♄	♃	♂	☉	♀	☿	☽
♈	Breast Arms	Neck Throat Heart Bowels	Head Bowels Eyes	Thighs	Reins Feet	Secrets Legs	Head Knees
♉	Heart Breast Bowels	Neck Shoulders Arms Bowels	Throat Reins	Knees	Secret- Members Head	Thighs Feet	Throat Legs
♊	Heart Bowels	Breast Reins Secrets	Breast Arms Secrets	Legs Ancles	Throat Thighs	Head Knees	Shoulders Arms Thighs Feet
♋	Bowels Reins Secrets	Heart Secrets Thighs	Breast Feet	Feet	Arms Shoulders Knees	Eyes Throat Legs Knees	Head Breast Stomach
♌	Reins Secrets	Bowels Thighs Knees	Heart Bowels Knees	Head	Heart Breast Legs	Throat Arms Shoulders Feet	Arms Shoulders Bowels
♍	Thighs Secrets Feet	Reins Knees	Bowels Legs	Throat Neck	Stomach Heart Bowels Feet	Head Breast Heart	Arms Shoulders Bowels
♎	Knees Thighs	Head Eyes Secrets Legs	Reins Secrets Feet	Arms Shoulders	Head Intestines	Throat Heart Stomach Bowels	Breast Heart Reins Bowels
♏	Knees Legs	Thighs Feet	Head Arms Secrets Thighs	Breast Heart	Throat Reins Secrets	Arms Shoulders Back Bowels	Stomach Heart Bowels Secrets
♐	Legs Feet	Head Thighs Knees	Throat Hands Thighs Feet	Heart Bowels	Arms Shoulders Secrets Thighs	Breast Heart Reins Secrets	Back Bowels Thighs
♑	Head Feet	Eyes Neck Knees Legs	Arms Shoulders Knees Legs	Back Bowels	Breast Heart Thighs	Stomach Heart Secrets	Reins Thighs Knees
♒	Neck Head	Arms Shoulders Breast Feet	Breast Heart Legs	Reins Secrets	Heart Knees	Heart Bowels Thighs	Secrets Legs Ancles
♓	Arms Shoulders Neck	Head Breast Heart	Heart Bowels Ancles Feet	Secrets Thighs	Neck Throat Bowels Legs	Reins Secrets Thighs Knees	Thighs Feet

HOW TO CORRECT A NATIVITY. Pag 1

In ancient times when Astrology was more generally believed in than at present, the the doctor or midwife saw to it that the moment a chi'd was born, or at least at the 1st cry, the hour and minut, day of month and year were set down. in the fam, ily record, and later in the church record This was done chiefly for the benefit of the Astrolger. Because the rising sign. at birth will influence the child as much as the sign he was born in. In fact the greatest factors in astrological influenes are:

1st - The sign a person was born in.

2nd - The degree of birth of the zodiac.

3d - The sign rising at birth or hour of birth.

4th - The sign the Moon was in at birth.

5th - The planet in the sign the the child was born in. If no planet is there the planet ruling the sign is next in power. If several planets are in the sign and the planet ruling the sign is there, of course, he is the ruling star of the child, influenced by others. If the Lord of the sign is not in tne sign but several others are, the planet nearest the degree of birth is the ruler of the child.

Some set up the claim that the time of conception is the proper time to figure from, but this is a great mistake, for this reason. If the planets have any effect on us at all it must be throu vibration of the atoms composing our physical system, set in motion to the harmony or inharmony of the planets at a given time. As the physical body of the child

HOW TO CORRECT A NATIVITY. Page 2

is yet a part of the parents, at conception, it is controled by their vibrations alone. Thus if you are tracing heredity the time of conception is the time. Because it is known that the habits and desires most manifest in the father three months prior to conception will be prominent factors in the child's nature. On the other hand the first five months after conception the mother is stamping her nature upon the child. The true student, however, recogizes the fact that the child exerts a powerful influence on the mother, causing tastes and desiers to be manifest that were dorment or, actually repugnant, yet indcpendant action of the child cannot take place until the child is an independent creature, of our atmosphere.

As a child enters our atmosphere the lungs become inflated, it sets the phytical machinery in motion and causes the child to cry out. He is then independent of the parents vibrations and has set up vibrations of his own.

Because the Moon governs the mating period of animal life, Butler, in his "SolarBiology" gives a discription of the thots, feelings, and emotions of the parents at time of conception, with something of the nature of the child, but as a whole the period to judge from is the moment of birth.

To do accurate work the hour and minut of birth should be known; yet very few know it. Even tho the hour of birth may be set down, according to some sort of time piece, but that time piece may vary quite materially with Sun time, as the Sun is continually gaining on the clock the fore part of the year and loosing with it the latter part, and now since we have Standard time we never know just what is ment when a time is given.

I have a system I have worked out which has proved very satisfactory. In a case where nothing what ever was known of the date of birth I have worked it out. The year, the month, day of month, hour of day and day of week and afterward prov-ed, by church records to be correct. With the best system we are not always shure of getting nearer than the rising sign, even this is a wonderful aid in writing a horoscope.

The system relying on personal discription, or date of past events, alone, will never, never do.

I have found all ordinary methods fail. I have had quite a number of horoscopes cast and no two got very near and not one got it right tho they were given all necessary information, and they got as far as five signs apart. This system will, easily give the ascending sign and generally the minute.

INSTRUCTIONS.

Take the chart before you, with the colored di-agram away from you, and the sign Aries to your left. Now remember what constitutes the houses is the divisions of the earth which correspond with the signs of the Zodiac. We must, also, remember the heavens seem to revolve around the earth, while in fact the earth's revolutions make it appear so, therefore we will call the signs on the bed piece houses. Aries the first house. Taurus the second house, and so on around to Pices the twelveth.

We will now take, for example, a person born March 21st, any year. This is at the spring equin- ox and the days and nights are of the same length. This is the natnral positon of the earth to the Zo- diac. From that day on the day lengthens at the expence of the night, untill the 21st of June, then they shorten untill December 23d, but it should be remembered that September 23d the days and nights are of the same length again. For this reason the divisions on the revolving disk are of unequal proportions. It is because ofthis position of the ear- th that gives you intercepted signs. The turning of the disk either way will throw Aries and Libra, on the disk, as interocpted signs, that is a whole sign and a part of two others in one house. I do not consider this of any great importance, but I speak of it that you may understand its meaning.

Supposing a person was born at eleven o' clock A. M. You place the bla k hand on the line of Aries, of the revolving disk, and moove it to the first de- gree of the first house. If our accompanying table tells you it is just six o' clock A. M. You turn the dial, with the hand, to the right. tnrou Pisces to

Aquarius, that is just two hours, or 8 o' clock, turn once again to Capricornus, that is 10 o'clock. Now one hour, or half way throu Capricornus to 11 o'clock (see clock dial on outer circle.) Now look back to the line of the Eastern horizon or Aries, on the bed piece and you find the 20 degree of the sign Gemini on the ascendent.

This gives an example where everything is even and the hour known.

Now let us take one born on the 15th day of August at 2 - 15 P. M. any year. By looking at the calander, any year, we find the Sun rises about 7 minutes after 5 A. M. This will not vary greatly in any locality between Latitude 22 an 55 where the greater number of pecple are born.

Now notice the circle of months just under the clock dial, place the black hand on the 15th day of August, on the bed piece and run the eye down to the inside er lower circle on the bed piece, you will find the degrees of the Zodiac, looking down on the inner side of the black hand and you find a person born August 15th was bern 24 degrees in Leo on the revolving disk. Now turn the disk so the 24th degree and the black hand come on the Eastern herizon er 1st degree of Aries, on the deb piece. We have found the Sun in its, apparant, daily revolutions every two hours passes throu one whole sign. By our table we found the Sun rises at 5 o' clock and 6 minuts therefor the first two hours brings you 7 o' clock and 6 minutes or the line of Aquarius - second move two hours more 9 o' clock and 6 minutes or the line of Capricornus, next two hours to the line of Sagittarius, next to Scorpio. Now we have to move forward one hour and nine minutes. We find under the clock dial or circle of spaces of 5 minutes each. As the clock dial cannot be shifted we must assume the figure 1 is two o' clock as we have already 6 minnts we advance 9 minutes more, as near as can be calculated, and we look to the Eastern horizen. on the bed piece and we find the 18th degree of Capricornus rising.

So far we have been figuring for a person where the hour of birth is known. Before we proceed let us understand the ascendant is all that space of 30 degrees under the Eastern horizon. Therefore the last example showes the person to be a Leo character, influenced by the 18th to 30th degree of Sagittarius and from 1 to 15 degrees of Capricornus. We will suppose the person had the Moon in Libra any where from 1 to 30 degrees and you will add a strong Libra nature. Thus by this combination its self we get a strong type of character without taking cognizance of the influence of the rest of the planets. Let us rember this as it will aid us in getting the rising sign where the hour of birth is not known.

We will now suppose we have to write a horoscope for one where the hour of birth is not known.

In such a case we should have the person with us to talk to, or a considerabl correspondence will be necessary, which would be the case with any system where proper data is not given.

Suppose the applicant says " I was born June 7 th 1872 but I do not know anything at all about the hour."

By the old system we look over the signs to see which, the best, discribes the personal apperance of the applicant; then to prove up our work we ask him the date of some accident. or death of the father, marriage, or any important event cf life, and then we figure by directions when these things ought to have taken place, and so by a slow and a tedious process we arrive at a conclusion which may be right or it may be wrong and I have more often found it wrong than right, and for my self, astrologers seldom hit the mark, nor do I say this system is infallib'e. But, I have becn able to get the ascending degree oftener than by any other means, and I do it in this way.

I know that each sign causes certain peculiarities in those born under a sign, or that has that specified sign rising or the Moon in that sign. So I say a person born June 7th was born full in the sign Gemini. I find the Moon was 11 degrees in Scorpio, so I know, he so far, has a Gemini Scorpio nature. I now tell him the different signs express their wn attributes when on the ascendant, so I read to him the atributs of the 12 signs and ask which strikes him nearest.

THE ATRIBUTES OF THE SIGNS.

ARIES produces one spirited, independent, very fond of music, but rarely a performer, but if one, is generally a good one. He is graceful, quick of step, neat in attire, generally slender built, sharp features, and long neck. He is fierce but forgiving. We fequently find Aries people with sandy or red hair, and often curley. Nearly always can show scars on the head or face. The eyes are bright but very often weak. When taken sick they first feel it in the head and stomach. Alamost invariably they have the squre and useful type of hand and the head line runs into the life line which shows a lack of confidence in themselves, early in life, and if born before noon they generally loose the father before ten years of age. If born between noon and midnight the native's friends are alamost shure to use influence to get him high position.

Physical temperment is, if born in a northern latitude, bilions-sanguine, if born in a suthern clime he is of nervous-bilious temperament.

The preceeding 8 pages of "How to correct a nativity." properly belong with the "Solor Bioscope" and the balance of the instructions will be found under the heading of "Influence of the twelve signs of the Zodiac."

One born by day light, in clasping the hands will place the right thumb over the left and those born in the dark hours place the left over the right.

THE TIME OF SUNRISE.

Time of Sunrise in the various localities is a very important matter to astrologers hence here is the time of Sun rise' within a few minutes, in the following named places. Mass. So. N. H. Vt. Con't. N. Y. Lower Mich. Wis So. Minn. So. Dak. Idaho. and Origon, and a few minutes later in Northen N. H. & N. Y. Upper Mich. Wis. & Minn. No. Dak. Montana, and state of Washington.

With our Solar Bioscope and accompanying tables, we make it possible, and quite easy to find the ascending degree and thereby the hour of birth, between latitude 22 and 55 where the great majority of people are born. Of course where the Long. and Lat. of birth is known 15 degrees of Lat. to the hour is easily calculated. The 8 pages "How to correct a nativity," refering to a chart, properly belongs to he Solar Bioscpoe, and Helio Ephemeries.

	JAN.	FEB.	MAR.	APR.	MAY	JUN	JUL.	AUG.	SEP.	OCT.	NOV.	DEC.
1	7 31	7 15	6 36	5 42	4 55	4 26	4 28	4 55	5 27	5 59	6 34	7 12
2	7 31	7 14	6 34	5 40	4 53	4 26	4 28	4 55	5 28	5 59	6 33	7 12
3	7 31	7 13	6 32	5 39	4 51	4 26	4 29	4 56	5 29	5 59	6 36	7 13
4	7 31	7 12	6 30	5 38	4 51	4 25	4 29	4 57	5 29	6 03	6 37	7 14
5	7 31	7 11	6 29	5 36	4 50	4 25	4 30	4 58	5 31	6 03	6 39	7 15
6	7 30	7 10	6 27	5 34	4 48	4 24	4 31	4 59	5 32	6 04	6 39	7 16
7	7 30	7 08	6 25	5 32	4 47	4 23	4 32	4 59	5 33	6 05	6 41	7 16
8	7 30	7 07	6 24	5 31	4 46	4 23	4 32	5 01	5 34	6 07	6 43	7 18
9	7 30	7 07	6 22	5 29	4 44	4 23	4 33	5 02	5 35	6 07	6 44	7 20
10	7 30	7 05	6 20	5 27	4 44	4 23	4 34	5 03	5 36	6 08	6 46	7 20
11	7 30	7 03	6 19	5 26	4 43	4 23	4 35	5 04	5 37	6 09	6 47	7 21
12	7 29	7 02	6 17	5 24	4 42	4 22	4 35	5 06	5 38	6 11	6 49	7 22
13	7 29	7 00	6 15	5 22	4 41	4 22	4 36	5 07	5 40	6 11	6 51	7 23
14	7 28	6 59	6 14	5 20	4 40	4 22	4 37	5 08	5 41	6 13	6 53	7 24
15	7 28	6 58	6 12	5 19	4 39	4 22	4 38	5 09	5 42	6 14	6 54	7 25
16	7 27	6 57	6 10	5 18	4 38	4 23	4 39	5 09	5 43	6 14	6 55	7 25
17	7 27	6 55	6 08	5 17	4 37	4 24	4 40	5 11	5 43	6 16	6 56	7 26
18	7 27	6 54	6 07	5 15	4 36	4 24	4 40	5 13	5 44	6 16	6 58	7 26
19	7 26	6 52	6 05	5 13	4 35	4 24	4 41	5 14	5 46	6 18	6 59	7 26
20	7 25	6 51	6 03	5 11	4 34	4 24	4 42	5 14	5 47	6 20	7 00	7 27
21	7 25	6 49	6 01	5 09	4 33	4 24	4 43	5 14	5 48	6 21	7 02	7 28
22	7 23	6 47	6 00	5 08	4 32	4 24	4 44	5 16	5 48	6 22	7 03	7 28
23	7 23	6 45	5 58	5 06	4 31	4 24	4 45	5 17	5 48	6 23	7 03	7 28
24	7 22	6 45	5 56	5 05	4 31	4 24	4 46	5 18	5 51	6 24	7 04	7 28
25	7 22	6 43	5 54	5 03	4 30	4 26	4 47	5 19	5 52	6 25	7 05	7 29
26	7 21	6 42	5 53	5 02	4 29	4 26	4 47	5 21	5 53	6 27	7 06	7 29
27	7 20	6 40	5 51	5 01	4 29	4 27	4 49	5 21	5 54	6 27	7 07	7 30
28	7 19	6 38	5 49	4 59	4 28	4 27	4 50	5 22	5 55	6 29	7 08	7 30
29	7 18		5 47	4 58	4 28	4 27	4 51	5 24	5 56	6 30	7 09	7 31
30	7 18		5 46	4 56	4 26	4 27	4 52	5 25	5 58	6 31	7 10	7 32
31	7 16		5 44		4 26		4 53	5 26	—	6 32		7 32

Lunar time 354⅓ days in a year, Solar time 365¼ days days. Astronomical or prophetic time 360 days "time, times and a half a time" 1260 Astronomical years.

STANDARD TIME AND SUN TIME.

To read the hour book properly we must use sun time. Standard time was adopted by the railroads at noon November 8th 1883. As the United States extends from 60 to 125 degrees West longitude and there is four minuts difference in time in each degree of longitude. It created confusion among railroad time peaces and so increased the dangers to railroad property and to the travling public. To overcome this the United States was devided in-to four time belts called meridians. The change in-to mean or sun time can be made as follows. For any place east of one of the standard meridians and taking that meridians time, subtract four minuts for evry degree of longitude east, and for any place west of the meridian add four minuts for each degree.

Fredric White published, in the Adept, the very usefnl table found on the next page.

EASTERN STANDARD, 75 DEG. W. OF GREENWICH.

Albany, N. Y.	add	5m.	Newport, R. I.	add	15m
Augusta, Me.	"	21	Philadelphia, Pa.	sub.	1
Bangor, Me.	"	25	Pittsburg, Pa.	"	20
Boston, Mass.	"	16	Portland, Me.	add	19
Baltimore, Md.	sub.	6	Providence, R. I.	"	14
Buffalo, N. Y.	"	16	Rochester, N. Y.	sub.	11
Concord, N. H.	add	14	Springfield, Mass.	add	10
Hartford, Conn.	"	9	Syracuse, N. Y.	sub.	5
Montreal, Canada,	"	6	Utica, N. Y.	"	1
Montpelier, Vt.	"	10	Washington, D. C.	"	8
New London, Conn.	"	11	Quebec, Canada,	add	14
New York City,	"	4			

CENTRAL STANDARD, 90 DEG. W. OF GREENWICH.

Burlington, Ia.	sub.	5m.	Leavenworth, Kan.	sub.	22m
Chicago, Illinois,	add	10	Louisville, Ky.	add	18
Cincinnati, Ohio,	"	22	Memphis, Tenn.	"	0
Cleveland, Ohio,	"	33	Milwaukee, Wis.	"	8
Columbus, Ohio,	"	28	New Orleans, La.	"	0
Dayton, Ohio,	"	23	Omaha, Neb.	sub.	24
Detroit, Mich.	"	28	Rock Island, Ill.	"	3
Des Moines, Ia.	sub.	14	St. Louis, Mo.	"	1
Dubuque, Ia.	"	3	Springfield, Ill.	add	2
Galveston, Texas,	"	19	St. Paul, Minn.	sub.	12
Indianapolis, Ind.	add	16	Toledo, Ohio,	add	26
Kansas City, Mo.	sub.	18	Topeka, Kansas	sub.	23

MOUNTAIN STANDARD, 105 DEG. W.

Albuquerque, N. M.	sub.	7m.	Prescott, Ariz.	sub.	30m
Denver, Colo.	"	0	Salt Lake City, Utah	"	28
Georgetown, Colo.	"	3	Sante Fe, N. M.	"	4
Helena, Mont.	"	27	Virginia City, Mont.	"	30
Ogden, Utah,	"	29	Minneapolis, Minn.	"	12

PACIFIC STANDARD, 120 DEG. W.

Carson City, Nev.	add	1m.	Salem, Ore.	sub.	11m
Grass Valley, Cal.	sub.	4	San Francisco, Cal.	"	10
Los Angeles, Cal.	add	7	San Jose, Cal.	"	7
Marysville, Cal.	sub.	7	Santa Barbara, Cal.	"	0
Oakland, Cal.	"	8	Stockton, Cal.	"	5
Olympia, Wash.	"	10	Seattle, Wash.	"	9
Portland, Ore.	"	10	Vallejo, Cal.	"	9
Port Townsend, W.	"	11	Victoria, B. C.	"	13
Sacramento, Cal.	"	6			

COMPARATIVE TIME.

EXPLANATION OF THE ABOVE CHARTE

The centeral figure of the cut is the clock dial stanbing 12 o'c. Noon at Washington D. C. The elock dials surr unding it show time of day at each of the named places under the dial. When it is noon at Washington it is 12 minuts after I2 at New York, the dial at the top. The second or next dial to the right is Chicago which stands 18 minuts after 11 A. M. the 3d following to the right is New Orleans which stanbs 8 minuts after 11 A. M. The 4 th to the right is San Francisco Cal. which stands 3 minuts to 9 o'c A. M. The next direct at bottom is Vianna Austra, the dial stands at 15 m to 6 o'c P. M. The 6 th dial is Berlin time 2 minuts. to 6 P. M. The 7 th is Paris time 17 m. after 6 P. M. The 8 th is London England, the dial stands at 10 iminuts after 5 o'c. P. M.

Outside of the circle of dials give the verses of the 49 th chadter of Genisis whre Jacob blesses his twelve s ns, in which he gives the atributes of the twelve signs of the Zodiac, all of which is explained in the book "Bible Astrology." This is a book of wonders, published by the Astrological publishing co. Still out side of that is a larger clock dial, with the storry of the Prodigal son as explained in the above mentioned book. This wonderfull book will show that astrological symbols are older than any written history, as they are found ingraved on the pyramids and obliska of Egypt and the temples of India, which antedate all written history including the Bible. It will also show that the circle crisent and cross are symbols of all religeon and that these symbols are astrological. It will also show astrologey is the baces of Freeemasonry and all other secret organizations. Astrology is also the father of the sun dial and clock dial, and that the christian religeon, including the trinity, the Father, Son and Holy Ghost and the 12 deciples are all to be found on the watch dial.

DIVISIONS OF TIME.

A calendar month varies from 28 to 31 days.

A mean lunar month is 29 days, 12 hours, 44 minutes, 2 seconds and a small fraction.

TRUE TIME.—There are two kinds of time: clock, or mean time; and apparent, or sun time. Clock time is always right, while sun time varies every day; the sun very seldom being on meridian at twelve o'clock. A Solar day differs in length, owing to the ellipticity of the earth's orbit, etc.; but a mean Solar day, as recorded by clock time, is 24 hours long.

An astronomical day begins at noon, and is counted from the first to the twenty-fourth hour.

A civil day commences at midnight, and is counted from the first to the twelfth hour.

A nautical day is counted as a civil day, but commences, like an astronomical day, at noon.

COMPARATIVE TIME FOR ONE-HALF WAY AROUND THE GLOBE.

When it is noon in Washington, the mean time in each of the cities will be given below.

	P. M.			A. M.	
Moscow, Russia,	7h.	38m.	Montgomery, Ala.	11h.	23m
Constantinople, Tur.	7	4	Nashville, Tenn.	11	21
Berlin, Germany,	6	2	Chicago, Illinois.	11	18
Rome, Italy,	5	58	Mobile, Alabama,	11	16
Paris, France,	5	18	Memphis, Tenn.	11	8
London, England,	5	8	New Orleans, La.	11	8
Halifax, N. S.	12	54	St. Louis, Mo.	11	7
St. John, N. B.	12	44	Davenport, Iowa,	11	6
Bangor, Maine,	12	33	La Crosse, Wis.	11	3
Portland, Maine,	12	27	St. Paul, Minn.	10	56
Boston, Mass.	12	24	Des Moines, Iowa,	10	53
Quebec, Canada,	12	23	Kansas City, Mo.	10	50
Providence, R. I.	12	23	St. Joseph, Mo.	10	49
Concord, N. H.	12	22	Galveston, Texas,	10	49
Montpelier, Vt.	12	18	Omaha, Nebraska,	10	44
Hartford, Conn.	12	17	Vera Cruz, Mexico,	10	44
New Haven, Conn.	12	16	Dallas, Texas,	10	41
Montreal, Canada,	12	14	Yankton, D.	10	39
Albany, N. Y.	12	13	San Antonio, Tex.	10	34
New York City,	12	12	City of Mexico,	10	32
Philadelphia, Pa.	12	8	Deadwood, D.	10	12
Baltimore, Md.	12	2	Cheyenne, Wy.	10	9
	A. M.		Denver, Colorado,	10	8
Richmond, Va.	11	58	Salt Lake City, U.T.	9	41
Raleigh, N. C.	11	53	Virginia City, Nev.	9	10
Charleston, S. C.	11	48	Prescott, Arizona.	9	38
Savannah, Ga.	11	44	San Diego, Calif.	9	19
Cleveland, Ohio,	11	41	Los Angeles, Calif.	9	15
Havana, Cuba,	11	39	Sacramento, Calif.	9	2
Detroit, Michigan,	11	36	San Francisco, Calif.	8	59
Atlanta, Georgia,	11	31	Seattle, W.	8	59
Cincinnati, Ohio,	11	30	Portland, Oregon,	8	58
Louisville, Ky.	11	26	Honolulu, Sand. Is.	6	37
Indianapolis, Ind.	11	24			

GOOD AND EVIL PERIODS.

Who has not noticed that he has periods when everything runs smooth and pleasant, then again strive as you will you cannot make headway and everything goes wrong?

Some overwise fellow says: "I don't believe in luck. I take hold and push and make my luck. There is no such thing as luck."

But let this man meet with a few reverses and he wil swear his failure was through no fault of his own, and he is ready to damn his bad luck, and make excuses for his failure.

Comercial statistics show that from 95 to 98 per cent of all business men fail soner or later. This is a terrible percentage. Why is it so? The answer is plain.

The moment a man sees things going wrong, instead of stopping and resting, he takes the advices of his friends, who are ignorant of the conditions, to push the harder, and he takes greater risks and loses all. Like a horse floundering in the quicksand, the more he struggles the deeper he gets.

What a lesson may be learned from occasional card playing for amusement.

Who that plays cards has not noticed how, at times, everything runs in his favor, he seems to win without half trying,. while at another time, he can't get a good hand of cards to save his neck. He changes the shuffle, he changes the cut, he changes partners, yet he cannot win a game. Would not a gambler be very unwise to continue to play when luck is against him? Yet he generally persists until he loses every cent before the luck turns. Just so with business men. Would it not be a grand thing to know when we may look for good and evil periods and wise to take advantage of them?

Good and evil periods may be classed as follows:

Good and evil hours of the day.

Good and evil days of the week.

Good and evil months of the year.

Good and evil years of a life time.

Good and evil cycles of 7 years each.

Every ninth year there is a change of circumstnces generally for the better, or turns out so in the end.

It is often said "History repeats itself."

The observer will notice, his life seems to run in circles; or conditions are ofttimes repeated, though not in just the same form as at first experienced.

The meaning of planitary influence is this: The universe is composed of elementary atoms and organic structures, and nobody is independent of all other bodies, but on the contrary, one body is effected more or less by every other body, according to bulk, distance, weight and directness of rays or vibration. Just as the sound is brought to your ear, the light to your eye, and heat to the system, through vibration of the ultimate atoms of surrounding mater and in your system, so are good and evil conditions caused by the harmonious or inharmonious vibrations of the ultimate atoms in your system, caused by changing positions of the heavenly bodies.

GOOD AND EVIL DAYS.

Why has Friday been generally considered an evil day? Because Christ was crucified on Friday and from time beyond record, Friday has been designated as hang man's day or day of execution of criminals. But Friday is no more an evil day than any other day, except for those born on Sunday. But a person born any other day of the week will experience his Friday the sixth day after birth and every seventh day thereafter.

A person born on Sunday, Friday and Saturday are his unfortunate days, Sunday and Wednesday his best days, though all days between evil days are called good. Those born on Monday, Saturdays and Sundays are the evil days, Mondays and Thursdays the best.

Born on Tuesday, Sunday and Monday are the evil days. Ask any Tuesday born person if Sunday is not a lonesome day and he will tell you yes. Tuesdays and Fridays are his best.

Born on Wednesday—Mondays and Tuesdays are the evil days and Wednesdays and Saturdays best.

If born on Thursay, Tuesdays and Wednesdays are the evil days and Thursday and Sundays the best days.

If born on Friday, then Wednesdays and Thursdays are the evil days and Fridays and Mondays the best days.

If born on Saturday, Thursdays and Fridays are the evil days and Saturdays and Tuesdays the best days. The reason given is because God finished His labors on the sixth day and rested on the seventh, hence man is always tired and does not feel so well on the sixth and seventh days after birth. But it is not unreasonable that man has his good and evil cycles. Though good may come on an evil day or evil on a good day, brought about by greater vibratory influences of changing planitary positions.

Sometimes one's own ruling planet may cause an evil day to be partly good and partly evil, or the good and evil days mentioned as belonging to a sign may come with the 1st, 4th, 6th and 7th days of birth so change the influence partly, but it is never safe to start an enterprise or take risks of any kind on the 6th or 7th dav after birth, while it is generally fortunate to take risks the 1st, 3rd and 4th days of birth, other things being equal.

INFLUENCE OF THE HEAVENLY BODIES ON THE DAYS OF THE WEEK.

From most ancient records Astrologers have claimed the days of the week are presided over by the heavenly bodies, and in some instances, as stated on page 2 of this book, these bodies were called angels and their names given as stated.

If every atom is a thinker, as modern occult scientists claim, all [illegible] bodies are kingdoms of thought of less or greater power than our own. Then it is not unreosonable to suppose the heavenly bodies are great bodies of thought which may be playing, each his part in the drama of Gods plan. Be that as it may, the Sun rules Sunday, and by the advice of an Astrologer Sunday is and has been a day of religious observance for nearly two thousand years. See quotation of Constantine's edict, in article on the Moon.

In nearly all languages, including our own, the days of the week are named after these planets. Sunday, after the Sun, and which is ruled by the Sun, which is the largest body of our Solar system and should rule the first day of the week. I have found it to be a fact that Sunday born people are generally dignified or else full of life or mental force and are generally more fortunate than those born on other days of the week.

Webster's Dictionary says MONDAY OR MOON'S day is so named after the Moon. Monday is ruled over by the Moon. Monday born people are generally very active and changeable, generally good talkers. Any person who is a great talker must have the Moon in a position to produce such an effect. If he be a reasoner, the Moon is assisted by Mercury, or Saturn. If a chater box the first two planets are evily aspected.

MARS rules Tuesday. In the English Tuesday is derived from the Anglo-Saxon *Tiwsdaeg*, or the day of Tiw, the God of war, which is identified with Mars, the Go of war.

TUESDAY born people are restless, active, aggressive, generally die by violence or accident or die suddenly, with no time to repent or pray.

WEDNESDAY is ruled over by MERCURY. Wednesday is derived from the Anglo-Saxon *Wednesdaeg*, and is atranslation of the Latin dies. *Mercurii*, Mercury's day, which was a day of marketing; rapid exchanges. Mercury was called the messenger of the Gods. The Astrologers call him a two-faced planet, because he acts good with a good planet and evil with an evil planet. How apprropriate to preside over a day of trade. Business knows no friends; he skins them all. WEDNESDAY born people are generally sharp traders, and successful in small business, or small advertising. This is a good day to trade, put out circulars and advertise.

THURSDAY is presided over by Jupiter, the God of wealth. Thursday is derived from the Norse word Thor, the Son of Odin, who presided over all the mischevious spirits of the air. He was considered the God of thunder. It is the same as the Greek and French *Juno* or Jupiter. Webster says: "From his name we get Thursday. Great wealth is generally amassed through trickery and pretentions of doing great public good. THURSDAY born people are next in god luck to Sunday born people, and they generally live to old age, if they live to middle life. In business they are most successful in large deals or enterprises. Their intentions are good, but if pressed their wealth comes in before honor.

FRIDAY is presided over by Venus the Goddess of love. Webster says: "The Goddess of marriage, equivalent to the Latin Juno, the wife of Odin or wooden. Frim this we get Friday, German Fridag or vrydag. FRIDAY—Both the strength and weakness of Friday born people is in their love and strong devotion or the other extreme, their fickleness.

SATURDAY is ruled over by the evil planet Saturn. Webster says: "Saturday derives its name from the name Saturn. Saturn in the Greek, Teetan, power; Chaladia, Sheetan; Babylonian, Saturn; finally Saten. The planet Saturn is a great spiritual planet, a tempter or developing planet. SATURDAY born people are generally hard workers or the other extreme, and will do no more than they have to. They seldom marry early in life or die young if they do. Saturday is said to be the most unfortunate day of the week to be born on, though not so bad if born before sunrise. SATURDAY born people are unusually bright, and of course sometimes fortunate, as neither an evil cycle, year, day or hour can be taken as a guide, alone, for one may upset the other or a very good or evil planetary position may in a measure interfere.

Further on will be found that the age of the Moon has something to do with a person's good or evil fortune through life, effecting the hours and days especially.

Before we discuss the good and evil years and cycles, I will present a perpetual calendar for getting the day of the week. For any day of the month from the adoption of the new style, 1752, to as long as the present system runs, or to eternity of past and future, by simply taking a date of the past or future and dividing by 28, using the accompanying tables as a guide.

Good and evil periods of short duration are produced by changing position of the Moon or transits of planets over their own positions at birth, called the radix, or over their own periods, called nodes.

As every heavenly body in our Solar system is in motion, all traveling in circles, or eliptical circles, they seem to pass over about the same position at regular periods. The Sun is said to make his circuit of the Zodiac in 25,920 of our Solar years, or 26,000 Zodiacal years. His North Node is the 1st degree of Cancer and his South Node the first degree of Capricornus, and it is believed by some of the world's best thinkers that the earth changes its poles twice in that length of time and civilization is blotted out. see "Bbile Astrology."

The Sun's satelites make their circuits around the Sun as follows:

MERCURY, in 87¾ days. Her North Node is 23 degrees of Taurus; her South Node is 23 degrees of Scorpio.

VENUS makes her circuit in 225 days. Her North Node begins the 17th degree of Gemini; South Node 17 degrees of Sagittarus.

MRS makes his circuit in 687 days and he begins his North Node 20 degrees of Taurus; his South Node 20 degrees of Scorpio.

JUPITER makes his trip in about 12 years. He enters his North Node 9 degrees of Cancer; his South Node 9 degrees of Capricornus.

SATURN makes his trip in 29½ years, and enters his North Node 22 degrees of Cancer, and his South Node 2 degrees of Capricornus.

URANUS makes his trip in 84 years, and enters his North Node 13 degrees of Gemini, and his South Node 13 degrees of Sagittarius.

NEPTUNE makes her trip in about 165 years and enters her North Node the 10th degree of Leo, and her South Node 10 degrees of Aquarius.

The planets do not return over exactly the same places at each circuit, but have their periods of return over approximately the same places when they produce similar effects.

The MOON makes her trip around the earth in about 27½ days, but her Node is continually moving backward, hence her period of getting back to the same place is 19 years. Mars period is also 19 years, so that any person born closely under the influence of the Nodes of Mars or the Moon will find 19 a very unfortunate number and every 19 years, or their 19th, 38th, 57th, 76th and 95th years very dangerous years. But it is not my intention to refer to good and evil periods which come irregularly, as they are not what I term certain or of definite force.

EXPLANATION OF PERPETUAL CALENDAR.

It was necessary to digress here to reach the explanation of the periods affecting man and to show the days of the week come on the some day of the month every 28 years. Thus it is possible to present a perpetual calendar as follows:

The table No. 1, or "Calendar of Years," contains the years in succession down the column from top to bottom, from 1753 to the year 2000. Run down the column of years until you find the year you want. Now notice at the left of the lines, running from left to right, the lines are numbered. Take the same number of line in which the year is on and go to table No. 2, or "Calendar of Months," with days of week under. Select the desired column and run down the column to the number of the line on which you found the year, and you will find the day of the week, the month stated on. Now go to table No. 3, or "Calendar of Days," and select the column which starts with the day of the week, the month started with, and run down to the day of month reuired and you have the day of week sought after.

EXAMPLE.—Look for the day of the week of April 2nd, 1843. You find 1843 in the 4th colmun, 23rd line; now go to 23rd line in "Calendar of Months" and run the eye out to the right to the column headed April and you find at the junction Saturday. Thus April started the month on Saturday. Now go to the 3rd table, or "Calendar of Days" of week and select the column headed Saturday and run down to the 2nd of the month and the day sought for was April 2nd, Sunday; so by dividing the years prior to 1753 or subsequent to 2000 by 28 this table can be used to all eternity of the past or future, according to our system of reckoning time. All of the years in the lines on which the letter L comes at the right of the calendar of years are Leap years, thus at a glance it is easy to find what years are Leap years, for all time, as the Leap years will always come on one of the Leap year lines.

Now to find what planet rules any given year, look for Su. for Sun, Mo. for Moon, Mu. for Mercury, Ve. for Venus, Ma. for Mars, Ju. for Jupiter, Sa. for Saturn. The planet rules the year by which these letters are found to the right of the year.

The Egyptian Cycle or Circle System, or in other words Astrological Periodicity is based on returning periods of the planets and days of the week which are also but another phase of repetition so often refered to as history repeating its self.

TABLE No. 1 OR CALANDER OF YEARS.

From 1753 to 2000, in 10 columns and 28 lines.

Every year on a line with the letter L is a leap year.

Cycles of planets and days of week. The 1-15-22-29 of any mo. comes same day of week.

No.									
1	1753—1781	....	1821—Su.	1849—Su.	1877—Su.	....	1917—Ju.	1945—Ju.	1973........
2	1754—1782	....	1822—Ve.	1850—Ve.	1878—Ve.	....	1918—Ma.	1946—Ma.	1974........
3	1755—1783	....	1823—Mu.	1851—Mu.	1879—Mu.	....	1919—Su.	1947—Su.	1975........
4	1756—1784	....	1824—Mo.	1852—Mo.	1880—Mo.	....	1920—Ve.	1948—Ve.	1976...L...
5	1757—1785	....	1825—Sa.	1853—Sa.	1881—Sa.	....	1921—Mu.	1949—Mu.	1977........
6	1758—1786	....	1826—Ju.	1854—Ju.	1882—Ju.	....	1922—Mo.	1950—Mo.	1978........
7	1759—1787	....	1827—Ma.	1855—Ma.	1883—Ma.	....	1923—Sa.	1951—Sa.	1979........
8	1760—1788	....	1828—Su.	1856—Su.	1884—Su.	....	1924—Ju.	1952—Ju.	1980...L...
9	1761—1789	1801-Ve.	1829—Ve.	1857—Ve.	1885—Ve.	....	1925—Ma.	1953—Ma.	1981........
10	1762—1790	1802-Mu.	1830—Mu.	1858—Mu.	1886—Mu.	....	1926—Su.	1954—Su.	1982........
11	1763—1791	1803-Mo.	1831—Mo.	1859—Mo.	1887—Mo.	....	1927—Ve.	1955—Ve.	1983........
12	1764—1792	1804-Sa.	1832—St.	1860—Sa.	1888—Sa.	....	1928—Mu.	1956—Mu.	1984....L...
13	1765—1793	1805-Ju.	1833—Ju.	1861—Ju.	1889—Ju.	1901—Mo.	1929—Mo.	1957—Mo.	1985........
14	1766—1794	1806-Ma.	1834—Ma.	1862—Ma.	1890—Ma.	1902—Sa.	1930—Sa.	1958—Sa.	1986........
15	1767—1795	1807-Su.	1835—Su.	1863—Su.	1891—Su.	1903—Ju.	1931—Ju.	1959—Ju.	1987........
16	1768—1796	1808-Ve.	1836—Ve.	1864—Ve.	1892—Ve.	1904—Ma.	1932—Ma.	1960—Ma.	1988...L...
17	1769—1797	1809-Mu.	1837—Mu.	1865—Mu.	1893—Mu.	1905—Su.	1933—Su.	1961—Su.	1989........
18	1770—1798	1810-Mo.	1838—Mo.	1866—Mo.	1894—Mo.	1906—Ve.	1934—Ve.	1962—Ve.	1990........
19	1771—1799	1811-Sa.	1839—Sa.	1867—Sa.	1895—Sa.	1907—Mu.	1935—Mu.	1963—Mu.	1991........
20	1772—1800	1812-Ju.	1840—Ju.	1868—Ju.	1896—Ju.	1908—Mo.	1936—Mo.	1964—Mo.	1992...L...
21	1773......	1813-Ma.	1841—Ma.	1869—Ma.	1897—Ma.	1909—Sa.	1937—Sa.	1965—Sa.	1993........
22	1774......	1814-Su.	1842—Su.	1870—Su.	1898—Su.	1910—Ju.	1938—Ju.	1966—Ju.	1994........
23	1775......	1815-Ve.	1843—Ve.	1871—Ve.	1899—Ve.	1911—Ma.	1939—Ma.	1967—Ma.	1995........
24	1776......	1816-Mu.	1844—Mu.	1872—Mu.	1900—Mu.	1912—Su.	1940—Su.	1968—Su.	1996...L...
25	1777......	1817-Mo.	1845—Mo.	1873—Mo.	....	1913—Ve.	1941—Ve.	1969—Ve.	1997........
26	1778......	1818-Sa.	1846—Sa.	1874—Sa.	....	1914—Mu.	1942—Mu.	1970—Mu.	1998........
27	1779......	1819-Ju.	1847—Ju.	1875—Ju.	....	1915—Mo.	1943—Mo.	1971—Mo.	1999........
28	1780......	1820-Ma.	1848—Ma.	1876—Ma.	....	1916—Sa.	1944—Sa.	1972—Sa.	2000...L...

TABLE No. 2 OR CALANDER OF MONTHS.

Multeply the year on any line by 28 and the days of the week will come on the same date of month, and this may go on to eternity.

	Jan.	Feb.	Mar.	Apr.	May	June	July	Aug.	Sept.	Oct.	Nov.	Dec.
1	Mon.	Thu.	Thu.	Sun.	Tue.	Fri.	Sun.	Wed.	Sat.	Mon.	Thu.	Sat.
2	Tue.	Fri.	Fri.	Mon.	Wed.	Sat.	Mon.	Thu.	Sun.	Tue.	Fri.	Sun.
3	Wed.	Sat.	Sat.	Tue.	Thu.	Sun.	Tue.	Fri.	Mon.	Wed.	Sat.	Mon.
4	Thu.	Sun.	Mon.	Thu.	Sat.	Tue.	Thu.	Sun.	Wed.	Fri.	Mon.	Wed.
5	Sat.	Tue.	Tue.	Fri.	Sun.	Wed.	Fri.	Mon.	Thu.	Sat.	Tue.	Thu.
6	Sun.	Wed.	Wed.	Sat.	Mon.	Thu.	Sat.	Tue.	Fri.	Sun	Wed.	Fri.
7	Mon.	Thu.	Thu.	Sun.	Tue.	Fri.	Sun.	Wed.	Sat.	Mon.	Thu.	Sat.
8	Tue.	Fri.	Sat.	Tue.	Thu.	Sun.	Tue.	Fri.	Mon.	Wed.	Sat.	Mon.
9	Thu.	Sun.	Sun.	Wed.	Fri.	Mon.	Wed.	Sat.	Tue.	Thu.	Sun.	Tue.
10	Fri.	Mon.	Mon.	Thu.	Sat.	Tue.	Thu.	Sun.	Wed.	Fri.	Mon.	Wed.
11	Sat.	Tue.	Tue.	Fri.	Sun.	Wed.	Fri.	Mon.	Thu.	Sat.	Tue.	Thu.
12	Sun.	Wed.	Thu.	Sun.	Tue.	Fri.	Sun.	Wed.	Sat.	Mon.	Thu.	Sat.
13	Tue.	Fri.	Fri.	Mon.	Wed.	Sat.	Mon.	Thu.	Sun.	Tue.	Fri.	Sun.
14	Wed.	Sat.	Sat.	Tue.	Thu.	Sun.	Tue.	Fri.	Mon.	Thu.	Sat.	Mon.
15	Thu.	Sun.	Sun.	Wed.	Fri.	Mon.	Wed.	Sat.	Tue.	Thu.	Sun.	Tue.
16	Fri.	Mon.	Tue.	Fri.	Sun.	Wed.	Fri.	Mon.	Thu.	Sat.	Tue.	Thu.
17	Sun.	Wed.	Wed.	Sat.	Mon.	Thu.	Sat.	Tue.	Fri.	Sun	Wed.	Fri.
18	Mon.	Thu.	Thu.	Sun.	Tue.	Fri.	Sun.	Wed.	Sat.	Mon.	Thu.	Sat.
19	Tue.	Fri.	Fri.	Mon.	Wed.	Sat.	Mon.	Thu.	Sun.	Tue.	Fri.	Sun.
20	Wed.	Sat.	Sun.	Wed.	Fri.	Mon.	Wed.	Sat.	Wed.	Thu.	Sun.	Tue.
21	Fri.	Mon.	Mon.	Thu.	Sat.	Tue.	Thu.	Sun.	Wed.	Fri.	Mon.	Wed.
22	Sat.	Tue.	Tue.	Fri.	Sun.	Wed.	Fri.	Mon.	Thu.	Sat.	Tue.	Thu.
23	Sun.	Wed.	Wed.	Sat.	Mon.	Thu.	Sat.	Tue.	Fri.	Sun	Wed.	Fri.
24	Mon.	Thu.	Fri.	Mon.	Wed.	Sat.	Mon.	Thu.	Sun.	Tue.	Fri.	Sun.
25	Wed.	Sat.	Sat.	Tue.	Thu.	Sun.	Tue.	Fri.	Mon.	Wed.	Sat.	Mon.
26	Thu.	Sun.	Sun.	Wed.	Fri.	Mon.	Wed.	Sat.	Tue.	Thu.	Sun.	Tue.
27	Fri.	Mon.	Mon.	Thu.	Sat.	Tue.	Thu.	Sun.	Wed.	Fri.	Mon.	Wed.
28	Sat.	Tue.	Wed.	Sat.	Mon.	Thu.	Sat.	Tue.	Fri.	Sun	Wed.	Fri.

TABLE 3 CALANDER OF DAYS OF WEEK.

After celecting the year desired note the number of the line, then take the line of the same number on 45 page or Calander of months, now celect the month and run down to the junction of the line the year was found on and you will find tne day of the week the month started on, now go to the column which starts with the same day the month startod with anb run down to the date of month and you will find the day of week saught for.

Sun.	1	Mon.	Tue.	1	Wed.	Thu.	1	Fri..	Sat..	1
Mon.	2	Tue.	Wed.	2	Thu.	Fri..	2	Sat..	Sun..	2
Tue.	3	Wed.	Thu.	3	Fri..	Sat..	3	Sun..	Mon.	3
Wed.	4	Thu.	Fri..	4	Sat..	Sun..	4	Mon.	Tue.	4
Thu.	5	Fri..	Sat..	5	Sun..	Mon.	5	Thu.	Wed.	5
Fri.	6	Sat..	Sun..	6	Mon.	Tue.	6	Wed	Thu.	6
Sat.	7	Sun..	Mon.	7	Tue.	Wed.	7	Thu.	Fri..	7
Sun.	8	Mon.	Tue.	8	Wed.	Thu.	8	Fri..	Sat..	8
Mon	9	Tue.	Wed.	9	Thu.	Fri..	9	Sat..	Sun.	9
Tue.	10	Wed.	Thu.	10	Fri..	Sat..	10	Sun.	Mon.	10
Wed	11	Thu.	Fri..	11	Sat..	Sun..	11	Mon.	Tue.	11
Thu.	12	Fri..	Sat..	12	Sun..	Mon.	12	Tue.	Wed.	12
Fri.	13	Sat..	Sun.	13	Mon.	Tue.	13	Wed.	Thu.	13
Sat.	14	Sun..	Mon.	14	Tue.	Wed	14	Thu.	Fri..	14
Sun.	15	Mon.	Tue.	15	Wed	Thu.	15	Fri..	Sat..	15
Mon	16	Tue.	Wed.	16	Thu.	Fri..	16	Sat..	Sun.	16
Tue.	17	Wed	Thu.	17	Fri..	Sat..	17	Sun.	Mon	17
Wed	18	Thu.	Fri..	18	Sat..	Sun.	18	Mon.	Tue.	18
Thu.	19	Fri..	Sat..	19	Sun.	Mon.	19	Tue.	Wed	19
Fri..	20	Sat..	Sun..	20	Mon.	Tue.	20	Wed	Thu.	20
Sat..	21	Sun..	Mon.	21	Tue.	Wed	21	Thu.	Fri..	21
Sun.	22	Mon.	Tue.	22	Wed	Thu.	22	Fri..	Sat..	22
Mon	23	Tue.	Wed	23	Thu.	Fri..	23	Sat..	Sun.	23
Tue.	24	Wed	Thu.	24	Fri..	Sat..	24	Sun..	Mon	24
Wed	25	Thu.	Fri..	25	Sat..	Sun.	25	Mon.	Tue	25
Thu.	26	Fri..	Sat..	26	Sun..	Mon	26	Tue.	Wed	26
Fri.	27	Sat..	Sun.	27	Mon.	Tue.	27	Wed	Thu.	27
Sat.	28	Sun.	Mon	28	Tue.	Wed	28	Thu.	Fri..	28
Sun.	29	Mon	Tue.	29	Wed	Thu.	29	Fri..	Sat..	29
Mon	30	Tue.	Wed	30	Thu.	Fri..	30	Sat..	Sun.	30
Tue	31	Wed	Thu.	31	Fri..	Sat..	31	Sun.	Mon.	31

STOWE'S MULTIPLICATION AND DIVISION TABLE—TO HELP YOU OUT IN FORGETFUL MOMENTS.

To multiply any number of the black figures on the left, by the figures in the top line in the same column to the right, the result will be found in the line below, or to divide any amount in the lower line by the column on the left, the result will be found in the top line.

	2	3	4	5	6	7	8	9	10	11	12	13	14	15	16	17	18	19	20	21	22	23	24	25
1																								
2	4																							
3	6	9																						
4	8	12	16																					
5	10	15	20	25																				
6	12	18	24	30	36																			
7	14	21	28	35	42	49																		
8	16	24	32	40	48	56	64																	
9	18	27	36	45	54	63	72	81																
10	20	30	40	50	60	70	80	90	100															
11	22	33	44	55	66	77	88	99	110	121														
12	24	36	48	60	72	84	96	108	120	132	144													
13	26	39	52	65	78	91	104	117	130	143	156	169												
14	28	42	56	70	84	98	112	126	140	154	168	182	196											
15	30	45	60	75	90	105	120	135	150	165	180	195	210	225										
16	32	48	64	80	96	112	128	144	160	176	192	208	224	240	256									
17	34	51	68	85	102	119	136	153	170	187	204	221	238	255	272	289								
18	36	54	72	90	108	126	144	162	180	198	216	234	252	270	288	306	324							
19	38	57	76	95	114	133	152	171	190	209	228	247	266	285	304	323	342	361						
20	40	60	80	100	120	140	160	180	200	220	240	260	280	300	320	340	360	380	400					
21	42	63	84	105	126	147	168	189	210	231	252	273	294	315	336	357	378	399	420	441				
22	44	66	88	110	132	154	176	198	220	242	264	286	308	330	352	374	396	418	440	462	484			
23	46	69	92	115	138	161	184	207	230	253	276	299	322	345	368	391	414	437	460	483	506	529		
24	48	72	96	120	144	168	192	216	240	264	288	312	336	360	384	408	432	456	480	504	528	552	576	
25	50	75	100	125	150	175	200	225	250	275	300	325	350	375	400	425	450	475	500	525	550	575	600	625

KEEP OUT OF DEBT

INTEREST ANNUALLY COMPOUNDED AT 100 YEARS

$1 At 1 per cent, ... 2.75

" " 2 " " 19.25

" " 6 " " 340.00

" " 10 " " 13,809.00

" " 12 " " 84,675.00

" " 15 " " 1,174,405.00

" " 18 " " 15,145,207.00

" " 24 " " 251,799,494.00

At 50 per Cent, it would eat up the world

THE BOOK-KEEPERS' MULTIPLICATION TABLE.

Large Figures on Left Multiplicand Figures on Top Line Multiplier Figures at Bottom the Result.

TABLE OF PLANETS RULING THE YEARS AND THEIR INFLUENCE.

SUN.	VENUS.	MERCURY	MOON.	SATURN.	JUPITER	MARS.
HONOR.	JUSTICE	TRAID.	FICKLE.	SLOW	FINANCE	WAR.
1800	1801	1802	1803	1804	1805	1806
1807	1808	1809	1810	1811	1812	1813
1814	1815	1816	1817	1818	1819	1820
1821	1822	1823	1824	1825	1826	1827
1828	1829	1830	1831	1832	1833	1834
1835	1836	1837	1838	1839	1840	1841
1842	1843	1844	1845	1846	1847	1848
1849	1850	1851	1852	1853	1854	1855
1856	1857	1858	1859	1860	1861	1862
1863	1864	1865	1866	1867	1868	1869
1870	1871	1872	1873	1874	1875	1876
1877	1878	1879	1880	1881	1882	1883
1884	1885	1886	1887	1888	1889	1890
1891	1892	1893	1894	1895	1896	1897
1898	1899	1900	1901	1902	1903	1904
1905	1906	1907	1908	1909	1910	1911
1912	1913	1914	1915	1916	1917	1918
1919	1920	1921	1922	1923	1924	1925
1926	1927	1928	1929	1930	1931	1932
1933	1934	1935	1936	1937	1938	1939
1940	1941	1942	1943	1944	1945	1946
1947	1948	1949	1950	1951	1952	1953
1954	1955	1956	1957	1958	1959	1960
1961	1962	1963	1964	1965	1966	1967
1968	1969	1970	1971	1972	1973	1974
1975	1976	1977	1978	1979	1980	1981
1982	1983	1984	1985	1986	1987	1988
1989	1990	1991	1982	1983	1984	1995
1996	1997	1998	1999	2,000	2001	2002

See instructions in "The effect of years." Stowe.

THE EFFECT OF THE YEARS.

The years the Sun rules will be noted for prolific growth of vegetation, but quick decay. Declaration of peace and dignity of government talked of.

Years of the Moon-rule are years of many changes of conditions, sudden failures or sudden fortunes made. Sudden and unexpected expressions of honesty or dishonesty, sudden attacks of ilness and sudden recoveires.

MERCURY years are very much like the Moon years, except more pronounced. They are noticeable years of invention, art, science, and literature.

MARS years are years of strife, labor strikes, rapid pushing of great enterprises, or battles if a war is in progress, a prolific year for animal production.

JUPITER years are years of starting great financial enterprises or financial agitation.

VENUS years are generally years of peace and good-will.

SATURN years are generally years of great spiritual development, and religious excitement, but otherwise evil, slow, bad conditions. Of course transits of the great planets through signs of the Zodiac should be taken into consideration where great events are to be considered. Thus the effects will be diminished or increased according to the strength of the influence.

GOOD AND EVIL YEARS.

It is said the family of European bankers and financiers of the world, who do business under the name of Rothschilds, depend upon their Astrologers as much as upon their bokkeepers. It is also claimed they will never, in any way, employ an unfortunate man; or take risks with one in business. Is it possible to take on the good fortune or misfortune of others?

Who will deny a healthy man may take a disease from a sick man, and yet never see how it is done?

Is it not admited that a person will take on disease much quicker at one time than at another?

Can the periods when man is most susceptible to disease or misfortune be determined? Certainly they can.

On another page will be found the natural evil years, that all men alike are more or less subject to. By watching the papers for the unfortunate, who suffer from accidents and crime, or from family difficulties which are aired through the press or in the courts, and it will be reaidly seen the mapority of them are pasisng through certain cycles or years called evil.

If a man is more susceptible to disease at one time than at another, he is also subject to good or bad luck or influence more at one time than at another.

If it is possible to determine when these periods come upon us, is it not also possible to avoid the evil and court the good?

If a man is not with a sick man during this evil period, he is not so liable to the evils of contagious diseases. If he know his evil periods will he not keep away from danger?

From this reasoning, if a man be in a fortunate period and his wife in an unfortunate period, it will pull him down, and in proportion lift her up. If both are in an unfortunate period it will be sad indeed. If both be in a fortunate year success and happiness are assured.

If a man in a fortunate year goes into business with one in an unfortunate year he must expect to experience hardships in busness. No man should start a new enterprise or make changes during an evil cycle or year.

A WORD TO JUDGES AND OFFICERS OF THE LAW.

Where two men are having differences to settle the one transiting an evil year is the more likely to be the aggressor if it is a mere quarrel, but if it be dollars and cents, and he is likely to be the loser, the other man is more than likely to be the aggressor.

Where a couple are seeking a divorce, the one who is in the evil year is the aggressor, nine times out of ten. Get them to agree to reason together for one year and the chances are there will be no divorce.

Let any person notice, when he is passing through an evil cycle, he will be more petulant, everything will seem to go wrong. In fact, I doubt any person is in his right mind, while transiting an evil cycle or year, consequently more kindness and leniency should be extended to the person who is transiting either an evil cycle or year, than to one who commits a crime during a normal period, and he that commits a crime during a fortunate year is certainly a depraved being.

The happiest years of any person's life are the Jupiter years, and suposed to be produced by the harmonious vibrations produced by Jupiter in his passage of his own radix or position at birth. These are the 12th, 24th, 36th, 48th, 60th and 72nd years. While other years not marked as evil are classed as good years the Jupitarian years are suposed to be the very best years. They are not all alike, as sometimes other planetary positions will add to the good vibrations, while at other times evil positions may so mar the good years as to show almost as much evil as good. Yet evil results are not so likely to follow the starting of an enterprise as it surely would if started during an evil year.

A litle observation will convince any reasoning man of the truth of this statement. A man would be worse than foolish to run for office during an evil year, if he can assertain his opponent is transiting a god or normal year.

An evil year commencing or closing an evil cycle will be far more malignant than otherwise or an evil year coming during a good cycle will hardly be felt in comparison to the former.

Of course a person born very fortunate must experience the evil years, but he will not feel them nearly so much as one who was born unfortunate.

To judge of the nature of an accused person, see influence of the sign of the Zodiac.

ADVICE TO BUSINESS MEN.

A long-winded article is not necessary in any case in conection with this mater, yet I do not want to cling to brevity at the expense of clearness of descriptive advice; either verbosity or brevity may marr the beauty and curtail the benefits intended. This litle bok is intended for the masses, who have not got the time to study Astrology in all of its parts. Under this heading I must refer to several departments of the book.

First—If in an evil cycle or year, take no more risks than can be helped. If you be in an evil year, let the wife atend to all important business matters, where it is possible. If she has been in the habit of handling the money, even in such things as buying household supplies, during her evil year she should turn everything into the hands of the husband, if he be not transiting an evil year. If both be transiting an evil year, have an understanding before the year begins to take effect, as to what you will do, then take no risks outside of that; do not buy or sell more than you have to, and, if possible, get a person who you know to be transiting a good year to transact business for you.

Avoid law suits at all times, but especially during an evil cycle or year.

If in business pertnership, let the partner, in a good year, transact all important business, as the one transiting an evil year is in a measure insane and his judgment cannot be depended upon. Do not dissolve partnership because of one being in an evil period, as the evil will follow you all the same. Neither go into business with a man who is transiting an evil period lest it ruin both.

If an employe be in an evil period do not discharge him unless he rfesue to listen and obey your wishes. He should be cautioned to do nothing of least importance of his own accord. On the other hand, if you be in an evil year and an employe be in a good year, you may ask the employe to assume responsible business matters, and seek his advice. But see that you pay him well for it, lest the greater evil come to you.

If you seek an employe for a certain purpose, read closely the influences of the Zodiac and judge his ability to perform your services from that, of course, after obtaining his date of birth. Or if you wish to judge of the nature of any person you will find his nature closely pictured under the influence of the signs of the Zodiac.

A WORD TO THOSE ABOUT TO MARRY AND TO THE MARRIED AND THOSE SEEKING DIVORCE.

If you wish to marry, ask an Astrologer when an opportunity is likely to occur, and whether suited to marry or not.

If seeking a divorce, first see a competent Astrologer and ask his advice.

If a man and his wife have differences, and one or both seem to have more temptations, and feel as if they cannot bear the other's presence, the chances are one or both are transiting an evil year or cycle, or the trouble began during one of these periods. If you have this litle book, go get it at once and assume all of the pleasing, coaxing ways you can assume and say: "Let us examine ourselves." If one be in an evil period and the other not, let the one in the evil period say: "I am in an evil period, be kind to me, bear with me, help me." If you cannot do it that way, say: "Let us read,' and read the above passage aloud. Then try to bear with each other, until the evil period is over. If angry expressions seem to bring on a quarrel let either one or both rush for glasses of water, each take a glass and without speaking, each go to the extreme ends of the house and drink it; then come back and read the passage.

If both are transiting an evil year, then call in an outside party, of judgment, who will read this portion of the book and talk kindly to both sides as a parent to children. Dear reader, we are not so far from the ways and feelings of children and a little kindly advice will go a long way to heal troubles. But never call in a relative or former friend of one. It were better it be a person of repute, but litle known by either. Dear friends, bear with one another when either trtnsit an evil year or cycle, for the best of us are insane in a measure at such periods. I have saved many a couple from divorce who afterward came and thanked me. Let every reader remember that divorced people are generally unfortunate, and misfortune follows them until a final sad downfall is sure to come. It is far beter you patch up your troubles. Look at the great Napoleon, from the time he divorced his Josephine, to marry the Austrian. His star went down. This is but one of thousands of instances you can refer to if you try.

A WORD TO THE DOCTORS AND NURSES.

Far be it from me to desire to give advice to doctors, as to the care of patients, except in so far as my profession may give me a knowledge, of which they do not understand, except they be also students of the great science.

Hypocraties, the father of Materia Medica, so-called, said: "A man is beter fited to be called a fool than a physician who does not understand astrology." I do not wish to declare any man a fool, but I am well satisfied that a little knowledge of astrology would be a great help to any physician.

A physician should first become familiar with the Zodiac, that he may diagnose a patient's troubles from the date of birth.

A physician should be able to tell at once, on receiving the date of birth, whether the patient be in a good or evil cycle or year.

He should know that disease will nearly always make itself manifest in that part of the body represented by the sign a person was born in, or that part of the body the sign represents which was rising at birth, or that the Moon was in at time of birth.

The physician should never look for a speedy recovery of a patient who is transiting an evil cycle or year, as he would during a good cycle or year, or even a normal year.

A surgical operation should never be permited during an evil cycle or year, or even started during a Mercury, Mars or Saturn hour, if it can be avoi ded, or when the Moon is in the sign representing that part of the body that is to be operated upon. The treatment that should be given to those born in various signs of the Zodiac, especially that of children, will be found under the name of each sign, and more particularly will the diagnosis of each degree be found in the second volume of this work.

A patient should be told if in an evil cycle or year, and while given encouragement he should be told the recovery is to be slow, that he may fortify against the long illness. Yet greater care should be exercised in breaking the news of great danger or long siege, to those born in the mental signs than to those born in the other signs. The most easily discouraged people are those born in the sign of Aries, Cancer, Virgo, Libra and Pisces. Those born in the vital signs, or that have the Moon in vital signs, or have vital signs rising are the quickest to recover from ill-health.

Many a physician is misled by finding the symptoms of disease being entirely different from its real nature and appearing in a different part of the body from which the disease is really located. Thus a wrong diagnosis is made. This is due to the patient having the Moon in a sign governing another part of the body from that in which the patient was born, or it may be due to the rising sign being different from that in which the patient was born. Therefore, to ask a patient for the date of his birth and then note the sign and part of the anatomy it covers, you will find where the disease will finally become seated, and what the disease is most likely to be and not be doctoring the symptoms instead of the disease.

The complications in the study of astrology are as great as the complications in the study of medicine and anatomy, and of course cannot be treated of to any extent in this little book, nor is it intended as an absolute guide to any branch of science, art or business upon which it treats. To thoroughly understand the benefits of astrology in its application to surgery and medical treatment one should become a thorough Astrologer, but as an assistant the physician applying the facts found here will find great aid, if in nothing else the knowledge of the length of time the effects of a disease is likely to hold a patient in its stubborn grasp.

To thoroughly understand the benefits of astrology in this direction one should understand the diseases belonging to the signs, houses and planets, and the mixed influences of changed positions of signs in houses and the mixed influence of the planets in the sign. For instance, the diseases of the signs are as follows:

ARIES—People are most subject to diseases of the head, eyes, ears, nose, mouth and stomach, nerves, headache, toothache, fevers (acute and chronic), catarrh, inflammation of the brain, epilepsy and apoplexy. Aries, Libra and Scorpio people are more subject to small-pox than those of other signs. Let it be understood that a disease may be manifest in that part of the body covered by the opposite sign or in that part of the body ruled by the sign the planet is in at birth, which also rules the sign of the birth. Let this be remembered for all signs. Thus Aries people will also show some of the symptoms and afflictions belonging to Scorpio, such as weakness of the generative organs, and troubles of kidneys, bladder and rectum. It is very rare that Aries people have more than two children, as it is a barren sign, while Scorpio people generally raise large families, it being a fruitful sign.

Children born in Aries are subject to nerve troubles and when teething are subject to worms and to water on the brain. Keep the brain cool and the child quiet and induce much sleep. A warm room and much sleep is the best medicine an Aries person can have, child or adult. Doctors should not let mock modesty stand in the way of their cautioning parents to watch the development of the sex functions in children born in any sign, much more so in the animal signs, and still more so in Aries and Taurus, lest an unnatural or morbid sex habit be developed. More constitutions are ruined by the abuse of these functions than by any other one thing. It is too often the case, where one or both married partners are walking shadows, nervous system destroyed, there seems to be no diagnosis that really fits their case. They have been over-indulging their passions.

Children will do beter sleeping alone, never should be allowed a close companion, exchanging homes and sleeping together, and the child should be gotten up as soon as it wakes up in the morning.

Some years ago I cast the horoscope of a friend and told him he would lose a member of his family. He asked: "Is it my oldest son?" Continuing, he said: "My oldest son has been ill for some time, and six of the best doctors of the place have given him up."

"What is the trouble?" I asked.

"Diabetes, they say," he replied.

"What is the date of his birth?" I next asked.

"He was 13 years old in April, and the doctors say he cannot live two weeks," he replied.

I went over and saw the boy and then went back to my office and erected a figure. I then said to the father: "Your boy has not got diabetes, or if he has it is not the first cause of his illness."

"What is the cause?" he asked.

"Perhaps I am like the doctors, I do not like to tell you, for fear you will be offended."

"No, I will not," said he.

"Very well, then, your son is dying from the effects of self-abuse."

"Impossible,' he cried, "he is too young; the functions are not developed."

"For several years your boy has had a close chum or companion and they frequently slept together."

"Yes," he replied.

"Well, just before your boy was confined to the house the other boy found another companion and stopped coming to your house."

"Yes." he replied.

"Well, by persistent practice they have developed unnatural sex passion."

"Why has it not hurt the other boy?" he asked.

"Your son was born in the sign Aries, with Venus the Goddess of love for a ruling planet, and it at an evil apscet. This weakens the boy in this direction, while the other boy was born in a vital sign with less danger of injury, hence he will last longer," was my explanation.

I saw my friend felt very bad and doubted me in this matter, but he went home and told his wife and she confirmed what I said by admitting she had caught the boy in the act. Then the boy was questioned and admitted the truth. My friend came back and told me.

These are unusually good and intelligent people. They asked me: "How long will he live?"

"For several months."

"What can be done for him?"

"I am not a physician. I have no right to prescribe."

This was the first week in December. The first week in February the boy was still alive, but failing rapidly. I was called over again, and asked: "How long can he live and suffer so?" He was suffering terribly with convulsions and nervous prostration.

"On February 20th Venus will reach a square to its own radix, evily aspected to Saturn. If it chances to be a cloudy, lowery or stormy day he will die before noon; if a clear day, with good care, he will recover."

I could say no more, for I felt there was no salvation. It proved a nasty, muggy day and the boy died at 11:20 noon.

I do not give exact dates for fear of attracting notice to the case and causing sorrow to a most estimable family.

TAURUS—People are most subject to throat troubles—croup, diphtheria, asthma, bronchitis, tonsilitis or glandular swellings. Being a vital sign they quickly recuperate from any illness. They are also subject to over-feeding and drinking, causing stomach troubles and later in life dropsy and heart troubles, as Venus rules Taurus and Libra, they will also have some trouble in the back and rines.

TAURUS children need much more care on account of their appetite and passions. Both sexes are too easily coaxed, and so led astray, by appealing to their sympathies, as they are very loving and sympathetic.

GEMINI people first feel illness through pains in the arms, shoulders and hands, and are subject to accidents to those members of the body. They are subject to nervous troubles, inflammations in arms, hands or breast, to biliousness, flatulency and pleurisy.

GEMINI children are generally quite healthy, but subject to delicate appearance, caused by extreme nervousness and often to over-study, for they are great students. They are apt to conceal their real feelings, and the girls as they become young ladies develop an unusual love nature, which in a measure they conceal, but are too apt to take the first offer in marriage or be led astray when very young, but this is easily overcome as they grow older.

CANCER people are most easily effected in the stomach, breast and lungs, to false pleurisy, to cancers, and to all tumorous affections of the breast, stomach and bowels, to dropsy, dyspepsia and to pulmonary consumption. False symptoms are of the opposite sign, of troubles of the knees and eyes. Persons born in any sign who have the planet Mars in Cancer at birth will suffer more or less with weak eyes.

CANCER children are subject most to stomach troubles and to worms, and when teething to summer complaint.

My mother never lost a patient who was suffering with summer complaint, even when called to attend those given up by most competent physicians, and she used a simple Indian remdy. She always insisted on perfect quietude for the child and she mixed a strong tea made of Red Roseberry leaves with the milk given to the child, which, if cow's milk, must always be scalded. It cannot hurt the child, will not bind it up too quickly, which if done, is dangerous, but keeps the bowls regular.

LEO people are affected in the back, shoulders, liver, heart, sides, stomach and lungs. Subject to rheumatic affections, palpitations and all other heart troubles, erruptive fevers, convulsions and fainting spells, especially to consumption. False symptoms are those of the troubles of Aquarius and to bleeding of the nose, lungs or diseased parts.

LEO children must be kept warm and their minds occupied in a harmonious manner. Colds should not be allowed to settle on the lungs, as they are especially weak in this part of the body.

If they have the influence of any other animal sign they are exceptionally weak in the sex functions.

VIRGO people are subject to diseases of the liver, stomach, bowels, intestines and rines. The diseases most prevalent with them are dyspepsia, colic, worms, diarrhoea and dysentery. After middle life to severe pains in the head and to apoplexy.

They are peculiar about their food and cannot eat it if the stomach says no, nor can they eat if angry or excited. False symptoms are usually of Pisces or Gemini diseases.

VIRGO children up to 10 years of age are generally delicate, and more Virgo children die under 6 years of age than of any other sign. It is very hard to raise them up to 10 years of age. They should have special care, be kept quiet, generally given pretty much their own way. Give them any kind of food their stomachs dictate, only limiting them as to quantity. Never urge them to eat something their stomachs rebel against. Their delicacy of nature subjects them, as children, to any disease prevalent. A great expression of love and harmony is their best medicine. Physicians should be very careful in giving Virgo people cathartics.

LIBRA people are subject to frequent spells of melancholy, to settling of diseases in the small of the back, reins, hams, small intestines, kidneys, bladder and generative organs, disease of the liver, back, lumbago, sciatica, and females to all female complaints.

These are the places where diseases are most likely to settle, though they often show symptoms of the diseases of Aries and Taurus, in the back, rines, generative and urinary organs.

LIBRA children are so much like Aries children I need say but little. Show them great sympathy and love and give them quiet and rest.

SCORPIO people are most subject to diseases of secrets, spine, rectum and groins; to diseases, rupture, gravel and to venereal diseases and of the sexual system. The ladies of this sign suffer terribly with female weakness.

As Scorpio people generally relish their food, in youth they often overload the stomach, and almost invariably suffer from stomach troubles. There is but one in forty born in Scorpio who are blonds and they suffer more wit stomach troubles than their darker skinned brothers and sisters. Scorpio, like Tarus and Leo, is a vital sign, so Scorpio people have more vitality and seldom remain ill long, but quickly recuperate.

SCORPIO children are men and women, and if the Scorpio nature be left unrestrained, they become shrewd and selfish, but let them once overcome this and they are most admirable people, as they are generally strictly honest, therefore the children need more care to cultivate their moral nature than the physical nature, except as to the overloading of the stomach. Their false symptoms are more likely to be of the diseases of Aries and Taurus.

SAGITTARIUS people first feel disease in hips and thighs or disease setles there. They are more subject to rheumatism and inflammatory diseases and to broken limbs, severe headaches and to symptoms of disease of Pisces and Gemini, and especially to those of the rising sign or to the sign the Moon is in at birth. These people suffer from diseases of intemperance.

SAGITTARIUS children need little special care except as to chose for them the proper vocation in life and to teach them the necessity of always telling the truth. They will sometimes lie when the truth would answer better and yet they do not intend to do so. Teach these children the great dangers of intemperance, as they or those born in Aquarius or Cancer are harder to reform than all others.

CAPRICORNUS people are most apt to have diseases setle in the knees and eyes. They very often have weak eyes. They are subject to inflammatory troubles, to sprains, broken bones and to all skin diseases, and often to the diseases belonging to Cancer people, so their symptoms here are liable to be the diseases of Cancer.

CAPRICORNUS people are more subject to the itch and all other eruptive skin diseases and when atending school should wear on the person a little bag of camphor and sulphur. This is an excellent disinfectant for keeping off all diseases of children, born in any sign, irrespective of what some wise doctors say. Parents should remember what has been said of animal signs and that this is the sign of the stubborn little goat and stubbornness is the greatest failing of these children.

AQUARIUS people find the weakest part of the body the leg below the knee to the foot. They are subject to nervous twitchings of the legs, and to many accidents to the lower limbs, to varicose veins and to gout and rheumatism, also to all blod diseases, and to all of the diseases of Leo, as well as to the symptoms. It being a vital sign there is no especial care concerning the health of AQUARIUS children, except to keep them balanced from going to extremes, as this is the highest and lowest of all of the signs, and if an Aquarius person became depraved they seldom reform.

PISCES people are most subject to diseases of the feet, of the nerves and head, and to gout, chilblain, corns, bunions and to cramps in feet. The symptoms are those of Virgo and Sagittarius.

PISCES children are subject more to whooping cough, croup and bronchial troubles. They should be allowed plenty of outdor air, as should all children, but those born in the quarter of labor—Capricornus, Aquarius and Pisces it is more necessary than to those of other signs, yet they should be kept warm and from unreasonable exposure.

Of course people of any sign are subject to diseases of all other signs, but these are not apt to be so malignant or dangerous as those belonging to the sign of the person is born in, as they are produced by planitary positions and the ascending sign. If a fiery sign be ascending the disease will be of a more feverish nature and of shorter duration. If an Earth sign be rising, the patient will become melancholy and the disease drift to chronic complaint.

If an air sign be on the ascendent, there is more danger of blood poisoning and of blood disorders hanging on, but fluctuating.

If it be a water sign rising, the diseases will proced from colds, moisture, disordered stomach and quickly yield to proper treatment.

Diseases arising in winter generally hang on much longer than those arising in summer.

Then, again, each planet influences diseases according to the house and sign that it was in at the patient's birth. But it requires the study of astrology in all of its parts to become familiar with this. To teach astrology is not the design of this litle book, but is intended rather as an aid to the proper diagnosing of diseases and care of the patient. Read the influence of the 12 signs of the Zodiac and t will aid in understanding the nature of the patient and how better to treat him.

If a jhysician find a disease does not yeild to treatment so radily as he thinks it ought, he should at once ascertain whether or not the patient be transiting an evil year or cycle and then tell the patient the reason why he does not recover as rapidly as he thinks he should and that the disease will require a slower treatment.

A disease once settled in that part of the body ruled by a sign a person was born in, may be kept under subjection or even seem to disappear for a time, but can never be cured. The least exposure is likely to bring its reappearance.

The good and evil cycles will be found under the influence of the 12 signs of the Zodiac, treating of the good and evil periods of those born under each sign of the Zodiac.

Besides the diseases spoken of as natural to the sign, planetary influences produce diseases and other evils that generally appear or have their rise during a natural evil year. These natural evil years are produced by the cycles of the planets, and are generally between the ages of 5 & 6, 13 & 14, 16 & 17, 19 & 21, 27 & 28, 33 & 34, 37 & 38, 41 & 43, 48 & 50, 54 & 55, 61 & 62, 69 & 70, 75 & 76, 79 & 80, 83 & 84, 89 & 90.

Sickness or trouble may come at other years, but it is never so malignant as that of evil years, hence you should not marry, travel, invest money, or take risks of any kind during an evil year. See good and evil cycles elsewhere.

Your good years are those between the evil ones, and your very best years those between 23 & 24, 28 & 29, 35 & 36, 39 & 40, 47 & 48, 59 & 60, 70 & 72.

Sometimes planetary influences start the evils a few months before the evil year begins and sometimes carry the evils over into a good year; in such cases, a change of business or residence will break or change the vibrations and bring better fortune. This will be better understood when you stop to think; there is no place of vacuum in the universe, and as all space is filled with atoms, and it is the vibration of the atoms that brings the light to your eye, the sound to your ear and the heat from the sun, so it is the harmony or in-harmony of these vibrations set in motion by the planets which gives you good or bad luck. Then get out of them by making a change. Just as you would get out of too much heat, light or darkness.

THE COMPLAINT OF AN OLD PHYSICIAN, who says- "When Jenner discovered cow-pox in England the world of science hurled an avalanch of fame upon him, but when the most scientific school of medicine in the world-that of Paris–published this recipe as a panacea for small pox it passed unheeded; it is as harmless as water as unfailing as fate, if taken acording to directions. It will prevent or cure small-pox though the pittings are filling and it will cure scarlet feaver."

Here is the formula. has it been tried and found wanting, or forgotten; or is it used by the docter and forgotten by the peopel?

The reason it is given here is that "I was told" it was discovered by a physician through astrology.

Here is the formula. Take one grain sulphate of zinc. and one grain digitalis(foxglove). Put this in a half tumbler of water and place in a pint bottle. Leave it stand twenty-four hours. Then put in a tablespoonful of Orleans or brown shugar. Shake well and fill up with rain water. A tablespoonful of this taken every morning will prevent the diseas, even though exposeb to it. When symptoms of small-pox, such as headach, pain in the back and feaver comes on, after exposier, a tablespoonful for an adult and a teaspoonful for children evry half houa will prevent the diseas, yet a physician should be called at once if the diseas is mistrusted.

PECULIAR PERIODS.

FATAL HOURS OF ILLNES. The hour of death has been recorded by leading physicans of Europe, and out of 2,880 cases of all ages and con. ditions it was found that the maximum hour of death is from 5 to 6 o'clock a. m., when it is 40 per cent, above the average; and the minimum during the hours from 9 to 11 o,cleck in the evening when it is 6 per cent. below the average. Thus the least mortality is during mid day hours-namly, from 10 till 3 o'clock; the greatest, during early mornitg hours, from 3 to 6 a, m. Fishermen say that the times of the ebb and fiow of the tides are always the most critical hours with invalids. Let it be here noticed the Moon is tne cause of the ebb and fiow of the tides, then is it not reasonable that the Moou exerts a tremendus influence on men, even to cause death, under certian conditions.

PERIODS WHEN MOST GENIUSES ARE BORN is said to be in April, fewest in January. The greatest actors were born in April the greetest number in October and november, The most tall people are born in July and October, the greatest number of short people are born in November and January. The greatest number of babys are born are born in the spiing months.

NO REAL DESTINY TO LENGTH OF LIFE

Varying occupations have much to do with life's length.

With regerd to the occupation which ensure longevity, it is the universal testimony that clergymen reach the highest age, being close run by gardeners and vine-dresser. Ordinary agricultural laborers, although their occupation is so largely in the open air, are not conspicuous as long livers, except in France, Sweden and England. People working in wood are longer lived than those whose occupations are with metals, and both attain a higher age than textile workers and workers in chemical industries. The shortest-lived are miners, except in England, where the superor mining regulations and abmirable sanitary arrangements have a benefical effect. In England and Norway sailors and fiishermen live to a far greater age than in Germany or France.

It is true, it might claimed, by the fatelist, that all conditions are fated and man simpley drifts to the place of his final destiny, as did the Turkish official who said to the sultan "I pray yonr magisty to send me to Smarna, at once for I fear if I stay here I shall be killed?" The sultan looked long and stady when the official asked "what does your majesty see?" The sultan replied "I see death and he says what is this man doing here I have orders to kill him at Smarns to night." It is said the official was killed in Smarna that verry night.

ASTROLOGY AND HEALTH OF MAN, BIRD, BEAST OR PLANT.

Though this matter has been discussed, let us recapitulate or discuss the subject from another standpoint.

When anything new is to be brought into the world, care should be taken to see that the seed or sire is in the best condition possible.

Next, it is necessary copulation should take place when the Moon is increasing in light, and at a time when the offspring will be brought into independent life, which will bring the best disposition and healthy body required. Of course, to do this to the best advantage possible one should understand Astrology in all of its ramifications, but what is given here will be of great help to the general public.

Every intelligent person should study well the signs of the Zodiac and their meaning and influences.

Those born in Aries are very wirey, of strong constitution, vitality backed up with tremendous elastic mental power. This is added to or lessened by the rising sign and position of the Moon or good aspect of planets. However, we need not go into all of that, but will only judge of the signs and age of the Moon, and position of Moon at birth, all of which can be judged in this book.

The brain is the most sensitive part of the system, and when the health runs down, it is manifest in the head, eyes, stomach, kidneys and nerves. Fevers and inflammatory complaints are apt to set in.

Plenty of sleep, light muscular exercise and fresh air is the best remedy.

TAURUS is a vital sign. Any vital sign gives a strong, robust constitution; in fact, an excess of vitality. The neck, throat and heart are the weakest points. Mankind is subject to dropsical affections, sometimes apoplexy. People of this sign begin to thicken up and grow fleshy about 30 to 40. This is a dangerous dropsical period.

They should be careful in diet and avoid anything of a fattening nature; also cultivate temperate habits and take plenty of exercise. They should act quickly, as those born in vital signs are generally taken ill very suddenly and either die or recuperate suddenly.

GIMINI is a neutral air sign, betwen the vital and mental. This sign produces a rambling, restless, active subject. Men born in this sign are rather wanderers, or anxious to carry on two or three kinds of business at one time. Horses and cattle will jump fences and wander; chickens and geese wander; trees and plants rapidly grow broad or tall; vines stretch to enormous length. That is, when born with the strongest Gemini influence, it will be most manifest. The strongest, of course, would be when born in Gemini, with the Moon in Gemini, and Gemini rising. Those born in this sign are long-lived. Of course, the sign rules the hands and arms, and human beings are more liable to accidents to hands and arms than other parts of the body. They are more subject to mental troubles and to afflictions of nerve disorders, worry, excitement, and to lung troubles than those of the vital signs. Avoid over-exercise, be careful of diet, and take plenty of rest and sleep, should be the orders of the attending physician.

CANCER is a mental sign and very weak in vital forces. Man or beast of this sign take on disease quicker than those of any other sign, especially through unhealthy conditions. The chest, stomach and lungs are the weakest points, and they are subject to cancerous and tumerous growths, especially where troubled with constipation. This being a mental sign, imagination plays a strong part in their illness, Both for man and animals. Be careful not to over-feed. And the physician should depend more on suggestive therapeutics with those of this sign than with any other sign.

LEO is a fire vital sign, ruling the heart; gives strong constitution, quick to yield to illness and quick to recuperate. To the people of this sign the lungs and heart are extremely sensitiv points. Fevers, inflammatory troubles, or sometimes extreme chills, are likely to suddenly seize them. Constipation is their worst enemy. Their best remedy is to be comfortably warm-housed, wholesome, nurishing food, temperate habits, cheerfulness and harmony.

VIIRGO is the second neutral sign of the Earth triplicity; gives a peculiar sensitive constitution, very weak in childhood, gaining strength as the child passes the eleventh year of age. Stomach, bowels and throat are the weakest points. Never waste money teaching a Virgo child vocal music, because by the evil year, 27 to 28, they invariably lose the power of the voice for vocal music. Stomach and bowel troubles, constipation and its evil eflects are the chief complaints; finally troubles of the head and apoplexy may cause death. Surrounding influences and good magnetism, plain diet and regular habits are the essential necessities for their health.

LIBRA, the third mental sign, an air sign, produces a wirey constitution, enabling a Libra person to mentally combat disease. The weakest parts are the rines, kidneys, bladder. In case of a running down of the system, stomach, head and blood disorders will set in. As these people are much given to spells of melancholy and sadness, congenial and harmonious surroundings, quiet, rest and sleep are necessary to their welfare.

SCORPIO is the third vital sign of the water triplicity gives a very strong constitution, with large store of vital forces, which if not wasted causes a quick recuperation from all diseases.

Most subject to gout, piles and all diseases of the rectum and generative organs, to blood disease and consequently the heart, this sign being square to Leo more of its people die of heart troubles than of those born in Leo which rules the heart.

This sign being a storehouse of magnetism Scorpio people should pay close attention to diet, fresh air and the cultivation of the magnetic forces through proper breathing—see breathing process elsewhere in first volum of "Periodicity." Scorpio people are natural magnetic healers.

SAGITTARIUS—3rd. Fire sign produces long lived people of great tenacity of purpose and conservers of the life forces. Gives a good constitution. The most sensitive part of the system is the nerves, lungs, sometimes producing consumption, sciatic rheumatism, will cause much lameness to hips also spinal troubles. This sign and its polar Gemini produces more accidents than any other sign. The weakness of Sagittarius people is a desire to over-do, over activity. While they must have plenty of fresh air and out-door exercise, they should cultivate regular habits and quietude, setting themselves to a reasonable amount of exercise and never allowing anything to force an increase above that fixed.

CAPRICORNUS being the polar of Cancer and answering to the knees of the cosmic man, its people must suffer as much by the weakness of Cancer as do Cancer people, though the knees and eyes are called the weak points of Capricornus people.

Sometimes through weakness of stomach, bowels and kidneys there is a tendency to rheumatism and complaints arising from chills, and exposure to colds. Capricornus people generally live to good old age, providing they keep in the harness, but let them retire from business and they seldom live more than a year or two. Avoid constipation, despondency and melancholy, cultivate cheerfulness.

AQUARIUS—The fourth vital sign gives strong wiry constitution. Being the polar of Leo more Aquarius people suffer from heart troubles and blood disorders than do Leo people.

Aquarius people are very liable to accidents of the legs from the knees down, to verrucose veins and blood poisoning.

Being in the active labor quarter they require much exercise and fresh air with careful concentration of thought and they require beautiful and harmonious surroundings.

PISCES gives a weak nervous constitution, subject to nervous dyspepsia and other stomach and nerve troubles, to swellings of the feet, sensitive feet and complaints arising from blood disorders, consumption and other lingering diseases. These people are cranks on cleanliness, a little dirt upsets them altogether. They are forever borrowing trouble over things that never happen. Therefore avoidance of cold, inharmony, uncleanliness and impure magnetism are essential to their health.

Let me call attention to the fact that Pisces, Aquarius, Sagittarius and Cancer people and those who have these signs rising or the Moon in these signs, should guard against the drink habit more carefully than those of other signs, as it is almost impossible to reform if once it becomes fixed. Again let me call the physicians attention that no surgical operation should take place when the dragon's head or tail, north or south node of the Moon, or the Moon are in the sign of birth, or when it is in the sign covering that part of the body in which the operation is to take place. For this see Moon tables of signs the Moon is in.

Through all forms of ill-health, the days when the Moon is in bad aspects to the sick person's degree of birth the patient will be worse; that is when the Moon is in the same sign the person was born in or three signs from it, or right opposite to it, or in the sign representing that part of the body the patient's trouble is in. (See Moon Tables.)

CONSIDERATIONS OF THE MOON'S EFFECTS FOR THE BENEFIT OF THE FARMER.

Astrologers have not given enough attention to the effects of the Moon in her changes and to the daily age of the Moon from new to dark.

Particularly should it be noticed what sign the Moon is in at time of each change, as the effects are quite different as the changes take place in the different signs.

The new Moon gives us the strongest phase, and the full Moon next.

When the change takes place in a mental sign, diseases of the brain are more negligent, and the mind of a healthy party will be more active; when the change takes place in Aries the mind of the intelligent man will run more in literature and scientific thought, than on other matters. If not of the intelligent type he will be more like the animal and the mind will run more to cohabitation or mating, especially if in the new Moon. (See paragraph on Procreation.)

If the change takes place in Cancer, the next mental sign, the mind will be more clairvoyant and drift to trade. If in Libra, the third, mental sign, the effect will be the same as in Cancer, but run more to mechanical lines or to gaming, especially horse-racing.

If in Capricornus, the mind will be strongly clairvoyant, imaginary and building air castles or to pushing business and to gaining and speculating.

If the change takes place in Taurus, the mind will be very sympathetic, and the vital forces good, this is about the same for all vital signs, except in Scorpio there will be more of an expression of selfishness, and if in Aquarius more activity, and desire to ramble. People suddenly leave their homes and cattle will stray away, this is decidedly the case with all of the air signs.

If the change takes place in Gemini the effects are much the same as if in Aquarius. But if in Virgo the effects are quite different, all persons are subject to cold and disturbances, stomach, bowels and lympathetic system. It is the worst sign of the whole 12 signs for changes to take place in, considering the welfare of man.

If it takes place in Sagittarius, religious excitement will increase, as well as temper and quarrels.

If in Pisces, it will tend to cause much news gathering, gossip and fickleness.

We will now reconsider the effects in the water signs under the head of procreation.

PROCREATION OR REPRODUCTION.

Under this head the fruitful, barren, masculine and feminine signs should be taken into consideration.

Let it be remembered that the changes of the Moon and especially the new of the Moon are the periods of animal heat or mating, and in serving animals the surest period is when the change take place in a fruitful sign. Cancer and Pisces are the best, and when a male offspring is desired wait until the next day when the Moon has reached the masculine sign Aries, or Leo, or Sagittarius, in the latter case of course if the change took place in Scorpio. If possible see that the dam is most agitated. If a female is wanted the sire should be first agitated, the dam most agitated. To assist the farmer in this matter I give table of

Periods of Gestation.

These periods are subject to slight variation caused by conditions, but are correct under favorable conditions.

Elephant—2 years.	Camel—12 months.
Horse and Ass—11 mos.	Reindeer—8 months.
Lion—5 months.	Bear—6 months.
Cow—9 months.	Sow—4 months.
Dog—9 weeks.	Cat—8 weeks.
Rabbit—4 weeks.	Guinea-pig—3 weeks.

Length of time a fowl sets.

Canary bird—14 days.	Swan—42 days.
Goose—30 days.	Turkeys and Pea Hen—38 days.
Ducks—30 days.	Common Hens—21 days.
Pigeons—14 days.	
Parrot—40 days.	

"I don't do my plantin' in the Moon, I do my plantin' in the ground, when it's ready."

"Of course you do and that's the reason you never got along any better, but you are not to blame, generations of educated asses have been talking the same nonsense; because their church had condemned all science."

Now, you skeptic, here is a good way to prove whether it pays to observe the Moon in doing your farming.

1st. Get a package of good peas and shake them up well so you know the package is all alike, or if some good and some bad they will be well mixed.

Now divide into four equal parts.

2nd. Prepare four pieces of ground just alike.

3rd. Number your packages of peas No. 1, No. 2, No. 3, No. 4.

4th. Look in the book "Astrological Periodicity" and plant your first package of peas, in the New of the Moon from first day to the fifth day, when the Moon is new, and if possible when in the sign Pisces-Aries-Taurus-Cancer or Scorpio.

You will get a plenty of straw and few blossoms and less peas.

5th. Now plant second package a day or two before or after the change of the first quarter and you will get plenty of blossoms, but not many peas yet. This is the time to plant flowers.

6th. Plant the third package from two days before the full to four days after the full of the Moon, but when the Moon is in the signs before mentioned and you will get a good crop of peas.

The nearer the full of the Moon the better.

7th. Now plant the last package as near the dark of the Moon as possible and when the Moon is in Aquarius, Leo, Virgo or Libra, if possible, and your peas will not come up from the ground very high.

I ran across a pretty successful farmer who said "Oh, Pshaw! I have tried all of that Moon business and I do not believe a thing in it."

"What was it you tried," I asked.

"Oh potatoes," said he.

"Well," I asked, "in what way did you plant by the Moon?"

"Why, in the New of the Moon, of course," he replied.

"What sign was the Moon in?" I next asked.

"I got the sign out of Peruna Almanac," said he.

"Which sign?" I repeated.

"I don't know now," said he. "But I tried it."

"You belong to the church do you not, and you believe in that?"

"I certainly do and a great deal more than I do in Astrology."

"Yes," said I. "And you will lie to support it."

"What do you mean?" he cried. "Seeming quite indignant, I answered, "Because you do not know one sign from another, and you say you got the signs from the almanac, whereas the common almanacs do not give the signs at all, they give the constellations instead of the sign. Many a person has been deceived by these overwise astronomers who work in the hands of these superstitious humbugs instead of in the interest of science. Even the virtuous newspapers have of late been publishing the story that Camille Flammarion, the great French astronomer, has of late been testing the matter and found there is nothing in it. I showed the clipping to this intelligent farmer and I called his attention to the fact that the announcement that Flammarion was going to put the matter to the test, and again that he had and found nothing in it, were dated only three months apart. So if Flammarion did test the matter in that length of time he is a hustler.

Now, said I, my friend, this is simply one of the thousands of religious lies to support a rapidly decaying old fossil, and yours is a lie of the same sort, because in the first place potatoes and all roots or things that mature in the ground should be planted in the old of the Moon, those that you require much stalk, in the New of the Moon, and those of which you desire much fruit in the full of the Moon.

He finally admitted he had lied and consented to give the matter a good trial, if I would tell him how.

RULES FOR PLANTING AND DOING OTHER THINGS.

Plant all things that bring their crops above the ground in the New of the Moon, and when it is in a fruitful sign if possible. Pisces, Cancer, and Scorpio are the fruitful signs. Gemini, Leo and Virgo are all called barren signs, and Aquarius is not good. Never plant when the Moon is in a barren sign.

Plants, vines, vegetables, trees do best if planted in the New Moon and when in a fruitful sign. Trees should be trimmed a little just before planting and always trim your trees you wish to thrive at the same time you would do your planting, for crops whose fruit matures above ground.

Never trim a tree or shrub in the old of the Moon and positively not when the Moon is in Leo unless you wish to kill it. Such as grubs, noxious weeds and thistles cut out when the Moon is in Leo and in the month of August if possible.

All plants which bring forth their kind beneath the ground should be planted in the old of the Moon, but if possible when in a fruitful sign. Do your harvesting, however, especially for your seed when the Moon is near the full.

Do all pruning, grafting and budding when the Moon is new.

Lay rail fence or foundation in the new of the Moon. If laid in the old of the Moon it will soon seem to sink in the ground and disappear and decay.

People who have no children and want them badly, should find out the age of the Moon and observe its influences.

Timber cut in the new of the Moon will warp or decay, that cut in the old of the Moon, when the Moon is in an air sign will dry out as hard as a bone.

Who has not noticed that at one time the meat you cooked seemed to expand and be juicy, while at another time it shrivels up and is very dry.

Anything killed before the full of the Moon will expand and be juicy, that killed in the old of the Moon, especially in an air or fire sign dries and shrivels up.

McDonald says to travel by land choose the new of the Moon. If by water go in the old of the Moon.

He also says "Letters asking favors are nearly always answered favorably if you write the request in the new of the Moon. I would add in the latter case always choose the time if posible, when the Moon or Mercury are in Gemini, because this is the sign of letters. It is the best time to send out circulars and to tackle all literary work.

A person born in Gemini or with strong Gemini influence, will do better in mail order business or get better satisfaction with correspondents than any other person. Let this be remembered by business people who employ typewriters or clerks to answer correspondence. Of course the more fortunate at birth the more satisfaction their work.

THE CORRECT KNOWLEDGE OF ASTROLOGY for best times for planting and harvesting is very simple and easily committed.

To be a successful agriculturist, first study the Zodiac so as to understand the symbols of the signs and of the Sun and Moon at least. Their influence on vegetable and animal life are then easily picked up. Here are the names of the signs and their influence:

ARIES—Is a masculine, movable, fire sign. Ruled by Mars. Its tendency is to produce much stalk, straw or top and fairly good for grain, if you plant when the New Moon is in this sign, very little fruit if in the old of the Moon unless of such stuff as matures in the ground.

TAURUS—Is a feminine, Earthy sign, governed by Venus, and is pretty good for all root crops, if you plant when the Moon is in this sign, and in the new Moon.

GEMINI—Is an airy barren masculine sign governed by Mercury. Seldom or never brings a good crop, but it is a good time to stir the soil and get rid of noxious weeds when the Moon is in this sign.

CANCER—A feminine fruitful movable water sign ruled by the Moon, and when the Moon is in this sign it is the very best sign to plant or start to do anything, but to get rid of noxious growth. It is bad for that, as the least stir of conditions will increase growth.

LEO—Is a barren masculine fiery sign ruled by the Sun. It is worse than folly to plant when the Moon is in this sign.

Neither plant or trim trees in the month of August or when the Moon is in the sign Leo.

Chop down grubs, hoe up thistles and weeds at such times, and they will surely die.

VIRGO—Is a barren feminine, earth sign, and is only good for the same as is Leo.

LIBRA—Is a masculine, movable air sign much like Aries, though it is better for the production of pith, pulp and roots and good for grain, it is next in value to a fruitful sign. Plant when the Moon is in this sign.

SCORPIO—Is a feminine, fruitful, water sign; it is next best to Cancer for planting, when the same rules are observed. Mars is its ruler.

SAGITTARIUS—Is a masculine, fiery sign ruled by Jupiter, and not very good to plant anything but a good time to cultivate.

CAPRICORNUS—Is a feminine moist, movable sign, will produce rapid growth of straw, stalk, pulp or roots. Not so good for grain. Stuff produced from planting in this sign decays easily.

Saturn is the ruler of Capricornus.

AQUARIUS—Is a masculine, air sign ruled over by Uranus, is much like Leo its polar. To plant when the Moon is in this sign is to throw away both seed and labor.

PISCES—Is a feminine, water, fruitful sign as good as Cancer or Scorpio for planting, if other rules are observed.

Other conditions might bring a bad crop if even these rules are observed. But generally speaking if these rules are observed you will get a good crop.

I live in Detroit, near the Eastern Market, and a few years ago I noticed the tomato crop was very small. I inquired of the gardeners the cause. They all admitted they did not know the cause, but said their vines were fine, but bore little or no fruit. I finally ascertained that nearly all of the gardeners bought their plants instead of planting the seed themselves. I also learned they bought them of the same man, and he knew nothing of taking advantage of the position of the Moon, while some of the farmers who lived away out and planted their own seed, happened to strike a good period and so had good crops.

Even where transplanting is necessary the proper time should be chosen as well as for planting, if you wish the best results.

FOR HARVESTING—Always gather your crops when the Moon is in an air sign if possible. Next best is a fire sign. But never gather fruit when the Moon is in a water sign, nor when the Moon is new as it surely brings early decay, or sprout.

Gather all fruit or vegetable for shipping, just before the full of the Moon. It will hold up fresh and plump, look fine in appearance and hold out in measure.

If possible gather seed at full of the Moon, and when it is in Aries, Taurus, Libra or Sagittarius.

A southern astrologer says that Taurus is the best sign for tobacco. Scorpio and Pisces are also good. But tobacco should be cut just after full moon to the old of the Moon. These same signs are best for cotton.

It seems of late years the south has paid more attention to the benefits of observing the Moon for planting, than the north has.

The following is a clipping from the St. Louis Republic:

AN OLD NEGRO'S DISCOVERY.

An old negro who has a 40-acre farm on Choctaw creek, near Sherman, Tex., claims that he makes a bale of cotton to the acre every year by topping the cotton stalks in the dark of the August Moon.

The topping is said to cause the plant to spread and to put on a heavier fruitage on the lower branches. If it bc established that his uniformly good yield is mainly due to summer pruning, this humble tiller of the soil on Choctaw creek has made as important a discovery in cotton planting as that made in cotton spinning by the mill operative who found out for himself that the thread came smoother and easier by wetting the raw cotton before spinning.—St. Louis Republic.

The above looks very reasonable to an astrologer for the reason that the clipping off the top of bush stopped all growth of the bush and threw the force into the cotton ball.

As we have given the treaty on animal and man and of vegetable matter, we now take up the subject of

---

THE MOON AND POULTRY RAISING.

ASTROLOGY AND POULTRY RAISING.

Notwithstanding the product of the American poultry yard is by many thousand dollars greater in value every year than that of the American wheat fields, we find neither the producer or consumer are reaping the reward, but the speculators and trusts get it all. They have their agents everywhere, and buying up the product, keep it in cold storage until not fit to eat and then get an enormous price for the half-spoiled stock.

There is no necessity for this state of things if the people will make the product so good and so plentiful that it will be impossible for the speculator to corner it.

How can this be done?

I answer, if the public in general will pay attention to these few pages the speculator may be driven from the field and both consumer and producer benefited.

Poultry and eggs are among the most substantial and wholesome of our food products and should be cheap to the consumer and yet profitable to the producer.

There is plenty of cheap land, and plenty of idle people who can turn their idle time into money.

It is true there are a plenty of books devoted to this subject, but they are all written above the heads of the people.

It is generally thought that it takes too long a time to develop your stock before you can reap a reward, and so does not pay.

That is true of the old way of raising and handling poultry, as they start the hens in March and spend the entire year before reaping a reward—from March to March raising and boarding a lot of chickens.

Of course on a farm, where little or no attention is paid to the chickens, this may do, but the stock is poor and generally not very saleable.

Now let us take the matter up in a scientific way.

Here is Mr. Brown. He has about twenty acres of ground, too much for a garden, not enough for a farm. He works out for a living, cannot spend too much time in the garden, so it grows up to grass and weeds. But he loves fowl. He also has a number of strapping big girls and boys, so he figures to set them at work and he talks over the matter together with his neighbor, and they conclude to send to the Agricultural Department at Washington, D. C., for books on chicken raising. The books come, they are beautifully illustrated, they are all that the printer's art can make them. While the books contain much useful information, there is not one word concerning the effect of Astrology in regard to chicken raising.

Someone gave Brown a pamphlet on the effects of the Moon on chicken raising. He shows it to Smith. Smith looks at it with contempt, saying: "Oh! what do those fortune-tellers know about chicken raising? The government has got all there is worth knowing." Both gentlemen went to work with a will. But Brown remembers his mother used to use the almanac in all such matters, until the "smart Alics" substituted the constillations for the signs, and then it did not work any more, so for years we have heard but little about using the almanac for such purposes.

Smith immediately fixed up his old barn for a hen-coop and bought a number of Plymouth Rocks and other fancy breeds of chickens. These are large, plump fowl; they are handsome, but not always the best paying stock. But, Smith was going for the best and as he said to Brown, "I am going into the business scientifically or not at all." Smith also got an incubator and as his hens laid he picked out all of the biggest eggs and said he would have no runtlings. Time made no difference to Smith; in fact, he knew nothing about a choice of time except to get there as soon as possible. Smith set his incubator going on the first day of January, and of course his chickens hatched—that is, all that did hatch—on the 21st and 22nd of January, when the Moon was in Gemini. Though a barren air sign, a few sickly chickens came out; he had very poor luck all around.

Smith did not know the hen moistened her eggs with dew and turned them over every morning, so he merely kept the incubator going until someone told him the eggs should be moistened and turned over. Then he moistened the eggs, but did not know the chemical difference between dew and water from the pump, so his chicks were scrawny, long-legged and restless, and because he used the long and large eggs most of his chicks were roosters. These he fatted and sold for springers in May. The pullets did not begin to lay until the next spring, because Smith fed too much grain and kept them too fat. He knew only what the books told him. Smith became discouraged and was about to give up in despair for with all of his product it did not pay the cost of each chick. Smith talked the matter over with Brown and asked him how he came out with his experiment.

"Well," said Brown, "here is what I did and here are my books.

"You know it was two years ago last fall we went into the business. We have had hardly time to establish ourselves and make ends meet.

"I first bought ten Black Spanish hens and a rooster, for which I paid 50 cents apiece, or $5.50. I bought the same number of Cochin Chinas and the same number of old-fashioned Dominics, which closely resemble the Plymouth Rocks, only they are smaller.

"You remember you laughed at me and said I had nothing but dung-hill stock. While my stock cost me $15, yours cost you $60.

"Of course I had more ground than you had. I had the twenty-acre lot, but you had five acres, which is quite enough; besides, you have your barn for a coop. I had to build mine, so I got some cheap lumber and built six coops, three feet wide and six feet long, three feet and a half high. The tops were built like a gable-roof house, to shed the rain, and on hinges so I can lift them up to take out the adjustable roosts and clean them and so that I can whitewash the inside of the coops. In this way I keep the coops free from vermin. At first I made drop-boards for each coop, but I soon found a better way, which was to put handles on each end of the coops, so my son and I can pick up a coop and move it a few feet and it is always on a clean piece of ground. No vermin can get a start in my coops. One side of each coop I built a tier of nests so I can lift a lid and get at the nests without going into the coops to frighten the birds. Though I make such pets of my birds this is hardly necessary, yet it is the best way.

"In the winter I placed the coops in a semi-circle, facing the south. I bought some old windows and made a regular hothouse, glass facing the south, of course. I also bought a load of sand and I always keep some on hand for the birds to scratch in, and it pays me just to see them roll and scratch and cover themselves with sand under the warm sunlight. The sand is dry; it will not freeze, so stormy and cloudy days the birds keep to their warm coops, but as soon as the Sun shines they enjoy themselves in the scratch-box, as we call it. I got a bushel of lime for whitewashing the coops, and I mix a little with the sand; this not only aids to keep the scratch-box clean, but furnished material for the shells of the eggs."

"That's all very nice," said Smith. "I know I made a mistake in not building more convenient coops, and I lost a number of birds from some disease. But what did all of this cost you?"

"Oh," said Brown, "the old lumber and windows, sand and lime, cost me $15, making $30 to start with."

"Yes," said Smith; "but your feed, what did you feed them?"

"Oh," said Brown, "you know it was September when we got our chickens. Well, I fed them such stuff as we had around the house, at first. You know I keep a cow and we often had lobbered, or thick milk; I found the birds thrive on that and it makes them lay like fun. I also was much surprised to see what a lot of grass and clover they will eat and I feed them that. This caused me to think, so I got a dozen old whisky barrels, for which I paid 50 cents each, or $6. I made silos of these and cut up cornstalks and clover and put a little salt on and let the stuff cure. This I did just before the full of the Moon, and when the Moon was in a water sign, so the nutriment ana moisture would not dry out of the fodder. My chickens loved this and thrived on it all winter. But hens need some meat, so I paid $7 for a grinder. I bought refuse, scraps and bones, at the butchers', until their charges for such stuff became as high as beefsteak, and then I thought of a better plan.

"I heard of a woman in Philadelphia who kept a boarding house and she raised 600 pounds of Belgian hares on ten feet square of ground in a back-door yard. So I noted in my books from Washington the information given there, and a year ago last spring I commenced to raise Belgian hares, not so much for market as for food for my chickens. I put them on the sand knoll and inclosed 60 feet square in wire fence. The whole enterprise cost me $25. But out of four does and a buck rabbit, in one year I kept up my stock and raised a thousand pounds of rabbit meat. The best of the rabbits I dressed for the market and sold 500 pounds at 6 cents a pound. The heads and feet I run through the grinder, as I did the bodies of some of the poorer hares. This gave my hens all the meat they required and furnished some better meat for my table than I could buy at the butcher's.

"I saved 100 rabbit skins, for which I got 8 cents apiece.

"Now we will get back to the chickens. Remember, it was two years ago last fall we started with thirty hens. October 1st I gathered my first eggs. October and November I got 1,200 eggs. December, none to speak of. In January I got over 600 eggs, so I averaged over 150 dozen of eggs. I could have sold these in town at an average of 20 cents per dozen, but I used some and sold some and kept the rest for the incubator.

"I first intended to hatch my chicks with the mother hen, instead of the incubator, but I found this would be unsafe business in winter time; besides, the hens I got were great layers but poor setters—that is, purposely I got breeds that were not given to setting every month and especially during winter months.

"To be most successful chickens should be hatched during the full Moon, and to hatch the day the Moon is in the sign Cancer. So year before last the full Moon occurred on January 28th and the Moon was in the sign Cancer, a movable sign, February 18th. So by placing the eggs in the incubator January 28th, we have 21 full days before bringing off the chicks. This hatched the chicks in February, which is not as good a month to bring them out in as is March. But we want to gain as much time as possible, so if we bring them out when the Moon is in the sign Aries or Cancer we will have good healthy chicks, but if we want good game cocks we want to bring them out when the Moon is in Aries, as we get the fighters from that sign. But we get more fruitful birds when the Moon is in Cancer.

"My brooder and incubator cost me $15 and was of the capacity of 200 eggs and I only lost ten eggs. This is remarkable, I admit, but it was largely due to the fact that I paid very close attention to the work.

"I got a dozen large red bottles and filled them with water and set them in the sun for several days. This vitalizes the water and causes it to more closely resemble morning dew. I sprayed the eggs with this every morning and turned them over as the mother hen does.

"You see I had 190 healthy chickens that grew like fun. I lost five small chicks, and it left me 185 good robust chicks. In May I sold fifty pairs at 60 cents a pair.

"My hens continued to lay well. In August my pullets joined the old hens in laying, so I had a hundred good laying fowl, and over four hundred chicks I was preparing for the market; so the first year my young stock paid for themselves in eggs. I do not have to wait until my chickens are a year old before getting eggs from them.

"The first year and a half I cleared $400 on my fowl and rabbits and have now added fancy stock and pigeons, and I expect to clear $1,500 this year beside furnishing my table, and I credit my great luck largely to the application of Astrology to poultry raising. This is simplicity itself.

"For good healthy stock I arrange to hatch my chicks from one to five days before the Moon fulls and when the Moon is in the sign Cancer. I do not use the common almanac for they are worthless, as they give the constillations instead of the signs.

"I select the sex of my chickens by selecting the eggs. The long, large eggs almost invariably hatch roosters and they are not so plump and saleable for table use as the pullets'. Eggs that will hatch the finest and best pullets are fair-sized, nearest to round eggs."

A person who is going to raise or deal in poultry should know the very best means of telling the exact age of an egg, so I give a method here that is said to be very accurate.

TESTING EGGS.

"A new and simple method for testing eggs is published in German papers. It is based upon the fact that the air chamber in the flat end of the egg increases with age. If the egg is placed in a saturated solution of common salt it will show an increasing inclination to float with the long axis vertical. A scale is attached to the vessel containing the salt solution, so that the inclination of the floating egg toward the horizontal can be measured. In this way the age of the egg can be determined almost to a day. A fresh egg lies in a horizontal position at the bottom of the vessel; an egg from three to five days old shows an elevation of the flat end so that its long axis forms an angle of 20 degrees. With an egg eight days old the angle increases to 45 degrees, and with one three weeks old to 75 degrees, while an egg a month old floats vertically upon the pointed end."

Now let us see if we cannot beat the cold storage speculator, so that every family can put down their own eggs.

I have used the following process in my family for years, except that I merely dipped the eggs in the solution and placed them back in the crate and they kept all right setting in my cellar.

Thrifty families can just as well preserve their eggs as their fruit, and the small dealer or chicken raiser can as well reap the harvest of winter prices for eggs as to give it to the cold storage speculator.

HOW TO PRESERVE EGGS.

"German papers state that it is possible to keep eggs fresh for any length of time by simply immersing them in a 10-per-cent solution of silicia of soda, commonly called 'liquid glass.' This produces the formation of a coating which renders the eggs perfectly air-tight and when so treated they retain their fresh taste for many months. The best proof of the efficacy of this process has been furnished by the fact that such eggs, after having been kept for a whole year, were hatched, and the chickens were strong and healthy. The preserving solution is best prepared by dissolving one pound of liquid glass in four quarts of cold water. The eggs are then immersed in this solution, which should be kept in a glazed earthenware vessel. If one of these preserved eggs is to be boiled, the shell must first be perforated, in order to prevent cracking."

TO TELL THE AGE OF AN EGG.

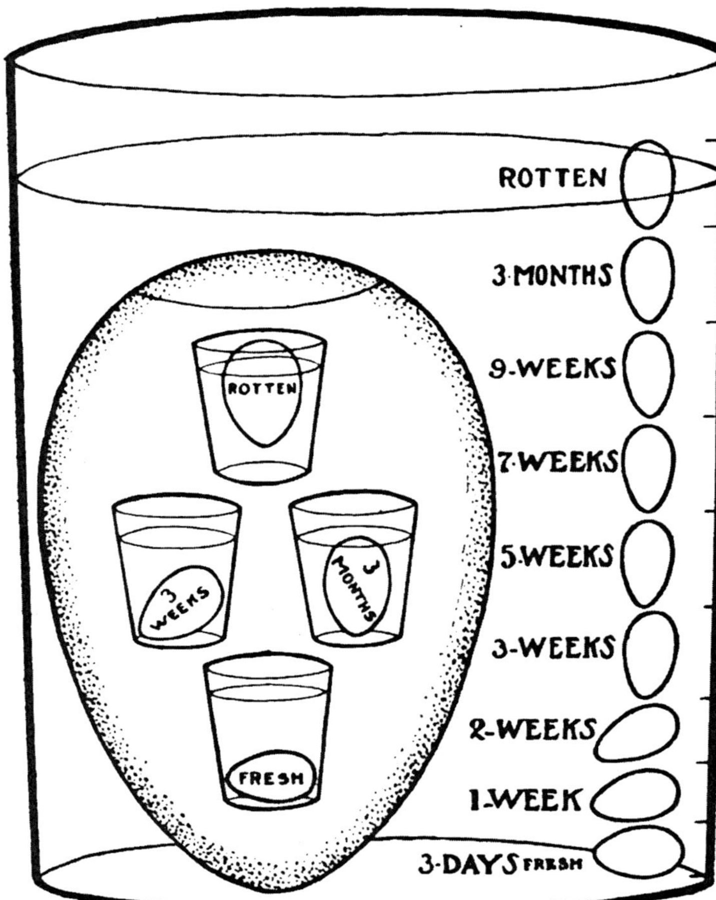

A fresh egg will sink when placed in water and rest on its side; if one week old there is a slight incline, which continues to increace as represented in the cut and in hot summer weather; in moderat or cool weather the decay is a little slower and can be arrested onlyby cold storage or by closing the pores of the shell.

TABLE OF NUTRITION AND GUIDE TO DIGESTION

THE TABLE SHOWS THE COMPARATIVE NUTRIMENT FOUND IN VARIOUS ARTICLES OF FOOD. THE FIGURES SHOW THE PROPORTION OF NUTRIMENT IN EVERY 1000 PARTS

CEREAL		ANIMAL FOOD		VEGETABLES		FRUITS & NUTS	
WHEAT	950	BEEF	260	POTATOES	120	PENUTS	700
BREAD	800	VEAL	250	BEETS	148	ALMONDS	656
RYE	792	PORK	240	CARROTS	98	WALNUTS	600
OATS	742	MUTTON	290	TURNIPS	42	APPLES	170
BARLEY	920	FOWL	275	CABBAGE	73	PEACHES	200
PEAS (DRY)	930	FISH (ABOUT)	200	CORN (GREEN)	180	PARES	190
BEANS (DRY)	890	EGGS	140	PEAS (GREEN)	160	CHERRIES	250
RICE	880	MILK	172	CUCUMBER	25	PLUMS	290
CORN (DRY)	960	RABBIT	260	MELLONS	30	STRAWBERRIE	120

LENGTH OF TIME OF DIGESTION IN HOURS AND MINUTS

ANIMAL FOOD	H.M.	VEGETABLES	H.M.	SUNDRIES	H.M.
BEEF (BOILED)	4.15	POTATOES	3.30	APPLES	2.30
BEEF (ROASTED)	3.20	BEETS	3.45	PEARS	1.45
LIVER	3.20	TURNIPS	4.00	PEARS	2.00
MUTTON (BOILED)	3.00	CARROTS	4.15	PLUMS	3.40
MUTTON (ROASTED)	3.15	ONION	2.05	BANANAS	1.45
PORK (BOILED)	4.15	PARSNIPS	3.30	BLACKBERRIES	2.35
PORK (ROASTED)	5.20	RADISHES	4.00	CHERRIES	2.00
VEAL	4.00	MUSHROOMS	1.20	CURRANTS	3.30
CHICKEN (BOILED)	4.00	BEANS (BAKED)	2.30	STRAWBERRIES	2.45
CHICKEN (ROASTED)	3.30	CABBAGE	4.30	FIGS	3.00
DUCK	4.00	ASPARAGUS	1.30	GRAPES	3.00
GOOSE	4.05	CAULIFLOWER	2.00	GRAPE SKINS	5.30
TURKEY	4.25	CELERY (UNCOOKED)	3.15	MELONS	3.00
RABBITS	4.30	CUCUMBER	4.45	NUTS	4.00
EGGS	3.00	HORSERADISH	4.00	PINEAPPLE	2.35
CHEESE	3.30	LETTUCE	3.00	ORANGES	2.45
MILK	2.30	RICE (BOILED)	1.30	MACARONI	3.00
BUTTER	3.00	PEAS (GREEN)	2.35	BREAD	3.30
FISH (SALT)	3.30	CORN (GREEN)	2.50	TAPIOCA	2.35
FISH (FRESH)	3.20	TOMATOES	2.05	OAT MEAL	3.05
LOBSTERS	4.00	GREENS	3.00	CORNMEAL	3.00
OYSTERS	2.35	BEETS (GREEN)	3.10	BEACON & HAM	4.00

The chart of "Right Hours to Success," on the opposite page, is the same as that used in our revolving disk. It may be used by calculation. As we always start at sunrsie, we set the symbol ruling the sign for a month, at sunrise, when the sign begins to rule. (See instructions.) We never change that, until the next sign begins its rule. The circle containing the days of the week also show the symbols of the planets ruling each day, and the planet ruling the day of the week also rules the first hour of the day, beginning with sunrise, then the planets follow in their order as found on the circle. Follow the eircle right around until the coil drops, worm like when you drop with it to the circle below. The revolving disk wil save much time and patience. Those paying $5. for the book should get all the charts mounted on card board which saves time and patience, and the inconvenience of stopping to calculate. For convenience, we have a small hour book of instructions, together with revolving chart for one dollar, extra charts fifty cents.

I feel sure any person who once uses this system of choosing the best time to do any thing will never again do without it, and go blundering his way throu the world.

PREFACE TO RIGHT HUROS. 1

The publishers had no intention of publishing an hour book, except as a part of "ASTROLOGICAL PERIODICITY. But many of our patrons desiring an hour book and table they could carry in the pocket, that it might be always handy to refer to, requested us to publish a small volume explanatory of the use of hours.

This we declined to do, as the field was well occupied with those books and tables already in use, and mentioned in this work. "The Little Mascot," by Prof Henry, of Boston, Mass., price $1.00, is a work every student should have.

The "Luck Dial," by Walter H. Lewis, of Manchester, N. H., price $1.00, is a beautiful dial, an ornament for any man's table.

The "Hour Iidicator," by Dr. J. MacDonald, of Binghamton, N. Y., a handy little dial for the pocket, price $1.00.

We have just heard of a small book published by the Portland School of Astrology, 226 Clay street, Portland, Ore. Price 25c.

While one dial or set of tables might be sufficient for any person's use, we might say the more we can learn of these things the better use we can make of them, so it is wise to purchase and compare all of these works.

While we have heard of the complaint of some authors, that their ideas have been purloined by others, we wish to say, there is no doubt that all authors have derived their information from the same source (i. e), the ancient astrologers, consequently the phraseology may seem much the same.

We know Mr. Stowe had no intention of copying from any other author and he says if any man will show him where he has done so, without giving credit, he will give due credit. If he has unconsciously copied from any one it is from Prof. Henry, of Boston. But there is no intended infringement here, and for fear any one would feel aggrieved, Prof. Stowe seeks to do him more good than evil by so advertising the best works in this line. Hence we mention other authors and advise the public to purchase.

We would have given Prof. Henry a special page the same as that given other astrologers. But, Mr. Stowe wrote him for his picture, but for some unknown reason up to time of going to press, he has received no answer.

It will be seen that Prof. Stowe's method of denoting the good and evil hours differs from all others in the use of the signs of the Zodiac in connection with planetary hours, this being the method of the old astrologers, and it is this fact that has casued our customers to urge the publication of a small volume of "Right Hours."

THE PROPER USE OF HOURS.

My excuse for presenting an hour book to the public is to correct the errors of former writers on this subject.

As the astrology of the ages has come to us in fragments and covered with literary cobwebs, the work of sifting out the truths and polishing the pure metal of facts that it may be distinguished from the baser metal is not the work of one author or searcher for truth; but we may all do our share and improve the work of one another, as some later writer may add to the truths I have uncovered in this little work. In fact, in a book I am now working on, entitled "Astrological Periodicity," I shall be able to add to modern astrology many wonders I have unearthed from the debris of ancient astrology.

The trouble of most of our writers on astrology is, they too often jump to conclusions and do not put their work to the test thoroughly enough before submitting it to the public.

Some years ago, while writing sketch horoscopes for a daily paper, I found in twenty successive cases of married couples that Venus, the goddess of love, was found in the sign of the married partner at birth. This was very strong evidence of an infallible rule of defining what sign a married partner would be born in. I was about to publish it as a wonderful discovery of a fixed rule, when lo and behold! I found nearly as many more consecutively where Venus was in no position to influence love affairs of the couples. This astounded me beyond measure, but it made me very careful of my claims in astrological truths.

I find Prof. Henry of Boston, and the late Earnest Green and others, in their hour books, divide the day and night hours, giving long hours for the day and short hours for the night, in summer, and vice versa for the winter months. This is all wrong; for if daylight and darkness has anything to do in the matter, a man in prison, shut out from daylight, could not be under the influence of the planets during the daylight hours. Then, again, the ancients did not so understand the matter—but the following is the language they use:

"Of the angels of the hours, according to the course of the days. The Sun, the angel Michael ruleth Sunday, the 1st hour of the day; Anael, Venus, 2; Raphael, Mercury, 3; Gabriel, Moon, 4; Cassiel, Saturn, 5; Sachiel, Jupiter, 6; Samael, Mars, 7; Michael, Sun, 8; Anael, Venus, 9; Raphael, Mercury, 10; Gabriel, Moon, 11; Cassiel, Saturn, 12.

"Angels of the hours of the night: Sachiel, Jupiter, 1 Samuel, Mars, 2; Michael, Sun, 3; Anael, Venus, 4; Raphael, Mercury, 5; Gabriel, Moon, 6; Cassiel, Saturn, 7; Sachiel, Jupiter, 8; Samael, Mars, 9; Michael, Sun, 10; Anael, Venus, 11; Raphael, Mercury, 12."

These are the names of the planets, called angels, who rule the hours of the day and night in their order, always starting with the Sun at sunrise on Sunday, as the Sun rules Sunday. The Moon rules Monday, and so starts Monday at sunrise, followed by Saturn, and so on in their order, as given in the accompanying tables. Mars rules Tuesday, and starts the first hour at sunrise. Mercury rules Wednesday;

3

Jupiter, Thursday; Venus, Friday. Saturn rules Saturday, and each start the day they rule at sunrise, followed by the next planet, as given.

Note what follows:

"But this is to be observed: that the first hour of the day, of every country, and in every season whatsoever, is to be assigned to the Sun,—rising. When he first appeareth rising on the horizon, and in the first hour of the night, is to be the thirteenth hour from the first hour of the day."

Be it observed, nothing here is said of long and short hours.

Where our friends have made their mistake in using the long and short hours, is this:

Noticing that all hours assigned to Mars or any one planet were not alke, and failing to observe the cause, they sought to find the cause; and so struck upon the theory that the Sun having more power upon us than any other body, they concluded the hours must be changed in length to match the day and night.

Instead of this, they should have noticed that the Zodiac is the basic work of all astrology, and that the signs of the Zodiac rule the hours of the day as much as the planets, commencing with Aries. From March 21st to April 19th, Aries rules the first hour of the day, Taurus the second, Gemini the third, and so on through the Zodiac, as presented in the tables. From April 19th to May 20, Taurus rules the first hour of the day, Gemini the second, and so on through the Zodiac. Thus each Zodiac sign rules during its term and as the Sun is strong while in a sign, the hours differ in their influence according to the sign the hour represents. Thus, a Jupiter hour will be much stronger in Pisces, Sagittarius, and Taurus, than in Capricornus or Scorpio—while fiery Mars will be softened in Taurus and Libra (see table of Influences). It will here be seen an Aries sun-hour would be quite different from a Capricornus sun-hour or during a sun-hour in any other sign.

4

The nature of a planet must be mixed with the nature of the sign it represents while it rules a specific hour.

It should not be claimed that any hour is good or bad, but that certain hours of the day will bring certain results, and are good for certain purposes and evil for other purposes. Besides, these cannot be arbitrarily fixed for every individual; but each individual should be watchful and test the hours for himself.

A person who had Mars for a ruling planet at birth might find a Mars hour excellent for him to execute a plan, if he is careful to avoid unpleasant controversy.

Then, again, if a man is in an evil year or cycle, a good hour might not bring as favorable results as if he were in a good period; even an evil transit culminating just in that hour might lessen the good or increase the evil af an evil hour.

THE OBJECT OF THIS BOOK IS TO GIVE THOSE WHO CONSULT ITS PAGES THE MOST FAVORABLE HOURS TO TRANSACT THE VARIOUS FORMS OF BUSINESS, such as consulting professional men or people occupying positions of dignity, making social calls, seeking employment, or for collecting money, writing letters or other documents.

That the planets do rule certain hours of the day will soon be made manifest to him who is careful and observant. To such a person will come the knowledge of the line of thought he or any other person is likely to follow during given hours of the day or night.

ℏ

DIRECTIONS.

First familiarize yourself with the influence of the signs, then with the influence of the planets; and their influence in the different signs of the Zodiac.

Aries is a positive, forceful, fiery, diplomatic, forgiving sign, and will exert that influence on a planetary hour during the reign of that sign. As example: The Sun rules honor and dignity if the Sun hour falls in Aries, that would take on the influence of Aries; and if you call on an errand, seeking the aid of a dignified person, he would appear austere, proud, obstinate, but if you appeal to his generosity and pride and kindly nature, he will be condescending. If it be in a Libra hour, you should appeal to his sense of justice; if it be in a Taurus or scorpio hour, appeal to his sympathy—and to his appetite, if possible; if it is in a Capricornus or Cancer hour, appeal to his business wisdom, ability, and business instincts; if it chance to be in a Pisces or Gemini hour, appeal to his intelligence and endurance; if in an Aquarius or Leo hour, appeal to his judgment; if in Sagittarius or Virgo, appeal to his religion or personal gain—these are the hours of bribery.

To recapitulate: the nature of ARIES is forceful, fiery, diplomatic, proud, austere, yet forgiving and kindly. Forceful argument should never be used—unless in a happy, kindly nature in an Aries or Taurus hour.

6

TAURUS influence is of a sympathetic, quiet, kindly nature, easily coaxed, but cannot be driven—stubborn. Take time to persuade.

GEMINI influence is of a nervous, anxious nature, all business and push, in a hurry to travel and get away; also intellectual, quick to perceive.

CANCER influence is of a quiet, plodding, thoughtful reasoning, home-loving, business nature.

LEO is of a forceful, inventive, mechanical nature; contrary, of the cat nature—coax me, pet me, but do not stroke the fur the wrong way. Appeal to the speculative.

VIRGO is of a jolly, good nature—give me my own way and I will do much more for you than if you make a bargain with me; yet if you offer me a bribe in a quiet, disinterested way, I'll take it.

LIBRA is of a balancing, reasoning nature. Appeal to reason and justice and intellectuality.

SCORPIO influences the appetite and religious sense of honor, but drives hard bargains, and is exacting in those bargains, and, like Virgo and Taurus, may be reached through the stomach. Also appeal to the speculative.

SAGITTARIUS is a fierce, fiery, forceful sign, influencing the morals, liable to be religious or hypocritical according to other conditions, especially in a Mars or Saturn hour.

CAPRICORNUS is all business, honor and dishonor, according to the planet in the sign.

AQUARIUS rules friends, and judgment and these matters are strongly influenced by the planet in the sign. Appeal to friendship in this hour.

PISCES rules enemies, but is an intellectual sign, slow and sympathetic, and may become your enemy or friend according to the planet in it. Curiosity plays a great part here; appeal to the intellectual and the curious during a Pisces hour.

INFLUENCE OF PLANETS.

As before stated, a person passing through an evil year or during an evil transit, will feel the evil hours more and the good hours less than one who was born fortnuate; or an unfortunate person will not feel the good hours so much as a fortunate person—so the fortunate person must always have an advantage over the unfortunate person. Yet the unfortunate person who understands how to take advantage of the good and evil hours may stand on a par with a fortunate man who does not understand how to make use of the hours.

The evil hours are those supposed to be ruled over by Saturn and Mars; those by Mercury are uncertain. The good hours are those ruled over by the Sun, Moon, Venus, and Jupiter, and the capital letters at the end of the name of each planet stand for: G, for good; E, for evil; B, for barren; C, for changeable; D, for doubtful.

But the following gives the influence of each planet, the expression, of course, to be modified by the sign ruling at the end of each line, or hour, and by the sign ruling the month you are working in. Thus, the first table runs from March 21st to April 19th. Aries then follows

Taurus, from April 19th to May 20th.

Gemini, from May 20th to June 21st.

Cancer, from June 21st to July 22d.

Leo, from July 22d to August 23d.

Virgo, from August 23d to September 23d

Libra, from September 23d to October 23d.

Scorpio, from October 23d to November 22d.

Sagittarius, from Nov. 22d to Dec. 22d.

Capricornus, from Dec. 22d to Jan. 20th.

Aquarius, from Jan. 20th to Feb. 19th.

Pisces, from Feb. 19th to Mar. 21st

SUN rules Sunday, and is strongest in Leo, next in Aries; the weakest in Libra and Aquarius.

A Sun hour is positive and apt to be barren of results unless special purposes are sought, such as consulting judges, dignitaries, people of wealth and power, or superiors, employers, or people of ruddy complexion, large bodies and heads, or those fond of honor, and so forth; then they should be approached with dignity and shown much respect—but to be judged by the sign the hour is found in at the end of the line to the right. Most favorable to application to people in power. It is good for business or to seek employment, but not to ask for money or loans.

Thoughts and conversation of this hour is apt to drift to governmental or political affairs, societies, or places of preferment, possibly to disease of the vital system. People born this hour are ruddy, forceful and commanding.

MOON is negative and movable. It rules Monday, and the first hour of that day she is most powerful in Cancer and Taurus, the weakest in Scorpio and Capricornus. It rules common and movable things, and to people who are shifting about much—to railroad people, travelers, and so forth. A Moon hour is a good time to go visiting or to receive visitors; and it is good for positive people to approach the wavering in a manner designated by the sign the hour is in.

PEOPLE BORN in this hour are apt to be unsteady of habits, and to be medium in size and of round features, pale or dusky complexions, full eyes, blue, gray or brown, with a restless, springy step. This is their hour; make no decisions in this hour; they are not likely to prove permanent.

9

THOUGHTS AND CONVERSATION will drift to travel or to removals and changeable matters, and matters of health to humors, neuralgia and all shifting diseases, including blood disorders—a very evil hour to visit the sick or to start on perilous journeys.

MARS rules Tuesday, and the first hour of that day. Mars is strongest in Aries, Scorpio and Capricornus, and weakest in Cancer and Taurus. Mars or Mars hours excites to energy, force, passion; it is a good hour to tackle a hard piece of labor, but expect accidents or breaking of tools. Be careful to avoid controversies, as this hour arouses evil propensities of men, especially the vicious; keep from dangerous places and avoid quarrels; trust no one; let everybody have his own way for the time, but put off matters until a more favorable period; buy nothing this hour.

People born this hour are likely to be of florid complexion, red or sandy hair, and high tempered. If other planetary influences are strong, of course this will be more decided.

THOUGHTS AND CONVERSATION of this hour are likely to be of war, law suits or contentions or argumentative and spirited, if not quarrelsome. To matters of health to accidents, fevers, acute pains or inflammatory troubles.

MERCURY is a swift, changing hour; is strongest in Gemini and Virgo, and weakest in Pisces and Sagittarius. It rules Wednesday and the first hour of that day. It is quite an uncertain hour. It relates to intellectual and literary matters. Thus it is good for all things that must be done quickly, as it will hasten matters.

PEOPLE BORN this hour are talkative and have a gift of language.

THOUGHTS AND CONVERSATION of this hour will drift to social or literary affairs in varied turn, according to the sign it represents, but always animated; illness coming on in this hour will take on a nervous form.

Things to do this hour: Make short calls, write letters, sign papers, buy books, deal with lawyers, printers, teachers, or literary people; juggle with numbers. A good hour to buy and sell in rapid exchange.

JUPITER is a slow, forceful, dignified planet, and rules Thursday and the first hour of that day. It is strongest in Pisces, Sagittarius and Cancer, and the weakest in Capricornus and Gemini.

It relates to wealth and position. The strength of the Jupiter hour depends upon the sign it represents at that hour of the day (see the right of the column the hour comes in; as with all other planets. It is supposed to be the best hour to do anything; but the person using this little book will quickly find the hours best suited to him for certain things. You may, however, have much confidence in whatever you do in this hour. It is a peaceful, generous hour.

This hour is good for all business transactions, especially in money matters and for asking favors; also for legal matters, and for handling vicious animals.

THOUGHTS AND CONVERSATION of this hour are likely to drift to speculation and money matters, to profits and losses, in all directions, and to pleasures of all kinds, especially of out door exercise and to horse races. The person who bets with firmness and confidence in this hour will win over the person who knows nothing of the hour matters.

Diseases of all kinds during this hour will take on a better turn, but effect the blood and liver.

VENUS is a negative feminine planet, and rules Friday, and the first hour of the day.

Venus is strongest in Gemini, Libra and Pisces, and weakest in Virgo and Scorpio. It rules all domestic and love affairs, art, music and dress. It is an hour for pleasure and to start on excursions and to places of amusement—to pop the question and to ask favors of the opposite sex.

11

THOUGHTS AND CONVERSATION in this hour are likely to rnn to matters of beauty, love and pleasure; the sick will improve, but the nature of illness contracted, already manifest, will assume a venereal or urinary form or symptom.

This is called the good hour for almost everything.

SATURN is a positive, cold, barren, yet spiritual planet; it rules Saturday, and the first hour of the day. It is strongest in Capricornus and Libra, and weakest in Aries and Cancer. It is called a very evil, treacherous hour; but it must be remembered, like all of the planets, its influence in the hour it rules partakes of the sign it represents of that hour. It relates to grief, sickness, death, and filthy things; yet, under favorable conditions, it is spiritual, and makes a good hour to engage in slow, measured or methodical matters, old or antique things.

I have found, however, it is, for me, an hour to accomplish much labor, especially in astrological literary matters.

THOUGHTS AND CONVERSATION will drift to history, war, things of the past, sorrows and worries; and if to diseases, it will be of old-standing and chronic complaints. The mind of the ill will be melancholy and gloomy.

TO BUSINESS MEN AND SPECULATORS.

During the different hours follow the following directions:

Sun hour, good—deal with matters of dignity and honor; but what you buy will remain with you long, unless the Sun be in Gemini, Libra or Aquarius.

VENUS, good—buy and sell rapidly. This is a very friendly hour; you can lead one less sophisticated into bargains through expressions of friendship.

MERCURY—good for rapid transactions and for exchange of papers; buy and sell through rapidity of presentation and brusk business manners. Read, study and mail circulars.

JUPITER—drive good bargains; look well to your holdings; things bought in a Jupiter hour must rise to a good profit if held long enough; stand on dignity.

MARS—if you win at all it will be by kindly expression of bravado and bluster. "I am all there is; buy of me or you won't get anything good." But this must be done in a kindly spirit.

SATURN—is not considered a good hour for business, for if one is successful he must be hypocritical.

A MOON hour denotes necessity for rapid exchange on an apparently friendly basis. You will find a general friendly expression and a desire to expressions of friendship; but if you wish to do business it must be done quickly.

In referring to the tables always use that one which encompasses the day of the month in which you use it. That is, use the Aries table between March 21st and April 19th, and so on through the twelve tables.

Persons who know their ruling planet, or the planet which influences them the strongest, may find the hour ruled by their planet, whether called good or evil hour, that may be beneficial to them.

Also, the Lord of the sign a person is born in will materially affect that person. Thus, I was born in Aries; Mars rules that sign; it is called an evil planet —but it often is quite beneficial to me.

Any ephemeries will tell you the name of your ruling planet and the Lord of your sign; or it can be had in your horoscope, written by us for $1.00.

THE ASTROLOGICAL PUB. CO.,

133 *Catherine St., Detroit, Mich...*

13

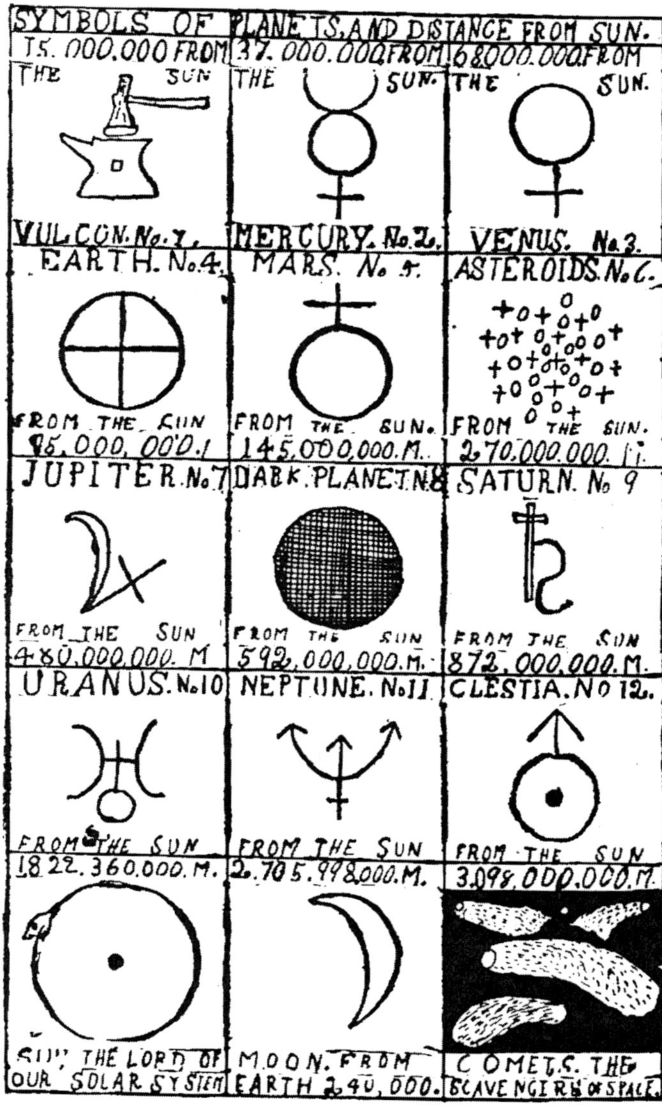
SYMBOLS OF PLANETS, AND DISTANCE FROM SUN.
15.000.000 FROM THE SUN
VULCON. No. 1.
37.000.000 FROM THE SUN.
MERCURY. No. 2.
68000.000 FROM THE SUN.
VENUS. No. 3.
EARTH. No. 4.
FROM THE SUN
95.000.000.M
MARS. No. 5.
FROM THE SUN.
145.000.000.M.
ASTEROIDS. No. 6.
FROM THE SUN.
270.000.000.M.
JUPITER. No. 7
FROM THE SUN
480.000.000. M
DARK PLANET. No. 8
FROM THE SUN
592.000.000.M.
SATURN. No. 9
FROM THE SUN
872.000.000.M.
URANUS. No. 10
FROM THE SUN
1822.360.000.M.
NEPTUNE. No. 11
FROM THE SUN
2.705.998.000.M.
CLESTIA. No. 12.
FROM THE SUN
3098.000.000.M.
SUN, THE LORD OF OUR SOLAR SYSTEM
MOON. FROM EARTH 240,000.
COMETS. THE SCAVENGIRS OF SPACE.

Page I3 gives symbols of planets and 14 symbols of the signs of the Zodiac. Notice the three symbols of astrelogy, the circle, criscent end cross, are the baces of the symbols of all religeon as well as all other astrological symbols.

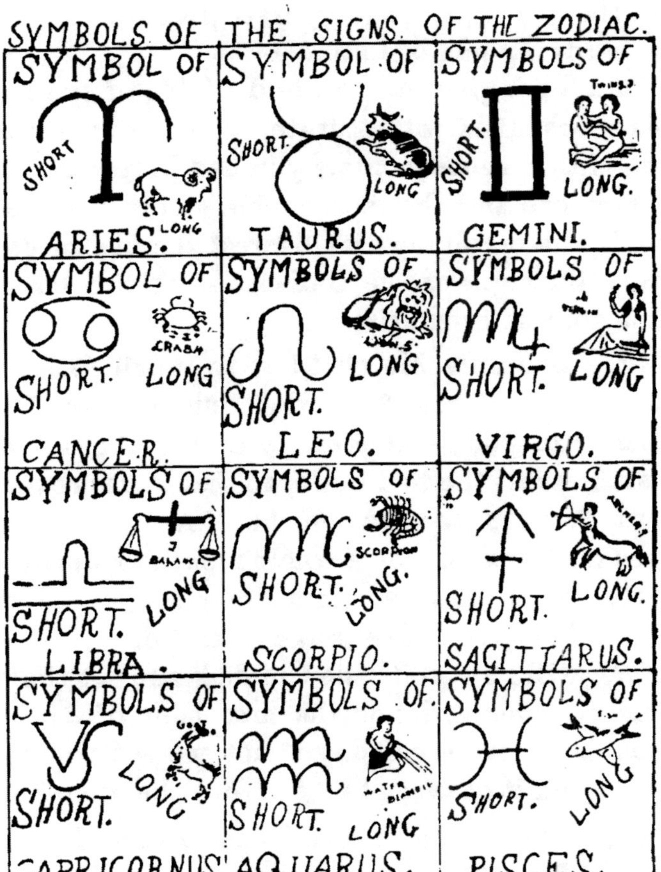

SPECIAL INSTRUCTIONS FOR THE USE OP THE REVOLVING DISK.

ls. If not familiar with the signsof the Zodiac and the planets, make yourself familiar with them by studying pages 13 and 14.

2nd. Though you will find a table of sun rise' in his book, it is not accurate, to the minute, for all localalities, censequentaly you had better get a local almanac and that will enable you to work closer,

3d The revolving disk nearest the bed piece contains the signs of the Zodiac, set this to cover the first hour after sunrise.

For example March 21st. to April 19th. Aries rules and March 21st. the Sun rises, in Detroit Mich. at 6oc., therefore you set the revolving disk, nearest the bed piece, so that Aries covers the hour from 6 to 7oc. A. M. Now remember this does not change, for a whole month or untill April 19th. when Taurus takes its place, and remains untill May 20t. See page 7 and 8.

We will now go to the top disk and set the word Sunday over Aries or the first hour of the day, that is if it be Sunday if not we set the day of the week it chances to be. Now the first hour of Sunday is a sun Aries hour, that is from Sun 6oc. to 7oc. then run as follows.

HOURS OF THE DAY.	HOURS OF NIGHT.
6 to 7 - ♈ - ☉ hour.	6 to 7 - ♈ - ♃ hour.
7 to 8 - ♉ - ♀ hour.	7 to 8 - ♉ - ♂ hour.
8 to 9 - ♊ - ☿ hour.	8 to 9 - ♊ - ☉ hour.
9 to 10 - ♋ - ☽ hour.	9 to 10 - ♋ - ♀ hour.
10 to 11 - ♌ - ♄ hour.	10 to 11 - ♌ - ☿ - hour.
11 to 12 - ♍ - ♃ - hour.	11 to 12 ♍ - ☽ - hour.
12 to 1 - ♎ - ♂ hour	12 to 1 - ♎ ♄ - hour.
1 to 2 - ♏ - ☉ hour.	1 to 2 - ♏ - ♃ hour.
2 to 3 - ♐ - ♀ hour.	2 to 3 - ♐ - ♂ hour.
3 to 4 - ♑ - ☿ hour.	3 to 4 - ♑ - ☉ hour.
4 to 5 - ♒ - ☽ hour.	4 to 5 - ♒ - ♀ hour.
5 to 6 - ♓ - ♄ hour.	5 to 6 - ♓ - ☿ hour.

It will be seen by this Monday starts with the Moon 6 to 7 and you have a Moon Aries hour then a Saturn Taurus hour and so following the worm circle on the disk. which gives you the planets ruling the hours and the signs they are in.

It is well to notice here, the disk bearing the signs is changed bnt once a month, or when the signs change. But, you must beare in mind the disk bearing the planets must be changed or set every morning, becaus the Sun rise is continually changing and there is a difference of 49 minutes betwen March 21 st. and April 19 th. Thus, a planitary hour may be found covering a part of two signs, this gives it two distinct influences or effects, for example, Mars is strong in Aries and weak in Taurus. Producing a firey austere influence while in Aries but mild and persuasive in a Taurus hour.

While the planetary hours can be used without the signs they cannot be judged so accurately as with the use of the signs.

I have found the use of long and short hours, as is done in some cases, rather hinders a perfect judgment than helps it.

The more assistence and greator the accuracy we can reach in the judgment of the use of hours, the greator the benifits we must derive. It is for this reason I have got out the revolving disk, as it gives the clock, the signs and the planets, and their influence, much more correctly than my plates, spoken of, which appear in "Astrological Periodicity," yet as they assist in the study of the work I leave them, but also adopt the revolving disk and beg the student to study every part of the book as well as the other books mentioned that he may perfectly understand the use and purpose of the work.

My revolving disk differs from all others, as I use the worm circle, so the planets may be followed in their order, without changing the disk, as in other dials.

Believeing it would be a great assistence to show

the conduct necessary to win the concent and influence of others, as well as what to do, I oppend the following explaination of planets in signs.

THE EFFECTS OF THE PLANETS IN THE DIFFERENT SIGNS.

SUN EXALTS IN ARIES—This hour excessively proud, austere, forceful, convey your message quickly, in dignified manner, use no argument, unless you feel your superiority greatly over another.

SUN IN TAURUS—Be dignified, but persuasive, kind of expression, be persistent, hang on for 24 hours, appeal to the stomach, treat if convenient, but do it carelessly.

SUN IN GEMINI—Be dignified but brusque, hurried in all business.

SUN IN CANCER—Always dignified. Do not hurry, be thoughtful, speak pleasantly of surroundings and home and on these grounds persuasive.

SUN RULES LEO—So is strong. Bend to dignity, show interest in mechanics, invention, and speculation, coax, flatter; but do not oppose or argue.

SUN IN VIRGO—Bow to dignity, show jolly good nature, do not be exacting, appeal to generosity, or offer inducements.

SUN FALLS IN LIBRA, is weak Sun hour. A person can be mre positive in this hour than in any other Sun hour, but he must show dignity and intellectuality.

SUN IN SCORPIO—This hour is very dignified and exacting, drives hard bargains, may be reached through the stomach, appeal to it while offering a bribe.

SUN IN SAGITTARIUS—Dignified, fierce, religious, look out for bribery or hypocrisy.

19

SUN IN CAPRICORNUS—This is an hour of rush, business and push, much honor expressed but not so much practiced, the planet in the sign at the time will give strong influence during this hour.

SUN'S DETRIMENT OR REST IN AQUARIUS—This hour will be more friendly, less dignified, but it is strongly influenced by the planet in the sign, seek friends and position.

SUN IN PISCES—Look out for trickery, enmity, excite sympathy and curiosity, in him you deal with.

THE MOON IS FIERY IN ARIES—This is a hot, passionate, fiery hour; what you do, do quickly; coax, do not argue, as no one has the time for argument in this hour.

THE MOON EXALTS IN TAURUS—This is a friendly hour, love of flattery, coaxing, but must be expressed in a diplomatic manner. Do not try to deceive.

THE MOON IN GEMINI—Excites too great activity, this is the hour to push business, mail letters and circulars, start on business trips; be quick with everything.

THE MOON RULES CANCER—Is strong, this hour is a good hour to receive, to do work at home, to buy things for the family or home, marketing, etc. It is also a good hour to pop the question.

THE MOON RULES LEO—This is a good hour for speculation, inventions, or mechanics, but be persuasive, yet quick.

THE MOON IN VIRGO—Is an hour of good nature, friendly, the best of the calling hours, but look out for bribery, or treachery in business matters.

THE MOON IN LIBRA—This is a pleasure loving-seeking hour, but reasoning and intellectual. Good to do any visiting, asking favors, if you appeal to good nature and reason.

THE MOON FALLS IN SCORPIO—This is a selfish hour, ask no favors, unless accompanied with promise or treat or some sort, or financial inducement.

MOON IN SAGITTARIUS—This hour is best for religious work of any kind or to seek a serving situation, act quickly and look out for hypocrisy.

MOON'S DETRIMENT IN CAPRICORNUS—This hour is good only to push business, already began, then appeal to business honor, but look out for dishonor.

MOON IN AQUARIUS—Appeal to friendship, especially to matronly ladies, deal with the rich and powerful and get a friend, a lady if possible to intercede for you.

MOON IN PISCES—This is a good hour to seek knowledge, money, trade, especially in liquids; appeal to curiosity. Look out for quick acts of an enemy. Any Moon hour is a dangerous hour for accidents.

In all Moon hours act quickly.

MERCURY IN ARIES—Appeals to the intellectual,

though a Mercury hour is called a very uncertain hour. I find it an excellent hour in all things pertaining to education, literary work, writing letters or marketing, or trading, no matter what sign is ruling. Yet it is best to observe and act upon the signs ruling the hours Mercury rules. In Aries one must be more forceful and dignified, can be very argumentative and forceful if you appeal to the intellectual.

MERCURY IN TAURUS—The same in all signs is tricky, but here works best when appealing to sympathy or the stomach. Deal in real estate or products of the earth.

MERCURY RULES GEMINI—Here he excites to great activity in all directions. If you are slow in action, you will fail. This hour is most excellent for all short journeys and for mailing letters, circulars and all literary matters.

MERCURY IN CANCER—Here again Mercury's influence is strongly to the intellectual, but acts slower than in Gemini. Appeal to the domestic side of life, good in all educational matters, and trade, good to deal in liquids, and air operations.

MERCURY IN LEO—This is the hour to begin a legal fight, or a battle, or an invention or mechanical job that requires mental work or much planning.

MERCURY IN VIRGO—Mercury also rules Virgo, or, properly speaking, it exalts here, is next most powerful in this sign. He creates mirth, and is very tricky in this sign, yet appeal to honor and sympathy and you can do much. It is good to start all matters that Mercury rules. But Mercury is a thief, if you do not watch him. Deal in matters of earth.

MERCURY IN LIBRA—Very intellectual, but appeal to passion and reason, good to start in matrimonial, musical, theatrical or literary matters.

MERCURY IN SCORPIO—Is likely to prove very tricky and uncertain, except in chemical matters or liquids, very bad to call a funeral at this hour.

MERCURY DETRIMENT IN SAGITTARIUS—Look out for accidents. It is a very uncertain hour, but is good for religious matters and to collect money for charity.

MERCURY IN CAPRICORNUS—This is another mental sign, and demands quick action and to deal in business matters, a god hour to speculate in real estate or products of the earth.

MERCURY IN AQUARIUS—It is a fair hour to appeal to friendship and to write and mail letters, circulars, etc., but beware of treachery.

MERCURY FALLS IN PISCES—Trust nothing to this hour, it may prove good or bad, more likely bad.

VENUS IN ARIES—Venus is a friendly hour, as good as Jupiter, but better for love-making and dealing with the opposite sex. A Venus hour is called a very lucky hour, and acts through the signs as followed in Aries, appeal to dress, and flashy appearance .

VENUS RULES TAURUS—Hence is strong in Taurus. This is the best hour for love-making or dealing with the opposite sex, and to ask favors in general, especially if you appeal to sympathy and kindness. In all Taurus hours let the opposite party think he is getting what he wants.

VENUS IN GEMINI—This influence simply hastens matters of the Venus influence, or Venus softens the events of the Gemini influence.

VENUS IN CANCER—Simply quiet Venus influence and makes it very domestic. It is an excellent hour to marry, or do work in the home.

VENUS IN LEO—Influences to dignity, dress, pomp, show, and is of a timid but friendly hour if you coax, do not try to drive.

VENUS IN VIRGO—Visit the sick, ask for charity, engage servants, but do not make love, unless you show the sweet heart wealth.

VENUS EXALTS OR RULES LIBRA—Make love, do business, select partners, attend to partnership, business, music, theatricals and all Venus matters.

VENUS IN SCORPIO—This is the hour that makes and heals jealousies, ask favors of the opposite sex, buy and sell chemicals, liquids and products of a southern clime, ask favors, but you are apt to pay for all you get.

VENUS IN SAGITTARIUS—This is excellent hour for church and society matters, to marry and do all Venus stands for.

VENUS IN CAPRICORNUS—Push all business matters with confidence, win business by kindly expression and appeal to honor.

VENUS IN AQUARIUS—This a good hour to make friends or appeal for favors.

VENUS EXALTS IN PISCES—Very strong. Do all things belonging to Venus and deal in products of the water, or vegetables, make friends, marry.

MARS RULES ARIES—This is the hour to commence or push a lawsuit, or battle, but avoid quarreling or making enemies, look out for accidents. Hold you own with firmness, but kindness. Do not buy, but push business, commend, good for hard work, but you may break tools.

MARS IS WEAK IN TAURUS—This hour is forceful and stubborn, but not so fiery as in other signs. A Taurus man with a strong position of Mars could not be defeated in war. This is a good hour to push business, labor once begun and to juggle with real estate and minerals, especially with iron, but do not take risks.

MARS IN GEMINI—This is a dangerous hour, beware of sudden impulse, temptation and passion, avoid all risks. But push work began.

MARS DETRIMENT IN CANCER—Does not exert great influence here, except as family quarrels are liable to begin, and divorces start in this hour, keep quiet and push work.

MARS IN LEO—His influence is much like that in Aries. Avoid trouble, but if forced into it push hard. Take no more risks than necessary, push work of a laborious kind.

MARS IN VIRGO—Causes sudden gains and losses. Take no risks from lawyers or other robbers, or of the health or bad hour for everything except what happens to come.

MARS FALLS IN LIBRA—Though Mars falls here he is very wicked in family affairs. This is a bad hour to get into a dispute of any kind, especially with the opposite sex. Robbery and murders are likely to be committed when Mars is in Aries, Gemini, Leo, Libra, Sagittarius or Aquarius. These are the most dangerous hours.

MARS RULES SCORPIO—This is an evil, dangerous hour; keep quiet, except to push laborious work.

MARS IN SAGITTARIUS—Danger of accidents. This hour is much like an Aries or Leo hour. It is a fiery but more likely to be a winning hour, especially for people born in Aries, Taurus, Leo. Virgi, Libra, Scorpio or Sagittarius and Capricornus, yet it is best to take no risks, but push what you undertake.

MARS EXALTS IN CAPRICORNUS—Do not buy, but sell, and push forcefully all things began, especially ordinary business.

MARS IN AQUARIUS—Makes a bad hour, avoid disputes or risks, but stick to labor, yet be careful to avoid accidents or breakage of tools.

MARS IN PISCES—Begets a vindictive, bad influence, take no risks in anything, work on unfinished work.

JUPITER IN ARIES—Jupiter hours are supposed to be the very best hours for any purpose, but they will vary, of course, being strongest when with the hour ruled by the sign Jupiter is strongest in. In an Aries Jupiter hour put on dress, dignity and politeness, almost to an extreme, and you are apt to win. This is the hour to enter politics.

JUPITER IN TAURUS—Makes a very successful hour, especially in all matters of speculation and trade, particularly so in dealing in real estate, copper, silver, tin, almsot any metals, and in mortgages, stocks and bonds. But be slow, deliberate and persuasive, and make your opponent think he is getting the best end of the bargain.

JUPITER IN GEMINI—Is of course best for letter writing, starting business enterprises which depend on advertising, and for travel, especially good for making contracts, but good for everything.

JUPITER EXALTS IN CANCER—This is a very successful hour, especially for all domestic matters and in trade, deal in products of water, and start factories.

Jupiter in Leo—Nobility of nature; speculative and good for invention.

JUPITER IN VIRGO—This is an hour of sudden losses or sudden gains, employ servants, call on the sick, ask favors of all kinds and deal in real estate or products of the soil.

JUPITER IN LIBRA—This is an especially good hour to form partnerships, start enterprise, musical, theatrical or educational matters, and for all matrimonial matters.

JUPITER IN SCORPIO—This is not a very good hour for anything except to make, break or execute wills and matters concerning insurance or goods of the dead. The most fortunate will win anyway.

JUPITER RULES SAGITTARIUS—This is a good hour for anything, especially for work of charity, religion, war, travel and invention.

JUPITER FALLS IN CAPRICORNIS—Consequently is not so strong here, and it is best not to put too much confidence in this hour, yet it would be well to push all ordinary business matters, and especially of real estate.

JUPITER IN AQUARIUS—Has no particular bearing except to ask favors of friends and to excite good and friendly feelings, and of course for general purposes.

JUPITER RULES PISCES—This is a powerful hour in all matters except to deal with opponents and enemies, or to ask favors of opponents.

SATURN FALLS IN ARIES—But as Saturn is called a very evil planet, except to a few who may have Saturn in a very good position at birth. In Aries he is stubborn, slow, bad for all diseases of the head; if starting in this hour. Give no medicine in any Saturn hour.

A Saturn hour is good for old affairs, of old people and old things. The best results I ever got at a spiritual seance was in a Saturn hour.

SATURN IN TAURIS—Is especially bad for real estate matters or money matters of all kinds, and for diseases attacking this hour especially of the throat, and of all other kinds.

SATURN IN GEMINI—This hour be very careful to avoid all letter writing or travel.

SATURN'S DETRIMENT IN CANCER—It is not likely to be a very bad hour, except for domestic affairs and tumerous complaints, or ordinary trade.

SATURN IN LIO—This hour is not so bad except for war, strife and heart troubles, or inventions.

SATURN IN VIRGO—It is ordinarily evil but not great, unless in matters concerning real estate, robberies, servants or sickness, especially bowel troubles.

SATURN EXAULTS IN LIBRA—This is a very evil hour for all things, especially concerning marriage, divorce and accidents that have their rise in this hour.

SATURN IN SCORPIO—A very evil hour, same as Libra, and for dangers from fire, storm, and the execution of all or any papers.

SATURN IN SAGITTARIUS—Especially avoid religious controversies, disputes and dangers from accidents.

SATURN RULES CAPRICORNUS—A strong hour, but very good for Saturn ruled people, especially for business people, and very dangerous for others.

SATURN IN AQUARIUS—Is a very bad hour, especially for treachery and making bad friends.

SATURN IN PISCES—This is a dangerous, sad hour; look out for enemies, and take no risks in anything.

A person born in this hour with Saturn in Pisces is almost sure to commit suicide.

PERSONAL DISCOVERIES.

1st. I find it to great advantage to arise in the morning with the Sun or within the hour ruling the the first hour after Sun rise, especially when that hour is a Sun, Moon, Venus, or Jupiter hour.

2nd. I find the planet ruling one's own sign will influence him more than other planitary hours.

3rd. A planet in its own sign at birth or strongly situated at birth may have a strong influence on its hour of the person who has it so situated. I know one man who is more fortunate in a Saturn than a Jupiter hour; of course this only occurs where Saturn is in an excellent position, ruling the native at birth, which rarely occurs.

4th. I have found the best time to start a journey is in almost any Moon, Mercury, Venus or Jupiter hour; the better the sign ruling the hour, the better the hour will be.

5th. I have discovered that the ancients were quite right in their methods of using the signs for the hours as well as the planets, and that the planets vary in the different hours ruled by the signs.

6th. One should know what kind of an hour he was born in and judge largely by that.

7th. The planet ruling the day of the week of birth is as essential to know as the ruling planet.

8th. I repeat, read this book over and over and become familiar with it if you wish to get the best results.

YOUR HOROSCOP OF CYCLES.

Else where I have given good and evil hours, goed and evil days of the week and good and evil years.

While certian years of life are good for nearly every person and other years are equally bad for all alike, yet good years in an evil cycle, may be so effected by the evil cycle as to appeer less good than other years not ealled good years. Again evil years in a good cycle may seem little less good than any ordinary year, while evil years in an evil cycle are apt to prove extremely evil, unless lighted up by very favorabl diretions, aspeets or transits, yet a good year, even in an evil cycle genearlly proves favorable for starting an enterprise. But one should never start an enterprise or take a risk, of any kind, during an evil year; especially if that evil year comes in an evil cycle.

In a lengihy, copy righted artical, by Ella, Wheeler, Wilcox. She asks" Did you ever notic that there are certian days when [saving your self] nobody but stupid and thotless peoqle are abroad?"

Then she sites a great number of calamities that are likly to befall you, if you start out on an evil hour.

At another day every thing goes like clock work. This is due to geting started right.

ɪ have before stated that every persn's good days are the day of the week of birth and the 3d and 4th days of the week after birth. The evil days are the 6th and 7th days after the day of the week of birth. The most eventful day of the week are for Aries, Tuesdays and Thursdays. For Taurus people, Mondays and Fridays. Gemini Wednsdays and Fridays. Cancer, Mondays and Fridays Leo' Sundays and Fridays Virgo. Mondays and wedensdsdays. Libra Fridays and Mondays. Sagittarius. Mondays and Thursdays. Capricornius, Wednesdays and Saturdays. Aquarius, Thursdays and Saturdays. Pisces, Fridays. Mondays and Wednesnays.

A German station says that the greatest number of accidents occur on Tuesdays, or Mar's day, which is 16 and 77 percent. On Monday, ruled by the Moon, the rate is 16 and 38 percent. Then follows Wedensdaya, ruled by Mercury 16 and 24 percent. Then Thursbay, ruled by Jupiter, 6 and 16 percent. Friday, ruled by Venus, the goddis of love, anb called the most unlucky day of the week gives us the least number of accidents except the day ruled by the Sun, Sunday, which produces less than 3 percent of the accidents, while Saturday, ruled by the great evil planet Saturn, stands even with Mars of Tuesday.

The 6th and 7th days of the week have been called good and evil days, since time imemmoral.

No doubt the basis for the idea of tho 6th and 7th days after birth bing evil days is that the Bible says God finished his work on the 6th and rested on the 7th days of the week. But the truth is that it all comes from astrology as Webester's dicton-naty admits the days of the week were named in honor or respect to the planets. The Bible being an astrological work makes frequent use of astrological nnmbers, espescially so of number 7.

Nearly 70 years ago. my father, Lyman Stowe senior, upon notcing the frequent use of the number 7 in the Scriptures, wrote the following poem.

In the old, Geocentric astrology, Satrun was counted the 7th heavenly body effecting our earth, including the Sun and Moon,

SEVEN IS A NUMBER MOST COMPLETE.

Seven is a number most complete,
Seven years composed the jubliee.
Seven days composed the christian's week,
Seven Attributes, the Deity.

Seven Orbs, we say revolve the sun.
Seven Colors do the rainbow grace,
Seven Wonders in the world were done
Seven Legions wire of Mary's race.

Seven Lamps contained the golden bowl;
Seven Pipes did shine from every one.
Seven Eys to Jashua shone on stone.
Seven Eys with zerubbabel's plumb.

Seven Priests 'round Jericho compassed,
Seven Trumpets of ram's horn's to sound,
Seven Days did bring a cirtain blast;
Seven brought the walls all to the ground.

Seven Churches ancient Asia graced;
Seven Candle-sticks therein were placed·
Seven Seals were once upon the book;
Seven were by Judah's Lion broke.

Seven Horns were seen upon the lamb.
Seven were the Heads the dragon bore,
Seven Angles flew at God's command,
Seven Viles of his wrath to pour.

Seven times with oil the sprinkling Priest
Sparkled before the throne of God.
Seven times that finger type of Christ
Sprinkled the mercy seat with blood.

The Moon makes her trip, a round the Earth, in about 28 days and her changes every 7 days. It is the changes of the Moon which effect our health so materially. Dr. Buchanan, a noted, Collge Professor and writer says, "Diseases show a tendency to relaps every 7 days." This, he attributs, to the Moon's changes. He then quotes, from the investigations of many, prominent, Medical men.

Prof. Reil, of Germany, said he thought the iregular periodicity of feavor to be due to some general law of the universe. This agreed with Kepler's idea. M. Brachet, a French savent, tested it experimentally, succesfually ad hering to the number 7.

Hippocrates, the Greok father of medical science said "The Lunar month has such special power over our bodies that not only births, but desease, death or recovery have a kind of dependency on su.h revolution."

One authorty says high tides and high feavers go togather.

Says Dr. Buchanan, "Galen, the great Roman physician discused the subject extensivly, in his writings. The influence af the Moon on cancers, was shown, in the London Medical Journal of 1785. and Culen aud Belfour endorsed this idea. Mead showed that the influence of the moon was greatest in apogeo and perigee.

Moderin astrologers have noticed the influnce of the sign cance and the 4th and 7th houses are strongly manifest in tho e afflicted with ulcers, cancers and tumors. It should be rembered the 4th house and cancer are ruled by the Moon.

Dr Buchanan figures the evil years of man to come every seven years. But, this does not exactly apply, as we find the regular occurence of evil years are not exactly in the sevens, yet as a whole they do. They occur betwen 5 and 6, 13 and 14, 19 and 21, 27 and 28, 33 and 34, 41 and 43, 49 and 50 54 and 55, 61 and 63, 69 and 70, 75 and 76, 83 and 84 89 and 90 The reason of this variation is due to regular, planitory influenees. The effect of good or evil years will be varied by the cycle one is transiting at the time.

An evil year that opens or closes an evil cycle will prove far more melignant than other evil years. For instance an Aries man's worst cycle is from his 49th to his 56th birth days, and his most dangrous years, in any way, especially, for business or accidents, is from 49 to 50 and from 54 to 55. He may not die for many years after, yet he is apt to contract the diseases, or harrass the mind with the things that will finally take him off.

The Jnpiter years are said to be the best years of a persons life time. These are years when Jupiter returns to the position it occupied at birth, which occurs every 12 years, or between 11and 12, 23 and 24, 35 and 36, 47 and 49, 59 and 60, 71 and 72. Of corse there are other good years, and years which may seem better than some years called good years, but an evil will not prove so malignent on a Jupiter year as on other years, and are less liable to occur on a Jupiter year than on other years. If a good year comes in a good cycle you may look for great success and happiness but if it comes while you are in an evil cycle it will merely prove less evil. Jupiter years, however, are the years in which we should establish our selves in business or position for the next 12 years.

THE CYCLES.

We must rembier that, it is claimed, every seven years, we change cvery partical of flesh, blood and bone in our, physical systems.

One thing is very clear, to the astrologer, every seven years there is a complet change in the direction of our affairs. Of course, to the casual observer, we may go on with our business as before but to our selves there will be a marked difference tho we may not, at the time, understand the real cau e. Whether it is due, as soem claim, to the influence of Uranus, who is seven years in a sign, or whether it is due to the influence of the signs of the zodiac, I am not prepared to say.

The 7 year cycles, however, are named after the signs of the zodiac.

Each cycle, not only, gives the influence of its own but it lends an influence of the opposite sign, thus Aries and Libra are polars. Taurus and Scorpio are polars. Gemini and Sagittarius are polars. Cancer and Capricornus are polars. Leo and Aquarius are polars. Virgo and Pisces are polars.

The ARIES cycle produces a cheerfu l, playful, lively influence, with Libra reflections of a sadness. This cycle is a good period to establish business or re build broken fortune .

There may be a tendency to fires or inflammatory troubles' reflected from Libra, but there is not likly to be failures, or bad luck in business while transiting the Aries cycl . If there be any ill luck you may look for a speedy recovery.

While transiting an Aries cycle, like the developing lamb, energy is on the increase, and force and push made mrnifest, therefore, extra, care should be taken, and all risks be avoided.

You may look for travel, presents, love of bus,-iness, and triumph over enimies.

THE TAURUS cycle is one of the most fortunate cycle of our life time, yet it is the polor of Scorpio, which is the worst cycle of our life time. Judging by this, we may look for some of the worst events of life to come in the midest of, unusual, good fortune, or viseversy. Yet as a whole both good and evil cycles hold good.

Another thing must be explained and that is the effects of thesign a person is born in is more than likely to be strongly manifest, when he reaches his polor or opposite sign.

During a Taurus cycle money comes easy and there is selbom a thot of worry, except during an evil year and even that is light. During this cycle every, possible, effort should be made to get established in, a permanent, business, and to lay up for a rainy day. During this period there is some danger from large animals and from offending friends in high places, and of the opposite influence of Scorpio in producing sudden losses.

THE GEMINI CYCLE is a period of great restlessness, and travle or a desire to do so. It is apt to bring many changes in our affairs, and it brings an increase of corrospondence or letters, according to ones time and station in life. Ii stirs the mind to activity, to reading and study. It is allmost sure to bring a change of circumstances genearally, for the better, tho it may bring discord among relatives. The polor influence of Sagittaruis is to dangers from accidents, war or contentions- or it may bring over religious zeal aud consequent mental disturbances, or unusual kindly expressions

THE CAPRICORNUS CYCLE is a quiet, contented, tho not a very fortunate cycle

Let me againa call attention to the fact that any person born under fortunate conditions will hardly percive the evil cycles or years, while one born under evil conditions will feel it heavly and hardly perceive the good periods. Then, again, one should have his horoscope to better read his transits.

It should be, farther, noticed that a child, a savage, or a very ignorant person would not percive these changes, as a bright successful person would.

During a Cancer cycle the mind is much upon the mother, home, married partner and children, tho it may bring activity, in business, travle of friends and relatives, succe s in business and danger of loss by water, or of drawning,

The polor influence is a danger from business temptations, and loss or gain of honor, also loss of friends by death or danger of your own death.

THE LEO CYCLE is also a home loving cycle. While transiting this cycle one is apt to experience unusual, expressions of love for the father, children and pleasurs, and if marriageable there will be good opportunities of marriage. It leads the mind to love of knowledge, education, machinery and invention. Of course, like all other cycles, the age one passes thru a cycle must be taken into consideration as it has something to do with the influence. While it brings attentions from the oppsite sex it also brings feelings of benevolance and favorable opportunities of expression. It is likly to excite organic heart troubles, and from the reflections of Aquarius, it may bring trou bles of the ankles, honor or disrepute, short journys, removals, many frienps and secret enemies.

THE VIRGO CYCLE is one of the best money making cycles of the whole 12 cycles, tho not of good for health, as there are great dangers of accidents, sickness, injuries from servants, and from the reflection of Pisces, it is liable to show sudden losses, some sadness and seems cruel enemies, yet altogether to ii is a cycle of advancemer.

THE LIBRA CYCLE is that of contradictions. It is apt to bring many admirers from the opposite sex, and if of proper age it will bring opportunities of marriage, and of business partnership, small or great dangers from fire or inflammatory diseases, expressions of high temper, which is likley to end in loss thru law suits, and may bring a change of circumstances or simelar conditions of the Aries nature or cycle. These may be good or bad according to the good or evil years you chance to be in.

THE SCORPIO CYCLE is the worst cycle of a life time. If death falls while you are in this cycle it is apt to prove a painful or frightful death. This cycle brings sickness, returns of old diseases, which were caused by carlessness or excesses, also look for treachery, bad friends and financial losses, and great dangers in every direction. It may bring sudden gains and the best luck of a lifetime, from the reflections of the poloar, but even if so, great care must be taken or the good luck is more than likely to turn to very bad luck.

THE SAGITTARIUS CYCLE is a very peculiar cycle, its polar, Gemini interchanges influences stronger than any of the other signs, or cycles. The tendency of the Sagittarius cycle is to produce a kindly, religious feeling, unless arroused in defence of a religious or moral principle, and then it arouses a warlike feeling and a desire to force matters. It is also liable to bring dangers to reputation thru disaprovals or scandles, according to the year you are transiting. It is, however, a good cycle for business, travel, courtship, literary work and mail order business.

THE CAPRICORNUS CYCLE, I have found to be a very treacherous cycle, bringing both good and bad influences according to the planets transiting the sign at the time. Planets transiting this sign, seem to exert more influence than in any other sign except Scorpio.

The Capricornus cycle is a cycle of great mental activity, in business matters, and in a social way, according to the age and station in life you are in when you transit this cycle. It is a better cycle for males than for females. It is likley to bring a break up in business affairs. and in the home, or by the reflection of its polor it may establish the home on a firmer foundation.

THE AQUARIUS CYCLE brings honor or disrepute and brings, many, good friends and some treacherous ones, and losses by them, and you may be ware of secret enemies. It brings travels, by short journeys, and removals.

From reflections of its polor it is likely to bring profits thru inventions or machinery. If born in May, August or November it is liable to brin heart troubles.

THE PISCES CYCLE is, said to be, the saddest cycle of a persons life time. It brings sickness, deaths, losses, afflictions, from enemies and, false, freinds, tho this cycle will be effected, for good or bad, by the years one is transiting, more than in any other cycle, and by the planitary transits, to a limited extent. When transiting the Pisces cycle one is, almost, sure to feel the reflection of its polar, Virgo, and sudden gains will, in a measure, compensate one for the sorrows he must endure.

YOUR CYCLE.

I will not put the reader to the trouble to figur out his particular cycle or good or evil periods, farther than to turn to it by looking for his sign and the good and evil periods of one born in the sign. **FOR THE BFNEFIT OF DETECTIVES OFFICERS OF THE LAW AND BUSINESS, MEN IN GENERAL** you have only to ascertain the date of birth and then look up the possibilities of yourself or the applicant for positisn, or the duration illness is likely to run. If death, or severe illness takes place at other times, or other troubles, except accidents and their effects, the first cause will be traced to one of these evil peroids.

I will now give the influence, effects and periods of each sign of the zodiac.

In regard to colors and gems I wish to explain, that their influence is due to their differing forms of vibrations, which produce differing results.

Why does the sunflower always keep turning to the Sun? Why does the, beautiful, four oclock always close its blossoms at four o clck in the afternoon?

Why does the morning glory open its blossom early in the morning and close it as soon as the sun begins to shine upon it?

Why are calculous and kidney diseases and nerve troubles worse at the new and full of the moon?

Why is the influenc of the moon greator at apogee, or perigee than at other times?

Why does the moon, at times, cause the tides, in the Bay of Funday, to rise to the height of 70 feet, and at other times not? Or if this is true, as Prof-essor Willis F. Moore, Chief of the United States Weather Bureau, admits it is, why can it not effect animal and vegetable life, which is from 70 to 90 percent water? It does.

Why is all vegetable life most full of sap at new and full of the moon?

Why are sexual excitements greator at new and full of the moon than at other times?

Why do more old people die at new and full of the moon than at other times?

Why will a bright moon light shining upon fresh poultry, veal or mutton soon spoil it?

Why will oxygen attack iron, and cause it to rust and why an alkali keep it off?

Answer me these questions and I will tell you why it is fortunate for some people to wear certian gems and unfortunate for others to wear the same gems?

Tell me why it is natural for the Mountin sheep to love and seek the rocks and mountin peaks, and for the antilope to seek the valleys and plains and I will tell you why it is natural for an Aries person to, explore, seak or hide himself or his plunder in new plowed feilds, mansions, small out buildings, and peculiar and out of the way places; and why it is natural for people of other signs to seek other places peculiar to othes not born in their sign.

Tell me why a diamond is harmonious for a person born in Aries and an opal good for one born in Libra and decidedly evil for most people born the sign Cancer?

If you will tell me why the magnet effects the needle, there by inabeling the marinor to guide his ship safely to harbor, or if mischievously placed may send his ship, to distrucion, with thousands of lives; tell me this and I will tell you why the vibrations of precious stones, or different colors effect different people in different ways.

It is clear that if the employer wishes a good man this will help him to choose one. If an officer is seeking a criminal this will help to find him, and help the officer to determine whether or not the person is naturally evil or is merely unfortunate.

We will give the influence of the zodiac,

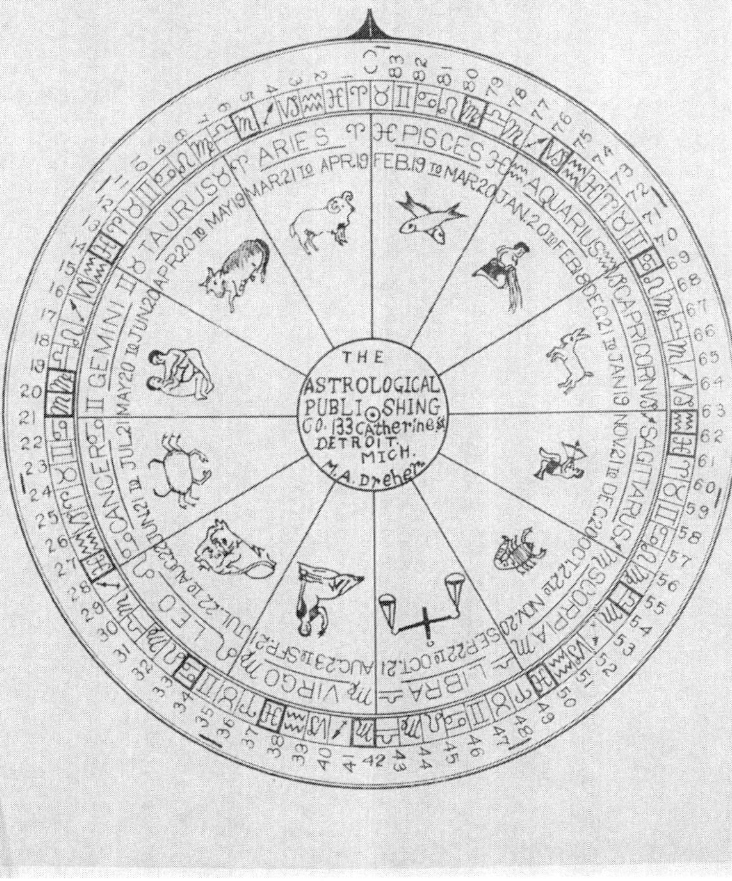
THE
ASTROLOGICAL
PUBLISHING
CO. 133 Catherine St
DETROIT.
MICH.
M.A. Dreher
ARIES MAR.21 TO APR.19
PISCES FEB.19 TO MAR.20
AQUARIUS JAN.20 TO FEB.18
CAPRICORNUS DEC.21 TO JAN.19
SAGITTARUS NOV.21 TO DEC.20
SCORPIA OCT.22 TO NOV.20
LIBRA SEP.22 TO OCT.21
VIRGO AUG.23 TO SEP.21
LEO JUL.22 TO AUG.22
CANCER JUN.21 TO JUL.21
GEMINI MAY.20 TO JUN.20
TAURUS APR.20 TO MAY.19

THE CYCLE CHART.

This chart has the years of birth from 1 to 84 years of age. Starting with Aries and running bac-kward throu the signs Pisces, Aquarius, Capricor-nus and so on the 85th year starts life over again.

As the years by the 12 signs keep repeating the-mselves down the left throu the signs, which stand as a seven year cycle each, the influence of each year is repeated except as is changed throu the cycle it is in. The 1st, 13th, 25th, 37th, 49th 61st, 73th and 85th years are Aries years and the print-ed matter under the head of Periodicity will expl-ain what each year stands for or means. Rember it it must be judged by the cycle it is found in, thus if born in Gemini the 1st year starts in Gemini, just so with every other sign or cycle. Each cycle runs seven years. An Aries year is quite different in an Aries cycle from that in any other cycle and so does the effect of every year differ according to the cycle it is found in and yet retains some of its orignal nature.

The years and cycles can be calculated from this chart, but we make it much easier understood and handier by cutting out the center and pasting it on card board then paste the outside on card board, after cutting the inner circle round fasten it on the outer circle with a flexible rivet, the center then becomes a revolving disk, so the sign a person was born in may be turned over the figur 1, making it easy to understand. Those paying five dollars for the book will get all af the appliances with it.

Astrological periodicity deals with the hours of the day. The days of the week. The months of the year., and the years of age of a person or thing, and their periods of life: which we consider as follows.

To judge of the proper hours of the day in which to do the various things that go to make up life. we use the hour book "Right Hours to Success." The same will be found in the book entitled "Astrological Periodicty."

To seclect the days of the week always count the day of birth a fortunate, day also the fourth day after. Whil ethe 6th and 7th days after birth are called evil days, or days when the native is most likely to meet with sickness, accidents or other troubles.

It must be noted, however' when these days come on the sign days, the effect will be increased or lessened as the case may be.

Kabalistic Astrology is based upon

mathematics, as calculated with planetary influences. The ancients understood this thoroughly; as no man has been able to add too or take from one prepositon of Euclid, they depend. much on figures.

The ancients devided the planets in-to octaves, as ruling the harmony of vibrations, and assigned them to the days of the week. as follows. The Sun assigned to Sunday and ruling Leo. The Moon rules Monday and the sign Cancer Mars rules Tuesday and the signs Aries and Scorpio. Mercury rules /Wednesday, and the signs Gemini, and Virgo. Jupiter rules Thursday, and the signs Sag ittarius and Pisces. Venus rules Friday, and the signs Taurus and Libra. Saturn rules Saturday and the sign Capricornus.

The Sun ruling Sunday and Leo, his home makes Sunday a very fortunate day, especially to those born in Leo, and in Aries, where he exalts.

The Moon is strong in Taurus and Cancer and because the Moon rules Monday, it is a better day for them born in those signs than for those born in other signs.

Starting with Aries, Mars rules Aries making Tuesday an eventful day for that sign, becaus Mars rules Tuesday and rules Aries, tho Sundays are the real fortunate days for Aries.

Taurus being ruled by Venus, which rules Friday, makes Friday both a fortunate and eventful day for Taurus people.

Gemini is ruled by Mercuy, which also rules Wednesday which makes Wednesday and Friday fortunate for Gemini people.

Cancer being ruled by the moon Monday should be its fortunate day, instead, Monday is its eventful day, showing both good and bad, while on accunt of Cancer being between Gemini and Virgo which are ruled by Mercury, Wednesday is the fortunate day for Cancer people. Thursday is, generally, a fortunate day for Cancer people, becaus Jupiter exalts in Cancer.

Leo is ruled by the Sun which makes Sunday the good day for Leo people.

Virgo is ruled by Mercury. As Mercury rules Wednesday, Wednesday is Virgo's eventful day but Monday is Virgo's fortunate day.

Libra is ruled by Venus which rules Friday and makes Friday the eventful day for Libra while Monday is the fortunate day, also the 21st of each month is fortunate for Libra people.

Scorpio is ruled by Mars; as Mars rules Tuesday it is both the eventful and the luckey day of Scorpio people,

Sagittarius is ruled by Jupiter so Thursday is its eventful day and Monday its fortunate day.

Capricornus is ruled by Saturn which rules Saturday and makes Saturday the eventful day and Monday the luckey day.

Aquarius is ruled by Uranus which has no day but Thursday is the fortunate day for Aquarius people·

Pisces is ruled by Jupiter, Thursday its eventful day. Wednesday, its luck day.

The best Months are generally considered the months sextile to the month of birth.

FORTUNATE Years. While there are other good years, the best years of any person's life are, supposed to be, the Jupiter years which are between 11 and 12-23 and 24-35 and 36-48 and 49-59 and 60 71 and 72-83 and 84-95 and 96. This is every 12 years, or what is called Jupiter years, that is when Jupiter returns to the same position he was in at time of birth. These often run over 24 to 26-38 to 41-47 to 49-56 to 61, especially if the person have good planetary influences or is transiting a good cycle.

The most evil years of any persons life are those between 5 and 6 - 13 and 14 - 16 and17 - 19 and 20 - 27 and 28 - 33 and 34 - 37 and 38 - 41 and 43 - 45 and 46 - 49 and 50 - 54 and 55 - 61 and 62 - 69 and 70 - 75 aud 76 - 83 aud 84 and to close of life. These often start a year before or run a year over, if a person is transiting an evil cycle, thus 19 to 21 - 33 to 35 - 41 to 43 - 54 to 56 - 61 to 64. Tho these evil years are found most easily, by the dark lines on the revolving disk, they must not be confounded with the sign years, which are used with the cycle.

The cycles run from the sign of birth around to the right, ccunting seven years to each cycle, as are found on our horoscope blanks pages 5 and 6.

The opposite cycle will always prove a vexious cycle, no matter what sign it represents. That is the polar sign to the one you were born in.

You can, generally, count cycles from the whole sign a person was born in, yet if a person be born in, the last 15 degrees of a sign the influence of the sign will extend over to 15 degrees of the next sign thereby mixing the influence of the cycles. This is not used, only in very clost work.

Scorpio and Pisces are considerde the most evil cycles, tho the polar or opposite cycle is but little less evil, and to those born in Scorpio, the Taurus cycle will prove the best and worst of their lives, and visevise, as will also the Virgo and Pisces. cycl. s prove to person born in them

As Virgo is one of the best money cycles Pisces will not prove as evil to Virgo people, so far as finance is concerned, as to people of other signs.

The Sagittarius cycle is an exceptionally fine cycle for money making, while Gemini, its polar, is a restless cycle.

The years runing throu Aries, Pisces, Aquarius, and so on backward throu the signs as placed upon the wheel from 1 to 84, must be judged according to the sign they represent and the cycle they are in. The house a person is passing throu, if known and understood, will aid in rendering judgment of each year of a life.

CYCLES. HOUSES AND SIGNS.

While the various writers on astrology explain the meaning of signs and houses, in a manner, let me explain here. The 12 signs of the zodiac are the 12 divisions of the circle of the heavens, extending 8 to 9 degrees each side of the ecliptic

The 12 houses are the 12 divisions of the earth corrosponding to the 12 signs of the zodiac. Geocentric astrologers often confound the two and cnfuse the student. The circle should always be drawn with the sign Aries to the left, as the ascendant, as the planets move from East to West. The Earth's revolutions bring its divsions throu the ascendent every 24 hours, a part of 2 signs may be in the same house at one time or visevis as you wish to call it, as the two are identicaly the same, or have the same meaning.

PERIODICITY. PAGE 8

The 1 st house represents character, dress, and form and Aries the first sign represents the same thing. The 2 nd house represents wealth and what comes of it. The sign Taurus or 2 nd sign represents the same thing. Gemini and 3 d house represents brothers and sisters, letters, and short journeys. Cancer and 4 th house deals with the mother and mother's estate. Of Leo and the 5 th house we judge of the father, children and pleasures. Virgo and 6th house deals with lawsuits, sickness and servents. Libra and 7th house rules affairs of the heart, love, courtship, marriage and business partnership. Scorpio and 8 d house covers deaths, wills, insurance and inheritence. Sagittarius and 9th house deals with accidents, wars, religeion, morals and is co ruler with Leo in all matters pertaing to invention and art. Capricornus and the 10 th house deals with honor, business and dishonor. Aquarius and the 11 th house are used to judge of all things concerning friends, new or old, fals or true. Pisces and 12 th house treats of enimies and of what comes of them, of sorrows and of long journeys.

In ordinary usage we must judge of the effect of planets in signs and houses and their aspects to each other and to each sign and house as well of the mixture of signs and houses, as it is often that one sign may be found, apart, in two diff-erent houses or visevis. In that case two planets might be in the same sign but in two different houses and visevis. (See Solar Biascope, our device for getting the hour of birth, when it is not known.)

While we do not use the planets with the Egyptian circle it is well to give their meaning here, and how they influence us.

Let us remember every thing is divisabl in-to atoms, and tho the atoms form molicules and organsims yet each atom holds its identity as does each molicule and organism. As plains of vibration make the different strains of music possible to us, which may be observed by watching the piano chord, when in use, so is every other sensation the result of vibration. Color, light, heat, smell, taste, feeling are known to be the result of vibration. As we well understand every organism effects every other organism, it is easy to see, as sure as the Moon, at times, raise the tides, in

Periodicity. Page 10.

the Bay of Funday, to 70 feet and at other times show much less effect, and as vegetable and animal matter are 70 percent water it is plain to be seen the vibrations set up by the heavenly bodies, in their, complicated, and changing positions is the instrument of nature on which God plays the music of the spheres, effecting all organisms and never creating two exactly alike.

Suppose the 6th house is found in the sign Taurus, which is the sign of wealth and represents the 2d house or house of wealth, would it not be plain that sickness would have something to do with wealth getting where the sign of wealth and house of sickness come together, or visevis?

When useing the planets we look to see what planets are in that sign and house and the aspects there-to. We do the same to judge other matters in other signs and houses.

With the Egyptian and Chaldiec Circle System we look for the year and the cycle you are transiting and form our judgment from that. It must be rembered the years and cycles are same as the signs and houses, tho the year on the bed piece stands for a whole years time. It must be noticed the first year starts with Aries and runs backward,

(The accompanying table showes the influence of planets in the signs and is properly called a key.)

The cycle years run as follows; see page 6. Starting with Aries, runing backward throu the signs.

Our revolving disk shows where each birth year comes in.

Thus if you were born Jan. 1st place, about, the third part of Capricornus at at figure one on the bed piece. Now by running your eye around the figures on the bed piece you can see, at a glance, what the year is and what cyele you are in, Supose you are 35, look for the figure 35 and it will show you, you are in a Gemini year, and the close of a Taurus cycle.

The meaning of each year or its influence will be found under the head of sign years, these must be mingled with the influence of the cycle a person chances to be in at the date examened.

Let the student notice the 18th year is given as a Leo year and the 21st year as a Scorpio year and the 26th year is given as a Capricornus year, and the 28th as a Pisces year, all of the rest of the years come in the regular rotation. This is because those years of life more closely resemble the years given than of the original way of judging the matter.

Now by refering to what each sign stands for and judging it as a year, while mixing the efects with those of the cycle one chance to be in you can clostly calculate what that year of life will bring to the person read for. It is well when giving a carful reading to read the years as they stand on the chart and then consider them as changed back the 18th to Scorpio, the 21st to Leo, the 26th to Pisces and the 28th to Capricornus. Remember and do not confound the years given as period years with those given as sign years.

THE SIGN YEARS,

As before stated must not be confounded with the good and evil years of the periods. Tho the cycle chart will give them in their order, except the 18th is a Scorpio year and the 21st a Leo year, the 26th Pisces year the 28th a Capricornus year in the sign years while as good and euil years they remain as they are.

The Aries years are as follows. From birth to one year - 12 to 13 - 24 to 25 -36

Periodicity. Page 13.

to 37 - 48 to 49 - 60 to 61 - 72 to 73 - 84 to 85. These are rebuilding years and are likely to bring any of the Aries effects combine with effects of the cycle one is passing through while in the Aries year.

Taurus years are betwen 11 and 12 - 23 and 24 - 35 and 36 - 47 and 48 59 and 60.- 71 and 72 - 83 and 84 - 95 and 96. These are generally good years for finance, tho in danger from robbers, swindlers and treachery of friends, or of falling out with friends. Yet may expect assistance or position throu friends. If a journey is taken it is likely to be a long and a profitable one, subject to dangers to self and married partner, from large animals.

Gemini years are those betwen 10 and 11 - 22 and 23 - 34 and 35 - 46 and 47 - 58 and 59 - 70 and 71 - 82 and 83.

Gemini years are very restless years and are likely to cause moving. traveling or changing of position. If in an opposite cycle, or a Scorpio or Pisces cycle the inclination should be held to quietude and avoid change. If in these cycles afflictions from secret enimies, loss of confidence of emplyers forsaken by friends or even persecution and enmity and possibly financial failures may be looked for.

In other cycles those restless years will be varied in their effects, sometimes rejoicing and happiness will follow, but the years must be judged, strictly by the cycle they chance to be passing throu

Caneer years are those between 9 and 10 - 21 and 22 - 33 and 34 - 45 and 46 - 57 and 58 - 69 and 70 - 81 and 82 - 93 and 94.

If not in an evil cycle these years may prove fortunate years in starting a business. tho assistance may not be expected and much up hill work may be looked for, dangers of accidents, falls or drowning, while on a business trip, may be expected. The family are liable to travel and inheritence or presents be received. Beware of complications in love affairs. Judge all of these things by the cycle the year is in.

Leo years are between 8 and 9 - 20 and 21 - 32 and 33 - 44 and 45 - 56 and 57 - 68 and 69 - 80 and 81 - 92 and 93.

Leo years are likely to lead the thots to invention and art. It is also likly to lead to business, harmony. love and marriage, with the marriageable, also treachrey and enemies, but if so it will bring providential assistance just at the right time from those well able to assist you, if you seek it, and it is likely to lift you to honor and preferment. Of course this must be judged by the cycle one is in.

Virgo years are those betwen 7 and 8-19 and 20 - 31 and 32 - 43 and 44 - 55 and 56 - 67 and 68 - 79 and 80. These seem to carry over the evil influences from Leo, so far as law suits and enmities are concerned and the native should be on his guard against everything and every body. he is subject to wounds sickness, his financial affairs are likely to go to extremes both ways. Much depends on the cycle one is transiting.

Libra years are those between 6 and 7 - 18 and 19 - 30 - and 31 - 42 and 43 - 54 and 55 - 66 and 67 - 78 and 79.

Libra years generally bring important changes, unpleasent relations with superiors, or people in high places, dangers of robery, fire and inflammatory troubles. To the marriagable it is a favorable period for love and marriage. All must be judged by the cycle one is transiting.

Scorpio years are those between 5 and 6 - 17 and 18 - 29 and 30 - 41 and 42 - 53 and 54 - 65 and 66 - 77 and 78 - 89 and 90. These are, generally, treacherous years in almost any thing, thou not classed with real evil years, they are years of more or the vexations, liable to bring sickness death. betrayal of friends, attacks of enemies, disasterous love affairs or domestic trials. Must be judged by the cycle in.

Sagittarius years are those between 4 and 5 - 16 and 17 - 28 and 29 - 40 and 41 - 52 and 53 - 64 and 65 - 76 and 77-88 and 89. These are generally most exelant years for matters of friendship and affection, to ask favors of people in high places and to establish enterprises, all of which you are likely to experience, but you are also likely to do foolish acts and bring down upon your head scandlous revelations, to come to the ears of those who should not hear it. See the cycle in.

Capricornus years are those between 3 and 4 - 15 and 16 - 27 and 28 - 39 and 40 - 51 and 52 - 63 and 64 - 75 and 76 - 87 and 88. These are good years to make or accept business propositions, to begin a law suit, to attack an enemy, to take a sea voyage or for fame, honor, success, love, and marriage and very likely to hear of the death of near friends.

Aquarius years are those between 2

Periodicity. Page 17.

and 3 - 14 and 15 - 26 and 27 - 38 and 39 50 and 51 - 62 and 63 - 74 and 75 - 87 and 88. These are restless years, liable to bring travel, gain and loss of friends, sickness or death of friends, threatened losses of position or wealth, unexpected assistance in the nick of time. This must be judged by the cycle you are in.

Pisces years are those between 1 and 2 13 and 14 - 25 and 26 exchanged with Capricornus at 27 and 29 (see instructions.) 37 and 38 - 49 and 50 - 61 and 62 73 and 74 - 86 and 87. These are very evil years, as a whole, producing failures, losses, animosities, illness and difficulties in many directions, also betrayals by friends. One should not travel, start law or business or make importent changes during these years, tho they must be judged by the cycle one is transiting.

Do not forget the inter changing years so you may judg both ways. Do not forget that a year representing a sign will partake of the sign opposite, thus Libra is opposit to Aries and when passing throu one you will experience some of the efects of the year sign oppsite. It is the same with the cycles,

THE CYCLES,

"ORDER IS GOD'S FIRST LAW."

The truth in the abov quotation is manifest in the precision in which the heavenlyi bodies moove. Every atom and evrey organic body is subject to God's imnutablelaws; and every atom of matter, as as every organic body is effected by every well other atom and every other organic body, according to bulk, weight, and distance apart; this is throu the laws of vibrátion, so if we study those laws we learn the harmony of the spheres and throu that our good and evil periods.

The chapter preceding this showes how the years of ones life are effected in accordance with the signs of the zodiac, but running backward from Aries to Pisces and so on throu the signs instead of Aries to Taurus and that way. Now we will notice the effect of the cycles that run for seven years each.

Always start with the cycle you were born in, suppos you were born in the sign of the goat which is between December 22nd and January 20th. You turn so the whole sign comes to the left of the first year, or exactly under the black point at the top. You then count down to the left, seven years to each sign or cycle, thus 7-14 - 21 -28 - 35 - 42 - 49 - 56 - 63 - 70-76-84. From 84 we always start over again.

If an evil year comes just before the starting of an evil cycle or just after it, it may caus that period to run 8 years, starting a year earlier or running a year longer, as the case may be.

Tho there may be some good years in a cycle the general effects are bad.

No. 1 or ARIES CYCLE.

If born in Aries you are shrewd calculative, a thinker. Love music, art and literature .You will want to do work in your own way, and be your own boss, and you cannot work as well in any other way. You are best adapted to brain work.

When a child is born in Aries, he is slow in mental development, tho physically quick andgraceful, loving sport and play, he will expand and grow rapidly or the other extreme, he will be very slow of growth, easily held back by some planatary influence. An older person, when transiting this cycle, will feel rejuvinated. sprightly, lamb like, more likely to love and be loved, but subject to accidents to the head and face, also to lower part of the body or back, and to inflammatory troubles, or fires. Rember that when in this cycle you will experience some of the effects of the 7th or Libra cycle.

No. 2 or TAURUS CYCLE

If born in Taurus, you are patient and induring in what ever profession or line of work you undertake. You are best adapted to a line of business that will, vigerously ,occupye mind and body at one and the same time.

This house, sign, or cycle deals with information concerning buisness transactions, success or failuer according to the year one is transiting, when passing throu the cycle, also, look for the possibility of inheritence or unlooked for sudden gains.

This is a fine cycle for money, tho during an evil year losses may come yet will not be so great as in other years.

Evil years bring the effects of the opposit cycle. If bad luck comes it will come throu thieives, robbers, or swindlers; or throu treachery from those supposed to be your best friends. Physical dangers threaten, especially from large animals or movable objects. This may come to the married partner. A profitable journey is likely if a Gemini year comes in this cycle.

No. 3 or GEMINI CYCLE.

If you were born in this cycle or between May 20th and June 21st you are best fitted where buisness push is needed, such as foreman, superintendent, or business of your own or a business of art, science or eaucational work. You are very likely to try to do too much, to carry a load on both sholders, or to try to do two things at one time. You should guard against too much excitability or over doing, at all times, and especially when transiting evil years and cycles. This sign, cycle or house deals, chiefly with brothers and sisters, and relatives in general, and with changes and travels in paticular. This is a very restless cycle, and if a Gemini year come in this cycle it will prove extreimely restless. This is a good period for a mail-order business, tho letters sent or receved should be scrutinized with greator care than at other times. In this cycle look for numerous changes, and for secret enemeies or enveous people who will persecute you and injure your reputation, and you will loos the confidence of employers and friends, and meet with sickness and loss.

No. 4 or CANCER CYCLE

If born in Cancer or between June 21st and July 22nd you will do best in some occupation where you can be home every day, such as commercial business, manufacturing or agriculture; and that home should be near some large body of water.

This cycle refures to parents, ancestors, family relations inheritence, legacies, and secrets where relativs are interested.

During this cycle there is great danger of injuries, from falls, physically or to character, also to severe illness and to drowning, if exposed. You are likely to some troubles of the affectioas. Be on your guard against every thing and every body, and give your whole attention to your busindss and you will make a successful cycle of it. unless it be an opposit cycle, and even then it will be benifited.

You will feel some of the effects of the opposit cycle.

No. 5 or LEO CYCLE.

If born between July 22nd and Aug. 23 you can adabt your self to alamost any position in life you chance to drop into,

You are naturally mechanical, speculative and inventive otherwise pushing and plodding, but destined to be successful.

During this cycle there is a tendency to travel and if a journey is taken it will be a profitable one. It brings new aquaintances, and affairs of the heart, and if marriagable there will be opprotunities of a marriage. You will manifest more than usual pride and meet with more than usual success. but with all of that, look out for treachery.

This is a cycle of presents and rewards and of children's success if any.

If troubbie comes, expect assistance, from the powerful, in the nick of time.

No 6 or VIRGO CYCLE.

The sign Virgo comes between Aug. 23 and Sept. 23d. It deals with sickness and servants. public aud private. If born in this sign you are best adapted for an editor, proof reader, leader of a reform, or painter. druggist, or general mixer, As your anayltical and critical powers are very accute.

This cycle brings heavy gains, and possible, heavy losses, as it is opposit to the very evil cycle Pisces. It is, generally, a money making cycle, and tho magnetic it is a bad cycle for health. One may recieve hard blows of fate, but he will succeed. financially, in the end. During evil years expect to be disappointed and wroged, especially by servants, public or private, and in good years to be benefited by them. Expect lasting enmities, and guard against every thing and every body.

No. 7 or LIBRA CYCLE.

the sign Libra comes between Sept. 23d and Oct. 22 nd rules love, marriage, partnership and law. As a cycle, like all the rest, it runs 7 years. If born in this sign you are best adapted for professional work or government employ, may be well adapted to the stage, or rostrum, or as a teacher. During this cycle we are likely tomeet with new experiences in love affairs, seperations and divorces, open enmities, and quarrels, with relatives.

There will be dangers of robbery, of fires or inflammatory troubles. While it i s a dangerous cycle, to life, the intuitions will be strong, the opporunities of successf ulpartnership and financial success, and of marriage, to marriagable, will be better than usual.

No 8 or SCORPIO CYCLE

The sign Scorpio runs from Oct. 22 to Nov. 22 nd. It deals with deaths, wills, insurance and inheritance. If born in this sign you are best adapted for a physician, chemist, banker, superintendant, foreman, or in government employ.

This is a cycle of gains and losses, deaths and betrayals, illness and dangers, of opportunities gained and lost. It is, generally, the worst cycle of ones life time. Tho in some respects, the Pisces cycle is worse. While transiting the Scorpio cycle old diseases are likely to return, painful accidents are almost sure to come. The loss of loved ones almost certian. About the only hope is of sudden gains, and if any, great care must be taken or great losses are sure to follow.

No, 9 or SAGITTARIUS CYCLE,

The sign Sagittarius runs from Nov. 22 to Dec. 23 rd, and rules morals, religion, wars and accidents. If born in this sign you are best adapted to work for others yet good in figures, a fair financier, skilful with your hands, good in music and a good and a safe leader of men. Like Gemini people, the polar you want to do too much and carry a load on each shoulder.

The Sagittarius cycle is a fine money makeing cycle, brings short journeys, successful enterprises, assistance, if called for, from high places. It brings new friends, and warm affections, tho it brings dangers of estrangments throu scandle.

Like Gemini, its polar, this cycle brings a change of circumstances, generally for the better, it also brings great activity and dangers of accidents.

No. 10 or CAPRICORNUS CYCLE.

The sign Capricornus runs from Dec. 22 to Jan. 20 th, and stands for business, honor and dishonor.

If born in this sign you are best adapted for organizing new enterprises, or better conditions in old ones. Whether your buisness be extensive or small, you will systeamtize every thing about it.

When transiting this cycle family afflictions are likely to trouble you and many anoyances take place, yet new business formes will be presented. This is a good cycle to push business, start new enterprises, take sea voyages and prosecute claims, great caution should be exercised to avoid slips and dishonor.

Periodicity. Page 27.

No 11 or AQUARIUS CYCLE.

This sign runs from Jan 20 th to Feb. 19th. It designates friends, good and bad and what comes of them. If you were born in this sign you are best adapted for any position, your station in life permits you to fill, if it leads you among the many, from President of the U. S. down to a waiter in a restaurant.

This is a cycle of activity of mind and body. Of warm friendships and of secret enemies, and of treachery and deceit; of interest in mechanics, arts and inventions; of short journeys, or removals and of assistance from people in high places, just in the nick of time.

No. 12 or PISCES CYCLE.

This sign runs from Feb. 19 to March 21 st, and is called the sign of sorrow, it designates enemies and what comes of them. If born in this sign your tastes and desires will lead you to occupations you are best suited to. You will do best to dwell near large bodies of water, and to deal in liquids or products of the water.

When transiting this cycle it brings obsticals, sorrows, quarrles, hatered, persecutions. It is evil for every thing. If any good comes to you while transiting this cycle you are fortunate indeed. Do not travel, start, new, business or take, unnecessary, risks of any kind while in this cycle, yet sudden gains may come.

Let it be rembered the years are merely the reflections of the cycles or the breaking up of the manifestations of the cycles in-to 12 parts, each part represents a year of the same nature of the cycle it stands for, with a mixture of the effects. of the year or cycle oposit. Each oppcsit cycle must always be carefully considered

While I do not claim infallibility for this work I do claim that if heed is given to the work the great percent of business failuers, which is said to be 98 percent, will be lessened, because men will push buisness when it is good and take no unnessary risks, during an evil period, when things are going backwards at every turn. It is a fool cry, "When business is bad push the harder," If yo do, like the floundering horse in the quick sand, you go deeper.

A carful study of this system will enable any person to learn his good and evil periods and how to take advantage of them.

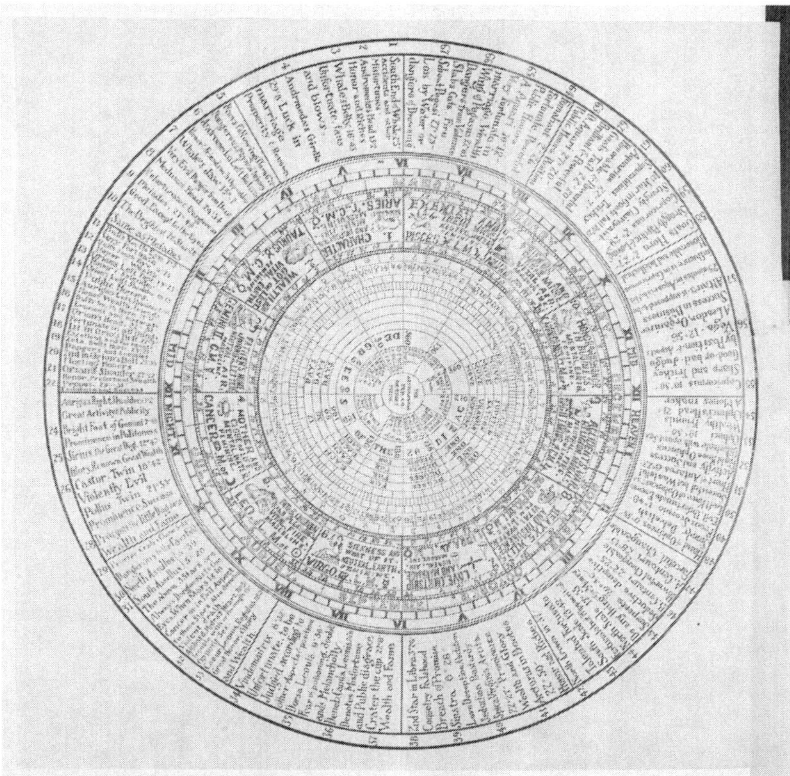

Instructions to Chart of Destiny 1.

EXPLANATIONS TO THE CHART OF THE ASTROLOGER'S GUIDE AND PERPETUAL HELIO CENTRIC EPHEMERIS.

This chart, though seemingly complicated, is very simple and when rightly understood becomes an invaluable aid to the old astrologer and of special value to the student beginning the study of astrology, because it brings the whole science before him at a glance.

The first two circles give places and number of the fixed stars, starting with No. 1-2 degrees of Aries and going down to the left around the circle to 62 or 27th degree of Pisces we give positions of fixed stars and their influence, when on the exact degree of ascension, or when a planet is under the exact degree of a fixed star.

It should be plain to any astrologer that there are few very strong characters, those extremely fortunate and those extremely unfortunate. In these cases we often find no reason, in ordinary astrology, for such extremes, where two are born but a few hours apart, and sometimes but a few minutes apart, except it can be found through the direct influence of the fixed stars.

One thing must be taken into consideration. It has generally been supposed the vibrations set up by each constellation of the name of the sign is the power which gives us the effect of that sign. Thus from March 21st to April 19th the earth is passing through Libra, the Sun in center seems to be passing through Aries, hence those born between those dates will show a decided Aries nature, except as it is effectfied by the rising sign and signs which the planets are in.

Now here comes the burning question. The constellations having moved 30 degrees west of the signs brings Aries under the constellation of Pisces. Then, why should not those born in Aries be affected by the constellation of Pisces?

The answer to the above must be drawn from one of two conclusions: either there is a power beyond these constellations still affecting our system or else, just as you strike a piano key and the cords vibrate for long afterward, so are the vibrations the effects of the fixed stars on our system in some direct manner. This is probably the case as the signs were once far more pronounced in their effects than at the present.

The tribe of Gad represented the sign Aries, and they were of a type so decidedly sandy of complexion or red-haired that it has been thought the Scotch were of that lost tribe.

The vibrations are losing their power and becoming mingled, mixing the effects of the signs or making them more general. This would account for the necessity of the exact degree of birth or of a planet to come under the direct degree or ray of a fixed star to show a decided influence. Thus a person born in exact two degrees of Aries, would be more subject to accidents than if born one or three degrees. Then again it would be more pronounced if the 2d degree of the first house were rising, or if Mars, Mercury or Saturn were in that degree or if any other planet chanced to be in that degree and at the same time afflicted.

Here necessitates an explanation of the houses. When the Sun gave birth to our earth, or it was torn off from the Sun, it was probably in the month of July and the Earth received the vibrations of the constilations as they stand in the Zodiac, when these vibrations discontinue the earth will be a dead body.

The 12 divisions of the earth corresponding to the 12 signs of the Zodiac are the 12 houses starting with Aries, the 1st house and numbering to the left around to Pisces the 12th house, thus if the

3rd division or Gemini comes on Aries, Gemini would be considered as in the first house and Aries the 11th house. The person born between March 21st and April 19th—say April 2nd, 1843, in Detroit, Mich., Sunday about 9:30 a. m., he would represent a strong Aries Gemini type, modified to some extent by influence of planetary positions.

As this would bring the Moon in Taurus, it would give a strong mixture of Aries, Taurus, Gemini, Leo nature. The Leo nature comes from the effects of the Sun's ruling Sunday and rules Leo. Mixed again with a Mars, Scropio nature as Mars is the Lord of Aries and Scorpio and is in Scorpio.

Thus the Geo. Centric system makes Aries always the 1st house and whatever division of the earth comes in that sign would be said to be in the 1st. house as the case above. Gemini is said to be the first house. Few know the exact moment of birth, and those who do, do not know how the clock stood with the Sun.

Our Solar Bioscope is almost indispensable to the true astrologer who wishes to get as near as possible to the degree of the ascending sign. (*See description of Solar Bioscope and other works.*)

Here it must be noticed that but twice a year the clock and the Sun agree, that is March 21st. and Sept. 23rd. as close as can be caloulated, then the days and nights are of the same length.

The clock dial on the chart is set for that time of year, so from Dec. 25th. to June 21st. the Sun is gaining on the clock continually; so the 21st. of March at 6 o'clock the Sun will be rising, but June 21st. it will be two hours high. Now it will begin to loose and loose until Deo. 22nd. and the clock gains on the Sun.

By this you always know the degree of the Zodiac, the Sun is in at sunrise as that degree is always on the ascendant or 1st. degree of Aries. As the Sun is two hours passing through a sign, it would be easy to keep track of the degrees past. As the Sun does not rise in all localities at exactly the same time, the time of Sunrise must be calculated by the longitude and latitude of the place of birth. Hence tables of houses have been figured, and the Solar Bioscope and a more simple method created.

The first circle below the clock dial divides the hours into 15 minutes or quarters.

After the clock dial comes the circles of the days of the month, by putting a hand on the dial with a straight edge on the day of the month and running the eye down to the fine divisions one inch below or just above the dignities of the planets in the large lighter circles, you will find the degrees numbered 5-10-15-20-25-30, etc.

The space between the days of the month and the degrees of the Zodiac are the names of the signs of Zodiac and instructions as to what you are to judge of, in each sign.

Thus with this person born April 2nd. with Gemini rising.

If a planet be in Aries you give it the influence of Aries and Gemini, just so for the other signs and houses give a planet the influence of the sign it is in and modify its influence by the sign the house represents which covers that sign, also by the dignities of the planets. Each 10 degrees of a sign is called a decan, and a planet in his own decan in any sign is stronger than in any other decan, or a person born in the 1st. 10 degrees of Aries will show a stronger Mars nature, the second 10 a Sun nature, the third 10 a stronger love or Venus nature, just so through all of the signs and decans. These in turn are mixed with the dignities of the planets, thus the 1st. 6 degrees of Aries are ruled by Jupiter, from 6 to 14 by Venus, 14 to 20 by Mercury, 20 to 26 by Mars, 26 to 30 by

INSTRUCTIONS TO CHART OF DESTINY 5.

Saturn. Thus the dignity of a planet must be considered as well as the decan. Now look down to next to the inside circle and you will find in what signs the planets are strong or weak. Thus the Sun rules Leo, exalts or is very strong in Aries, has his detriment, or is not very strong in Aquarius. Has his fall or is very weak in Libra. Just so with all of the other planets and this must be taken into consideration, when figuring the positions of each planet.

POSITIONS OF PLANETS.

We now come to the getting of the position of planets.

Start with the 1st degree of Aries and run 30 degrees in a sign, so where it is marked degrees at the 3rd circle from the center, you will find at the last degree of each sign, in large figures, the number of the degrees of the Zodiac running 30-60-90-120-150-180-210-240-270-300-330-360.

These are also found in smaller figures just above the circle of degrees.

As the swift moving planets require more space for figuring than the slow ones we have reversed the order and put Neptune in the smallest circle near the center, and Mercury on the outside.

Let the student here understand, the Moon does not revolve around the Sun except as it goes with the Earth, consequently while the Earth is a whole month in a sign the 12 signs focus on the Earth as they focus on the Sun, therefore the Moon passes through the whole 12 signs of the Zodiac every month, while in one sign with the Earth.

See illustration of Earth's Zodiac on page of description of planets.

The position of the Moon is given in a separate set of tables.

INSTRUCTIONS TO CHART OF DESTINY 6.

After drawing your map of the Zodiac turn to the Moon tables and get the position of the Moon and place it in the Zodiac circle in the sign you found it, and mark the degrees.

Now turn to the table which bears the degree you want; we have figured the 2nd of April, 20th degree of Gemini, rising, latitude 42° 20′, longitude 82° 58′, or Detroit, Mich., the year 1843. As the table run from 1825 to 1920 it is easy to turn to the year wanted, we find Mercury Jan. 1st 18 degrees in Capricornus. We now count the days 31 days in January, 28 in February, 31 in March and 2 of April, which added together make 92 days. As Mercury goes round the Sun in about 88 days, you leave the hand at 18 degrees of Capricornus, or swing it round once. Take 88 from 92, which leaves you 4 days. Now you may move your hand forward one space in the circle of Mercury for each day. This brings Mercury within 4 degrees in Pisces. As we started at noon Jan. 1st we must calculate we travel 4 degrees a day in Pisces (see table of speed of planets in each sign so you can easily determine the place of Mercury by counting back the number of degrees Mercury travels in the sign he is found and then figure from noon). In this case the birth being about 9:30 a. m., we must figure Mercury 2 degrees in Pisces.

If you get within one degree of position with this planet you are nearer than is generally reached.

We found the Moon 14 degrees in Taurus. We now place Mercury 2 degrees in Pisces. Had our date been Dec. 2nd we should have had to swing our hand three times around, and then place Mercury where we found him, and then move him forward 60 days or spaces.

Always add the number of days in each month and divide by 88—it leaves the number of days or spaces to move Mercury forward from where you found him. Then to be absolutely accurate, count 87¾ days.

We now find Venus Jan. 1st, 1843, 15 degrees in

INSTRUCTIONS TO CHART OF DESTINY 7.

Cancer. We move that one space or one and one-half degrees for each day or 92 spaces. The circle of Venus is just above the name which is in the circle of Mars for convenience of space. That leaves him 6 degrees in Capricornus.

As Venus makes her trip in 225 days the positions might be found where you would have to swing the hand clear around the dial once and then have 140 days or spaces to move forward, which would be equivalent to 210 degrees.

In counting the number of days it is easy to add the days in each month together and then subtract. If you have to swing the hand around the circle once or more.

If you do not readily remember the number of days in each month, commit to memory the following verse and it will always call it to mind quickly:

Thirty days hath September,
April, June and November,
All the rest have 31.

Excepting February 28 alone, or excepting leap year, then's the time February has 29.

After Venus, we come to our Earth.

As before stated, place the hand on the day of the month and follow it down to the degrees, and it shows you what degree the Sun is in, in appearance. The Earth will be found in the degree exactly opposite.

If reading from Helio Centric, which you must if reading from these tables, you should count the 1st degree of Libra as the ascendant, and count your aspects from the Earth, though you may use the houses if you wish to. In either case you always give the attributes of the signs given in the month or the Geo system, and if using Geo Centric tables you figure your aspects from the Sun or rather the degree of birth, which is the same thing.

We now find Mars Jan. 1st, 1843, at noon, was 24 degrees in Virgo. We move him forward one space for each 10 days. As we had 92 days we must move him forward 9 spaces, and as he travels half a degree per day and we have two extra days, we move him one degree farther. You will see by the tables the planets do not move through each sign exactly the same, and in Helio Centric Astrology a degree is near enough, as there is not one case out of a thousand where you will find a person who knows the exact time of day of birth, and where Astrologers claim to figure it out exactly, you may take it with a large grain of salt. I have never found one yet who could do so.

I do not pretend this system of ephemeris will get places of planets to a minute, but if you wish to figure down very closely it will aid you to do so in a much quicker way even than the Geo-Centric tables will permit.

Next is Jupiter, we find 12 degrees in Aquarius. As we move him forward but one degree for each twelve days, and as 12 is in 92, the number from Jan. 1st to April 2nd, it is 7 2-3 degrees, or 19 degrees and 40 minutes in Aquarius.

Next is Saturn 16 degrees in Capricornus. Saturn moves one degree for each 30 days, or about two minutes per day. So we find Saturn in Capricornus 19 degrees and about 4 minutes.

Next is Uranus, we find 29 degrees in Pisces, and as he moves one degree for each 90 days, we find him on the cusp of Aries.

Neptune we find 15 degrees in Aquarius. As Neptune moves but 1 degree in 180 days, he has moved but half a degree.

Now we have our map made and ready to judge the horoscope.

As this is merely an Ephemries it is not intended as a book of instruction for judgment. You will have to refer to our Universe or other works for that purpose.

The Moon tables are all the farmer requires; the tables of planets are intended for use in casting horoscopes alone.

Position of Planets Each Year

JAN. 1.	☿ IN	♀ IN	♂ IN	♃ IN	♄ IN	♅ IN	♆ IN
1825	18 ♈	20 ♈	5 ♓	11 ♌	11 ♊	14 ♑	4 ♑
1826	9 ♋	22 ♐	14 ♍	9 ♍	24 ♊	19 ♑	7 ♑
1827	22 ♍	14 ♋	3 ♈	8 ♎	7 ♋	23 ♑	9 ♑
1828	8 ♏	3 ♓	2 ♎	9 ♏	20 ♋	26 ♑	11 ♑
1829	15 ♐	22 ♎	28 ♈	8 ♐	2 ♌	0 ♒	13 ♑
1830	19 ♑	8 ♊	15 ♎	6 ♑	13 ♌	4 ♒	16 ♑
1831	15 ♓	24 ♑	22 ♉	8 ♒	25 ♌	8 ♒	18 ♑
1832	23 ♉	3 ♍	15 ♏	10 ♓	7 ♍	12 ♒	21 ♑
1833	13 ♌	23 ♈	14 ♊	14 ♈	19 ♍	17 ♒	23 ♑
1834	12 ♎	0 ♐	7 ♐	15 ♉	2 ♎	21 ♒	25 ♑
1835	22 ♏	20 ♋	5 ♋	18 ♊	14 ♎	25 ♒	27 ♑
1836	27 ♐	2 ♓	1 ♑	19 ♋	26 ♎	0 ♓	29 ♑
1837	6 ♒	15 ♎	28 ♋	16 ♌	8 ♏	4 ♓	1 ♒
1838	24 ♒	5 ♊	27 ♑	13 ♍	20 ♏	8 ♓	3 ♒
1839	5 ♊	20 ♑	17 ♌	12 ♎	1 ♐	13 ♓	5 ♒
1840	17 ♌	4 ♍	24 ♒	13 ♏	12 ♐	17 ♓	8 ♒
1841	14 ♎	16 ♈	6 ♍	12 ♐	23 ♐	21 ♓	10 ♒
1842	3 ♐	3 ♐	23 ♓	10 ♑	4 ♑	25 ♓	13 ♒
1843	18 ♑	15 ♋	24 ♍	12 ♒	16 ♑	29 ♓	15 ♒
1844	5 ♓	29 ♒	20 ♈	14 ♓	28 ♑	4 ♈	17 ♒
1845	11 ♉	16 ♎	15 ♎	18 ♈	10 ♒	8 ♈	19 ♒
1846	0 ♌	4 ♊	14 ♉	19 ♉	26 ♒	12 ♈	22 ♒
1847	2 ♎	24 ♑	10 ♏	22 ♊	8 ♓	16 ♈	24 ♒
1848	16 ♏	9 ♍	7 ♊	22 ♋	21 ♓	20 ♈	26 ♒

Position of Planets Each Year

JAN. 1.	☿ IN	♀ IN	♂ IN	♃ IN	♄ IN	♅ IN	♆ IN
1849	25 ♐	24 ♈	2 ♐	19 ♌	4 ♈	24 ♈	28 ♒
1850	10 ♒	10 ♐	0 ♋	16 ♍	17 ♈	28 ♈	0 ♓
1851	2 ♈	24 ♋	24 ♐	15 ♎	30 ♈	2 ♉	3 ♓
1852	5 ♊	5 ♓	10 ♋	14 ♏	13 ♉	6 ♉	5 ♓
1853	20 ♌	24 ♎	23 ♑	13 ♐	25 ♉	10 ♉	8 ♓
1854	18 ♎	5 ♊	18 ♌	11 ♑	7 ♊	14 ♉	11 ♓
1855	5 ♐	20 ♑	19 ♒	7 ♒	14 ♊	15 ♉	15 ♓
1856	2 ♎	7 ♍	2 ♍	9 ♓	27 ♊	19 ♉	17 ♓
1857	29 ♒	20 ♈	16 ♓	13 ♈	11 ♋	23 ♉	19 ♓
1858	30 ♈	8 ♐	21 ♍	16 ♉	24 ♋	27 ♉	22 ♓
1859	16 ♋	20 ♋	12 ♈	19 ♊	8 ♌	2 ♊	24 ♓
1860	27 ♍	1 ♓	6 ♎	20 ♋	21 ♌	6 ♊	27 ♓
1861	13 ♏	17 ♎	2 ♉	20 ♌	5 ♍	10 ♊	29 ♓
1862	22 ♐	7 ♊	29 ♎	17 ♍	17 ♍	14 ♊	30 ♓
1863	0 ♒	23 ♑	2 ♊	15 ♎	29 ♍	19 ♊	3 ♈
1864	20 ♓	20 ♍	22 ♏	11 ♏	11 ♎	24 ♊	4 ♈
1865	2 ♊	23 ♈	24 ♊	10 ♐	23 ♎	27 ♊	7 ♈
1866	26 ♌	9 ♐	16 ♐	10 ♑	5 ♏	2 ♋	9 ♈
1867	22 ♎	24 ♋	16 ♋	11 ♒	17 ♏	6 ♋	12 ♈
1868	1 ♐	2 ♓	11 ♑	14 ♓	28 ♏	11 ♋	14 ♈
1869	8 ♑	26 ♎	6 ♌	17 ♈	9 ♐	15 ♋	16 ♈
1870	21 ♒	7 ♊	8 ♒	20 ♉	20 ♐	20 ♋	18 ♈
1871	13 ♈	25 ♑	25 ♌	23 ♊	1 ♑	24 ♋	21 ♈
1872	9 ♋	10 ♍	3 ♓	13 ♋	12 ♑	29 ♋	23 ♈

Position of Planets Each Year

JAN. 1.	☿ IN	♀ IN	♂ IN	♃ IN	♄ IN	♅ IN	♆ IN
1873	22♍	25♈	14♍	23♌	23♑	4♌	25♈
1874	8♏	11♐	3♈	21♍	4♒	8♌	28♈
1875	16♐	25♋	3♎	19♎	16♒	13♌	30♈
1876	22♑	11♓	28♈	16♏	27♒	19♌	2♉
1877	14♓	27♎	23♎	15♐	9♓	22♌	4♉
1878	21♉	10♊	23♉	15♑	21♓	26♌	6♉
1879	12♌	26♑	14♏	16♒	3♈	1♍	9♉
1880	10♎	11♍	13♊	18♓	15♈	6♍	11♉
1881	22♏	23♈	6♐	22♈	28♈	11♍	13♉
1882	0♑	12♐	8♋	26♉	11♉	15♍	15♉
1883	11♒	26♋	28♐	27♊	24♉	20♍	17♉
1884	6♈	11♓	28♋	28♋	8♊	25♍	19♉
1885	28♊	25♎	27♑	27♌	21♊	29♍	22♉
1886	11♍	9♊	18♌	25♍	5♋	5♎	24♉
1887	0♏	21♑	24♒	22♎	18♋	9♎	26♉
1888	9♐	12♍	6♍	20♏	2♌	14♎	29♉
1889	18♑	28♈	21♓	19♐	16♌	19♎	1♊
1890	3♓	14♐	26♍	19♑	29♌	23♎	3♊
1891	26♈	27♋	19♈	20♒	12♍	28♎	6♊
1892	28♋	12♓	15♎	23♓	24♍	3♏	8♊
1893	5♎	24♎	15♉	27♈	6♎	7♏	10♊
1894	18♏	13♊	6♏	0♊	19♎	12♏	12♊
1895	25♐	28♑	8♊	2♋	0♏	16♏	14♊
1896	4♒	14♍	28♏	2♌	11♏	21♏	16♊

Position of Planets Each Year

JAN 1.	☿ IN	♀ IN	♂ IN	♃ IN	♄ IN	♅ IN	♆ IN
1897	29 ♓	29 ♈	0 ♋	0 ♍	23 ♏	25 ♏	19 ♊
1898	13 ♊	15 ♐	22 ♐	29 ♍	4 ♐	30 ♏	21 ♊
1899	9 ♍	26 ♋	20 ♋	27 ♎	16 ♐	4 ♐	23 ♊
1900	23 ♎	12 ♓	16 ♑	24 ♏	26 ♐	9 ♐	26 ♊
1901	5 ♐	25 ♎	8 ♌	23 ♐	7 ♑	14 ♐	28 ♊
1902	11 ♑	8 ♋	14 ♒	22 ♑	18 ♑	18 ♐	1 ♋
1903	24 ♒	21 ♑	0 ♍	24 ♒	29 ♑	22 ♐	3 ♋
1904	24 ♈	12 ♍	11 ♓	27 ♓	10 ♒	27 ♐	5 ♋
1905	20 ♋	28 ♈	18 ♍	30 ♈	22 ♒	1 ♑	7 ♋
1906	26 ♍	14 ♐	7 ♈	3 ♊	3 ♓	5 ♑	9 ♋
1907	13 ♏	27 ♋	7 ♎	5 ♋	15 ♓	9 ♑	11 ♋
1908	18 ♐	12 ♓	3 ♉	5 ♌	27 ♓	13 ♑	13 ♋
1909	27 ♑	24 ♎	27 ♎	3 ♍	9 ♈	18 ♑	16 ♋
1910	11 ♓	13 ♊	28 ♉	2 ♎	22 ♈	22 ♑	18 ♋
1911	20 ♉	28 ♑	19 ♏	29 ♎	4 ♉	26 ♑	21 ♋
1912	15 ♌	14 ♍	21 ♊	28 ♏	18 ♉	1 ♒	24 ♋
1913	13 ♎	19 ♊	11 ♐	26 ♐	1 ♊	5 ♒	27 ♋
1914	24 ♏	15 ♐	12 ♋	27 ♑	15 ♊	9 ♒	0 ♌
1915	0 ♑	26 ♋	6 ♑	29 ♒	28 ♊	13 ♒	3 ♌
1916	2 ♐	7 ♓	3 ♋	17 ♓	11 ♋	17 ♒	5 ♌
1917	4 ♑	20 ♎	27 ♐	18 ♈	24 ♋	22 ♒	7 ♌
1918	12 ♒	2 ♊	20 ♋	16 ♉	7 ♌	26 ♒	9 ♌
1919	6 ♈	14 ♑	19 ♑	15 ♊	19 ♑	1 ♓	11 ♌
1920	20 ♊	27 ♌	7 ♌	15 ♋	2 ♍	5 ♓	13 ♌

INSTRUCTIONS TO MOON TABLES

These instructions have been corrected and the tables designed for general use, particularly for the Helio system, and for use with "Astrological Periodicity," because that system does not require so close and accurate work as the Geo system.

It is well known that the Moon exerts an influence of the sign it just emerges from as well as the sign it is about to enter, before leaving the one or entering the other. Therefore, for general use such as the farmer and business man would put it to, or for the practice of Helio Astrology, this system is all right. Again, the Geo tables are only made out from year to year, while you may ascertain the position of the Moon, by this system, a hundred years hence, or as far as you please.

To get the place of the Moon at any particular period—say April 2nd, 1843—turn to index table on page 335 and look for the year 1843. You find it on line one, column six; the lines run from left to right and are the number of tables, which are 19.

The columns are the years from top to bottom; 1843 is in column six, hence 1843 is in the first table. Now, by referring to the first table, the days of the month run from top to bottom on the left hand; therefore, April 2nd, 1843, the Moon was from 14 to 27 degrees in Taurus, according to time of day and locality. If you wish to work very accurate for close aspect work, remember the ephemries are made out for noon of each day, at Greenwich time, and for such work the Geo ephemries are best, but still you

INSTRUCTIONS FOR MOON TABLES. Page 2

won't care for such work when you thoroughly understand this system, or Astrological Periodicity.

Now to get the phases or age of the Moon.

This is very simple. Especially if you have our Solar Bioscope. By placing the hand on the day of the month and then look down to the inner circle it gives you the degree the Sun is in for any day of the year. Or if you get the place any other way, it is the same. The Earth is always right opposite to the Sun. The sign and the degree the Moon is in will always determine its age (see pages 23 to 26).

The instructions for these tables for the first edition were somewhat in error, and do not need the calculations of a day, hence this correction; besides I did not refer to pages 23 to 26, which ought to have been done to make the work perfect.

Re member, the Moon travels about thirteen degrees per day, and when in the same sign with the Sun it is dark or old Moon until it passes the Sun; then it is a small crescent, or new Moon, and by the eighth day is about equal distance between the Sun and Earth, or first quarter; when in conjunction with the Earth (i. e., in exact degree and sign with the Earth) it is full; and then it wanes as it nears the Sun again. Thus, 13 degrees from the Sun it is one day old, and so on, add the days until re-born a new Moon. The Moon makes its circuit of the Earth about every 28 days, a little less.

INSTRUCTIONS TO MOON TABLES.

The following twenty tables give the dates of the phases of the Moon, for the 19th. century as they stand. But, for the 18th.century or from 1700 to 1800 you should deduct one day. Thus, when a change takes place, at any stated place, say New York July 2nd. 1786, you would say July 1st. But if it be July 2nd 1968, or any other year of the 20th. century you would say, July 3d. thus adding a day. to the day of the month given.

To repeet that there may be no miss understanding, rember 1700 to 1800 you take one day from the day of the month given and from 1800 to 1900 the tables stand as they are, from 1900 to 2000, you add one day and from 2000 to 2100 you add 2 days and to 2200 add three days and so keep on addsng a day to eadh century. to etrnity.

The same index and the same instructions are to be observed in the use of the second lot of tab.es, or the tables showing the signs the Moon is in at any given date.

An example,- supose you want to know the age of the Moon and the sign it was in April 2nd. 1843 you turn to the index of Moon tabls page 335 and you find the table runs lengithwise the page with the numbers of the tables, from 1 to 19 run across the page. We now look for the year 1843, we find it in the first column running lngithwise the page and we find it at the top of the sixth column running crosswise of the page; this tells us we must look to table number one, we turn to that table and we ffind the last new moon previous to that date on March 29 th. We now count to April 2 nd, and we find the Moon was five days old, and by looking to table number one of the signs the Moon is in, page 336, we find the days of the month in the, first column to the left and April is the 4 th column to the right, thus April 2 nd we find the Moon is in the sign Taurus 19 degrees. This is 6 degrees farther than it was April 2nd 1843,; this is the greatest difference found; so for use in Heleo-Centric astrologey or for all other purposes except very clost work in Geo-Centric astrologey, and it is as clost as the majority of them figure. These tables are all that is necessary.

Aftr you have found the age of the Moon turn to page 31 to 35 and you will see the meaning of the age of the Moon at birth.

It is necessary to get the age and the sign the Moon is in for planting and for other purposes but the methued is all the same. and the index is the same.

INDEX TO MOON TABLE 128

	1	2	3	4	5	6	7	8	9	10	11	12	13	14
1	1748	1767	1786	1805	1824	1843	1862	1881	1900	1919	1938	1957	1976	1995
2	1749	1768	1787	1806	1825	1844	1863	1882	1901	1920	1939	1958	1977	1996
3	1750	1769	1788	1807	1826	1845	1864	1883	1902	1921	1940	1959	1978	1997
4	1751	1770	1789	1808	1827	1846	1865	1884	1903	1922	1941	1960	1979	1998
5	1752	1771	1790	1809	1828	1847	1866	1885	1904	1923	1942	1961	1980	1999
6	1753	1772	1791	1810	1829	1848	1867	1886	1905	1924	1943	1962	1981	2000
7	1754	1773	1792	1811	1830	1849	1868	1887	1906	1925	1944	1963	1982	2001
8	1755	1774	1793	1812	1831	1850	1869	1888	1907	1926	1945	1964	1983	2002
9	1756	1775	1794	1813	1832	1851	1870	1889	1908	1927	1946	1965	1984	2003
10	1757	1776	1795	1814	1833	1852	1871	1890	1909	1928	1947	1966	1985	2004
11	1758	1777	1796	1815	1834	1853	1872	1891	1910	1929	1948	1967	1986	2005
12	1759	1778	1797	1816	1835	1854	1873	1892	1911	1930	1949	1968	1987	2006
13	1760	1779	1798	1817	1836	1855	1874	1893	1912	1931	1950	1969	1988	2007
14	1761	1780	1799	1818	1837	1856	1875	1894	1913	1932	1951	1970	1989	2008
15	1762	1781	1800	1819	1838	1857	1876	1895	1914	1933	1952	1971	1990	2009
16	1763	1782	1801	1820	1839	1858	1877	1896	1915	1934	1953	1972	1991	2010
17	1764	1783	1802	1821	1840	1859	1878	1897	1916	1935	1954	1973	1992	2011
18	1765	1784	1803	1822	1841	1860	1879	1898	1917	1936	1955	1974	1993	2012
19	1766	1785	1804	1823	1842	1861	1880	1899	1918	1937	1956	1975	1994	2013

TABLE I PAGE 129

SIGNS THE MOON IS IN FOR EACH DAY OF THE MONTH GREENWICH TIME. EXACT FOR 1881 AND WITHIN 6 DEGREES FOR ALL OTHER YEARS ON I LINE ON INDEX TABLE

DAYS OF MONTH	JAN	FEB.	MAR	APR	MAY	JUN	JUL.	AUG	SEP	OCT.	NOV	DEC.
1	♑24	♓17	♓25	♉14	♊17	♌1	♍3	≏19	♐8	♑16	♓10	♈18
2	♒9	♈1	♈9	27	29	13	15	♏2	22	♒0	24	♉2
3	24	15	23	♊9	♋11	25	27	15	♑6	15	♈8	15
4	♓9	28	♉6	21	23	♍7	≏10	28	20	29	22	28
5	23	♉11	19	♋3	♌5	13	23	♐12	♒5	♓14	♉6	♊11
6	♈6	23	♊1	15	17	≏1	♏6	26	20	29	19	24
7	19	♊5	13	27	29	14	19	♑11	♓5	♈13	♊3	♋6
8	♉2	17	25	♌9	♍11	28	♐3	26	20	27	15	18
9	14	29	♋7	21	23	♏11	18	♒11	♈5	♉11	28	♌0
10	26	♋11	19	♍3	≏6	26	♑3	27	19	25	♋10	12
11	♊8	22	♌1	15	19	♐11	18	♓12	♉3	♊8	22	24
12	20	♌4	13	28	♏3	24	♒3	27	17	20	♌4	♍6
13	♋2	16	25	≏11	17	♑9	18	♈11	30	♋3	16	18
14	14	29	♍7	25	♐1	24	♓3	25	♊12	15	28	≏0
15	26	♍11	20	♏8	16	♒[illegible]	18	♉8	25	27	♍10	12
16	[illegible]	23	≏[illegible]	22	♑10	24	♈2	21	≏7	♌8	22	25
17	20	≏6	16	♐6	♍15	♓8	16	♊4	18	26	≏5	♏8
18	♍2	19	29	26	29	22	[illegible]	16	♌0	♍2	17	21
19	14	♏2	♏12	♑4	♒14	♈6	♉12	28	12	" 14	♏0	♐5
20	26	15	26	19	20	19	25	♋10	24	" 27	13	19
21	≏9	29	♐10	♒2	♓12	♉2	♊7	22	♍6	≏9	27	♑4
22	22	♐13	24	17	25	15	19	♌4	18	22	♐11	18
23	♏5	27	♑8	♓1	♈9	28	♋1	15	≏1	♏5	25	♒3
24	19	♑11	22	15	22	♊10	13	27	13	18	♑9	18
25	♐3	26	♒6	29	♉5	22	25	♍9	26	♐2	24	♓3
26	17	♒11	20	♈12	18	♋4	♌7	21	♏9	15	♒8	♓17
27	♑2	26	♓5	26	♊1	16	18	≏4	22	29	22	♈1
28	17	♓10	19	♉9	13	28	♍0	16	♐5	♑13	♓6	15
29	♒2		♈3	22	25	♌10	12	29	18	27	20	28
30	17		17	♊5	♋7	21	24	♏12	♑2	♒11	♈4	♉12
31	♓2		♉1		19		≏7	25		25		25

TABLE 2 **PAGE 130**

SIGNS THE MOON IS IN FOR EACH DAY OF THE MONTH
GREENWICH TIME. EXACT FOR 1882 AND WITHIN 6 DEGREES
FOR ALL OTHER YEARS ON 1 LINE ON INDEX TABLE

DATE OF MONTH	JAN.	FEB.	MAR.	APR.	MAY.	JUN.	JUL.	AUG.	SEP.	OCT.	NOV.	DEC.
1	♊7	♋23	♌2	♍17	♎19	♐6	♑13	♓6	♈30	♊7	♋24	♌27
2	20	♌5	14	29	♏2	20	27	21	♉14	20	♌7	♍9
3	♋2	17	26	♎11	15	♑4	♒12	♈6	28	♋3	19	21
4	14	29	♍8	23	27	18	26	20	♊11	16	♍1	♎3
5	27	♏11	20	♏5	♐11	♒2	♓	♉4	24	28	13	14
6	♌9	23	♎2	18	24	16	25	18	♋7	♌10	25	26
7	20	♎5	14	♐1	♑7	♓0	♈10	♊1	19	22	♎6	♏9
8	♍2	17	26	14	21	15	24	14	♌1	♍4	18	21
9	14	29	♏8	27	♒5	28	♉7	27	13	16	♏0	♐4
10	26	♏12	21	♑11	19	♈13	21	♋10	25	28	13	16
11	♎8	24	♐4	24	♓4	27	♊4	22	♍7	♎10	25	30
12	20	♐7	17	♒8	18	♉11	17	♌4	19	22	♐8	♑13
13	♏2	21	♑0	23	♈2	24	♋0	16	♎1	♏4	20	27
14	16	♑5	14	♓8	17	♊8	13	20	12	16	♑3	♒11
15	29	20	28	22	♉1	21	25	♍11	.25	28	17	25
16	♐13	♒5	♒13	♈7	15	♋4	♌7	22	♏7	♐11	♒0	♓9
17	27	20	28	22	29	16	20	♎4	19	23	14	23
18	♑12	♓5	♓13	♉6	♊12	29	♍2	16	♐1	♑6	28	♈7
19	27	20	28	20	25	♌11	13	27	14	20	♓12	21
20	♒12	♈5	♈14	♊4	♋8	23	25	♍10	27	♒3	26	♉5
21	27	20	28	18	21	♍5	♎7	22	♑10	17	♈11	19
22	♓12	♉4	♉14	♋0	♌3	17	13	♐5	24	♓2	25	♊3
23	27	18	26	13	15	29	♏1	18	♒8	17	♉10	17
24	♈11	♊1	♊10	25	27	♎11	14	♑1	23	♈1	24	♋1
25	25	14	22	♌7	♏3	23	26	15	♓8	16	♊9	14
26	♉9	26	♋5	19	21	♏5	♐9	23	23	♉1	22	27
27	22	♋8	17	♍1	♎3	18	23	♒14	♈8	16	♋6	♌10
28	♊4	20	29	13	15	♐1	♑7	29	23	♊1	19	22
29	17		♌11	25	28	15	21	♓15	♉8	15	♌2	♍5
30	29		23	♎7	♏10	28	♒6	♈0	23	28	15	17
31	♋11		♍5		23		21	15		♋11		28

H A DREHER

TABLE 3 PAGE 131

SIGNS THE MOON IS IN FOR EACH DAY OF THE MONTH GREENWICH TIME EXACT FOR 1883 AND WITHIN 6 DEGREES FOR ALL OTHER YEARS ON 1 LINE ON INDEX TABLE

DATE OF MONTH	JAN.	FEB	MAR	APR	MAY	JUN	JUL	AUG	SEP	OCT	NOV	DEC
1	♎10	♏24	♐2	♑19	♒26	♈19	♉28	♋20	♏8	♎11	♏25	♐28
2	22	♐7	15	♒3	♓10	♉4	♊12	♌3	20	23	♐7	♑10
3	♏4	19	27	17	25	18	26	16	♎2	♏4	19	23
4	16	♑2	♑11	♓1	♈10	♊3	♋10	29	14	16	♑1	♒5
5	29	16	24	16	25	18	24	♍11	26	28	13	18
6	♐12	♒0	♒8	♈1	♉10	♋2	♌7	24	♏8	♐10	26	♓2
7	25	15	23	16	25	16	21	♎6	19	22	♒9	15
8	♑8	30	♓8	♉1	♊9	29	♍3	18	♐1	♑4	22	29
9	22	♓14	23	16	24	♌12	16	29	13	17	♓5	♈13
10	♒6	29	♈8	♊1	♋8	25	28	♏11	26	30	19	28
11	21	♈14	23	15	21	♍8	♎10	23	♑8	♒13	♈4	♉12
12	♓5	29	♉8	29	♌4	20	22	♐5	21	27	19	28
13	19	♉13	22	♋13	17	♎2	♏3	17	♒5	♓11	♉4	♊12
14	♈4	27	♊6	26	29	14	15	♑0	19	26	19	27
15	18	♊10	20	♌8	♍12	25	27	13	♓3	♈1	♊4	♋12
16	♉2	23	♋3	21	23	♏7	♐10	27	18	26	19	26
17	16	♋6	16	♍3	♎5	19	22	♒10	♈2	♉11	♋4	♌10
18	30	19	29	15	17	♐1	♑5	25	17	26	18	23
19	♊13	♌2	♌11	27	29	14	18	♓9	♉2	♊11	♌2	♍6
20	21	14	24	♎9	♏11	26	♒2	24	17	25	15	19
21	♋10	27	♍6	20	23	♑9	15	♈8	♊2	♋9	28	♎7
22	23	♍9	18	♏2	♐5	22	30	23	16	23	♍10	13
23	♌5	21	30	14	17	♒6	♓14	♉7	30	♌0	23	25
24	18	♎3	♎12	26	♑0	19	28	21	♋13	19	♎5	♏7
25	♍0	15	23	♐8	13	♓3	♈12	♊5	26	♍1	16	18
26	13	26	♏5	20	26	17	26	19	♌9	14	28	♐0
27	25	♏8	17	♑3	♒9	♈1	♉10	♋3	22	26	♏10	12
28	♎6	20	29	16	23	15	24	16	♍4	♎8	22	25
29	18		♐11	29	♓6	29	♊8	29	17	19	♐4	♑7
30	♏0		23	♒12	20	♉14	22	♌12	29	♏1	16	20
31	12		♑6		♈5		♋6	25		13		♒2

M A BREHER

TABLE 4

PAGE 132

SIGNS THE MOON IS IN FOR EACH DAY OF THE MONTH GREENWICH TIME EXACT FOR 1884 AND WITHIN 6 DEGREES FOR ALL OTHER YEARS ON 1 LINE ON INDEX TABLE

DATE OF MONTH	JAN.	FEB.	MAR.	APR.	MAY.	JUN.	JUL.	AUG.	SEP.	OCT.	NOV.	DEC.
1	♒15	♈6	♉1	♊24	♌2	♍20	♎24	♐8	♑22	♒25	♈14	♉21
2	29	20	15	♋8	15	♎3	♏6	20	♒4	♓8	29	♊7
3	♓12	♉4	29	22	28	15	18	♑2	17	22	♉13	22
4	26	18	♊13	♌5	♍11	27	29	14	♓0	♈6	28	♋7
5	♈9	♊2	27	19	24	♏9	♐11	26	14	20	♊13	.22
6	23	17	♋11	♍1	♎6	21	23	♒9	27	♉6	28	♌7
7	♉7	♋1	25	14	18	♐3	♑5	22	♈11	19	♋13	21
8	22	15	♌8	27	♏0	14	17	♓5	25	♊4	28	♍5
9	♊6	29	22	♎9	12	26	30	18	♉9	19	♌12	18
10	21	♌12	♍5	21	24	♑8	♒12	♈1	24	♋3	25	♎1
11	♋5	26	18	♏3	♐5	21	25	15	♊8	17	♍8	13
12	20	♍9	♎0	15	17	♒3	♓8	29	22	♌1	21	26
13	♌4	22	12	27	29	15	21	♉13	♋6	15	♎4	♏8
14	18	♎4	25	♐9	♑11	28	♈4	27	20	28	16	20
15	♍1	17	♏7	20	23	♓11	18	♊11	♌4	♍11	29	♐2
16	14	29	18	♑2	♒6	24	♉2	25	18	24	♏11	13
17	27	♏11	♐0	15	18	♈8	16	♋10	♍2	♎7	23	25
18	♎9	22	12	27	♓1	22	♊1	24	15	19	♐5	♑7
19	21	♐4	24	♒10	15	♉6	15	♌8	28	♏2	16	19
20	♏3	16	♑6	23	28	21	♋0	22	♎11	14	28	♒1
21	15	28	19	♓6	♈13	♊6	15	♍6	23	26	♑10	13
22	26	♑11	♒1	20	27	21	26	20	♏6	♐8	22	25
23	♐8	23	14	♈4	♉12	♋6	♌14	♎3	18	20	♒4	♓8
24	20	♒6	28	19	27	21	28	15	30	♑2	16	20
25	♑3	20	♓12	♉4	♊12	♌6	♍12	28	♐12	14	29	♈3
26	15	♓4	26	19	28	20	25	♏10	24	26	♓11	17
27	28	18	♈11	♊4	♋13	♍3	♎7	22	♑5	♒8	24	♉1
28	♒12	♈2	25	19	27	17	20	♐4	17	20	♈8	1·5
29	25	16	♉10	♋4	♌11	29	♏2	16	30	♓3	22	29
30	♓9		25	18	25	♎12	14	27	♒12	16	♉6	♊15
31	22		♊10		♍8		26	♑10		♈0		30

TABLE 5 PAGE 133

SIGNS THE MOON IS IN FOR EACH DAY OF THE MONTH GREENWICH TIME. EXACT FOR 1885 AND WITHIN 6 DEGREES FOR ALL OTHER YEARS ON 1 LINE ON INDEX TABLE

DATE OF MONTH	JAN.	FEB.	MAR	APR	MAY	JUN	JUL	AUG	SEP	OCT	NOV	DEC.
1	♋15	♍7	♍15	♏4	♐7	♑21	♒24	♈10	♉30	♋9	♍2	♎10
2	♌0	21	29	16	19	♒3	♓6	23	♊14	23	16	23
3	15	♎5	♎11	29	♑1	15	18	♉6	28	♌7	30	♏6
4	30	18	26	♐11	13	27	♈0	20	♋12	21	♎13	19
5	♍13	♏1	♏8	23	25	♓9	13	♊3	27	♍6	26	♐1
6	27	13	21	♑5	♒6	22	26	18	♌12	20	♏10	14
7	♎10	25	♐3	17	18	♈4	♉10	♋3	26	♎4	23	26
8	22	♐7	14	28	♓1	18	24	18	♍11	18	♐5	♑8
9	♏5	19	27	♒11	13	♉1	♊9	♌3	25	♏1	18	20
10	17	♑1	♑9	23	26	16	24	18	♎9	14	♑0	♒2
11	29	13	21	♓5	♈9	♊0	♋9	♍3	23	27	12	14
12	♐10	25	♒3	18	23	15	24	17	♏6	♐10	24	26
13	22	♒7	15	♈1	♉7	♋0	♌9	♎1	19	22	♒6	♓8
14	♑4	19	27	15	22	16	24	15	♐2	♑4	18	20
15	16	♓2	♓10	29	♊7	♌1	♍9	28	14	16	30	♈2
16	28	14	23	♉13	22	15	23	♏11	26	28	♓12	15
17	♒10	27	♈6	28	♋6	30	♎7	24	♑8	♒10	24	28
18	22	♈10	20	♊12	21	♍14	20	♐6	20	22	♈7	♉11
19	♓5	24	♉4	27	♌6	27	♏3	18	♒2	♓4	20	25
20	17	♉7	18	♋11	21	♎10	15	♑0	14	16	♉3	♊10
21	♈0	21	♊2	25	♍4	23	27	12	26	29	17	25
22	13	♊5	16	♌9	17	♏6	♐9	24	♓8	♈12	♊2	♋10
23	27	19	♋0	23	♎0	18	21	♒5	21	25	16	25
24	♉10	♋3	14	♍7	13	♐0	♑3	18	♈4	♉9	♋1	♌10
25	24	18	28	20	21	12	15	30	16	23	16	25
26	♊9	♌2	♌13	♎4	♏8	24	27	♓12	30	♊7	♌0	♍9
27	23	17	27	17	21	♑6	♒9	24	♉13	21	15	23
28	♋8	♍1	♍10	29	♐3	18	21	♈7	27	♋5	29	♎7
29	23		24	♏12	15	♒0	♓3	20	♊11	20	♍13	20
30	♌8		♎7	24	27	12	15	♉3	25	♌4	26	♏3
31	23		21		♑9		27	16		18		16

TABLE 6 PAGE 134

SIGNS THE MOON IS IN FOR EACH DAY OF THE MONTH GREENWICH TIME. EXACT FOR 1886 AND WITHIN 6 DEGREES FOR ALL OTHER YEARS ON 1 LINE ON INDEX TABLE

DATE OF MONTH	JAN	FEB.	MAR	APR	MAY	JUN	JUL.	AUG.	SEP	OCT.	NOV.	DEC.
1	♏28	♑14	♑23	♓7	♈9	♉27	♋4	♌27	♎20	♏27	♑14	♒16
2	♐11	26	♒5	19	22	♊11	18	♍12	♏5	♐10	27	28
3	23	♒8	16	♈1	♉5	25	♌3	27	18	23	♒9	♓10
4	♑5	20	28	13	18	♋9	18	♎11	♐2	♑6	21	22
5	17	♓1	♓10	26	♊2	24	♍3	25	15	18	♓2	♈4
6	29	13	22	♉9	15	♌8	17	♏9	27	♒0	14	16
7	♒11	25	♈4	22	29	23	♎1	22	♑10	12	26	28
8	23	♈7	17	♊5	♋13	♍7	15	♐5	22	24	♈8	♉11
9	♓4	20	29	19	28	21	29	18	♒4	♓6	20	24
10	16	♉2	♉12	♋3	♌12	♎5	♏12	♑0	16	18	♉3	♊7
11	28	15	25	17	26	19	25	13	27	30	15	21
12	♈10	28	♊3	♌1	♍10	♏2	♐8	25	♓9	♈12	28	♋5
13	23	♊12	22	15	24	15	21	♒7	21	24	♊12	19
14	♉6	26	♋6	29	♎8	29	♑3	19	♈3	♉6	25	♌3
15	19	♋11	20	♍14	22	♐12	16	♓0	15	19	♋9	17
16	♊3	26	♌5	28	♏6	24	28	12	27	♊2	22	♍1
17	18	♌11	20	♎12	19	♑7	♒10	24	♉10	15	♌6	15
18	♋2	26	♍4	27	♐3	19	22	♈6	22	28	20	29
19	18	♍11	19	♍11	16	♒1	♓3	18	♊5	♋12	♍4	♎13
20	♌3	26	♎4	24	28	13	15	♉0	18	26	18	27
21	18	♎11	18	♐7	♑11	25	27	13	♋2	♌9	♎3	♏1
22	♍3	25	♏[illegible]	20	23	♓7	♈9	25	15	24	17	25
23	18	♏8	16	♑3	♒5	19	21	♊8	29	♍8	♏1	♐8
24	♎2	21	30	15	17	♈1	♉4	22	♌14	23	15	22
25	16	♐[illegible]	♐12	27	29	13	16	♋6	29	♎7	29	♑5
26	30	17	25	♒9	♓11	25	30	20	♍14	22	♐13	17
27	♏13	29	♑7	21	23	♉8	♊13	♌5	29	♏7	26	♒0
28	25	♑11	19	♓3	♈5	21	27	20	♎14	21	♑9	12
29	♐8		♒1	15	17	♊5	♋12	♍5	28	♐5	22	24
30	20		13	27	♉0	19	27	21	♏13	18	♒4	♓6
31	♑2		25		13		♌12	♎6		♑1		18

TABLE 7 PAGE 135

SIGNS THE MOON IS IN FOR EACH DAY OF THE MONTH GREENWICH TIME EXACT FOR 1887 AND WITHIN 6 DEGREES FOR ALL OTHER YEARS ON 1 LINE ON INDEX TABLE

DATE OF MONTH	JAN	FEB	MAR	APR	MAY	JUN	JUL	AUG	SEP.	OCT.	NOV	DEC.
1	♓30	♉14	♉23	♋10	♌18	♎11	♏20	♑11	♒28	♈1	♉15	♊19
2	♈12	27	♊5	24	♍2	25	♐4	24	♓10	13	27	♋1
3	24	♊9	18	♌8	16	♏10	18	♒7	22	24	♊10	14
4	♉6	23	♋1	22	♎1	24	♑1	19	♈4	♉6	22	27
5	13	♋7	15	♍7	16	♐9	15	♓1	16	18	♋4	♌10
6	♊2	21	29	22	♏0	23	28	13	28	♊0	17	23
7	15	♌5	♌13	♎7	15	♑6	♒11	25	♉9	12	30	♍7
8	23	20	28	22	♐0	20	23	♈7	21	25	♌13	21
9	♋13	♍5	♍13	♏7	14	♒3	♓5	19	♊4	♋7	27	♎5
10	27	20	29	22	28	15	18	♉1	16	20	♍11	19
11	♌12	♎5	♎14	♐6	♑12	27	29	13	29	♌4	25	♏4
12	27	20	29	20	25	♓9	♈11	25	♋12	17	♎10	19
13	♍11	♏4	♏13	♑3	♒7	21	23	♊8	25	♍2	25	♐3
14	26	18	28	16	19	♈3	♉5	20	♌9	16	♏10	18
15	♎10	♐2	♐11	29	♓1	15	17	♋3	23	♎1	25	♑2
16	24	15	25	♒11	13	27	30	17	♍8	16	♐10	16
17	♏8	28	♑8	23	25	♉9	♊12	♌1	23	♏2	24	♒0
18	22	♑11	20	♓5	♈7	21	25	15	♎8	17	♑9	13
19	♐5	23	♒2	17	19	♊4	♋9	30	23	♐2	22	26
20	18	♒5	14	28	♉1	17	23	♍14	♏8	16	♒5	♓8
21	♑1	17	26	♈10	13	♋0	♌7	29	23	♑0	18	21
22	14	29	♓8	22	26	14	21	♎14	♐7	14	♓0	♈2
23	26	♓11	20	♉4	♊8	27	♍5	29	21	27	13	14
24	♒8	23	♈2	17	21	♌11	20	♏13	♑5	♒10	24	26
25	20	♈5	13	29	♋4	25	♎4	27	18	22	♈6	♉8
26	♓2	16	25	♊12	17	♍9	18	♐11	♒0	♓4	18	20
27	14	28	♉7	24	♌1	23	♏3	25	13	16	♉0	♊2
28	16	♉10	20	♋7	14	♎7	17	♑8	25	28	12	15
29	♈8		♊2	20	28	22	♐1	21	♓7	♈10	24	27
30	20		14	♌4	♍12	♏6	14	♒3	19	21	♊6	♋10
31	♉2		27		26		28	16		♉3		23

H A DREHER

TABLE 8 — PAGE 136

SIGNS THE MOON IS IN FOR EACH DAY OF THE MONTH GREENWICH TIME EXACT FOR 1888 AND WITHIN 6 DEGREES FOR ALL OTHER YEARS ON 1 LINE ON INDEX TABLE

	JAN.	FEB.	MAR.	APR.	MAY	JUN.	JUL.	AUG.	SEP.	OCT.	NOV.	DEC.
1	♌ 7	♍ 28	♎ 22	♐ 16	♑ 23	♓ 11	♈ 14	♉ 27	♋ 12	♌ 15	♎ 4	♏ 12
2	20	♎ 12	♏ 7	♑ 0	♒ 6	23	26	♊ 9	24	28	♎ 19	28
3	♍ 4	27	22	14	19	♈ 5	♉ 8	21	♌ 7	♍ 12	♏ 4	♐ 13
4	18	♏ 11	♐ 6	27	♓ 2	17	19	♋ 4	20	26	20	28
5	♎ 2	25	20	♒ 10	14	29	♊ 1	16	♍ 4	♎ 11	♐ 5	♑ 13
6	16	♐ 9	♑ 4	23	26	♉ 11	13	29	18	26	20	28
7	♏ 0	23	17	♓ 5	♈ 8	23	25	♌ 12	♎ 2	♏ 11	♑ 5	♒ 12
8	14	♑ 7	♒ 0	17	20	♊ 5	♋ 8	25	17	26	19	25
9	28	20	13	29	♉ 2	17	20	♍ 9	♏ 2	♐ 11	♒ 3	♓ 9
10	♐ 13	♒ 3	25	♈ 11	14	29	♌ 3	23	16	25	16	21
11	27	16	♓ 8	23	26	♋ 11	16	♎ 7	♐ 0	♑ 9	29	♈ 4
12	♑ 11	29	20	♉ 5	♊ 8	24	29	21	15	23	♓ 12	16
13	24	♓ 12	♈ 2	17	20	♌ 6	♍ 13	♏ 5	29	♒ 6	25	28
14	♒ 8	24	14	29	♋ 2	19	26	19	♑ 12	20	♈ 7	♉ 10
15	21	♈ 6	26	♊ 11	14	♍ 2	♎ 10	♐ 4	26	♓ 2	19	22
16	♓ 4	18	♉ 8	23	27	16	24	18	♒ 9	15	♉ 1	♊ 4
17	16	♉ 0	20	♋ 5	♌ 9	29	♏ 8	♑ 2	23	28	13	16
18	28	21	♊ 2	17	22	♎ 13	23	16	♓ 6	♈ 10	25	28
19	♈ 10	24	14	30	♍ 6	28	♐ 7	29	19	22	♊ 7	♋ 10
20	22	♊ 6	26	♌ 13	19	♏ 12	22	♒ 13	♈ 1	♉ 4	19	22
21	♉ 4	18	♋ 9	26	♎ 4	27	♑ 6	26	13	16	♋ 1	♌ 4
22	16	♋ 0	21	♍ 10	18	♐ 12	20	♓ 10	26	28	13	16
23	28	13	♌ 4	25	♏ 3	27	♒ 4	22	♉ 8	♊ 10	25	29
24	♊ 10	26	18	♎ 9	18	♑ 12	18	♈ 5	20	22	♌ 7	♍ 12
25	23	♌ 10	♍ 2	25	♐ 4	26	♓ 1	17	♊ 2	♋ 4	19	25
26	♋ 6	24	16	♏ 10	19	♒ 10	14	30	13	16	♍ 2	♎ 8
27	19	♍ 8	♎ 1	25	♑ 3	23	27	♉ 12	25	28	15	22
28	♌ 2	23	16	♐ 10	18	♓ 6	♈ 10	24	♋ 7	♌ 10	29	♏ 6
29	16	♎ 8	♏ 2	25	♒ 2	19	22	♊ 5	20	23	♎ 13	21
30	30		17	♑ 9	15	♈ 2	♉ 4	17	♌ 2	♍ 6	27	♐ 6
31	♍ 14		♐ 2		28		16	29		20		21

H. A. [illegible]

TABLES — PAGE 137

SIGNS THE MOON IS IN FOR EACH DAY OF THE MONTH GREENWICH TIME. EXACT FOR 1889 AND WITHIN 6 DEGREES FOR ALL OTHER YEARS ON 1 LINE ON INDEX TABLE

DATE OF MONTH	JAN.	FEB	MAR	APR.	MAY	JUN	JUL.	AUG	SEP.	OCT.	NOV	DEC.
1	♑6	♒13	♓6	♈24	♉27	♋11	♌14	♎1	♏22	♑1	♒24	♈1
2	21	♓11	19	♉6	♊9	23	26	14	♐6	15	♓8	15
3	♒5	25	♈3	18	21	♌5	♍9	28	20	29	21	27
4	20	♈8	15	♊1	♋2	17	21	♏11	♑4	♒13	♈4	♉10
5	♓3	20	28	12	14	29	♎4	25	19	27	18	22
6	17	♉3	♉10	24	26	♍12	18	♐10	♒3	♓11	♉1	♊4
7	30	15	23	♋6	♌8	25	♏1	24	17	25	13	17
8	♈12	27	♊5	18	20	♎8	15	♑9	♓2	♈8	26	28
9	25	♊9	16	♌0	♍3	22	♐0	24	16	22	♊8	♋10
10	♉7	20	28	12	16	♏6	15	♒8	30	♉5	20	22
11	19	♋2	♋10	25	30	21	30	23	♈13	17	♋2	♌4
12	♊0	14	22	♍8	♎14	♐6	♑15	♓7	27	30	14	16
13	12	27	♌4	22	28	21	♒0	22	♉9	♊12	25	28
14	24	♌9	17	♎5	♏13	♑7	15	♈5	28	24	♌7	♍10
15	♋6	22	♍0	20	28	22	29	19	♊4	♋6	19	22
16	·18	♍5	13	♏4	♐13	♒6	♓13	♉1	16	18	♍1	♎5
17	♌1	18	27	19	28	21	27	14	28	29	14	18
18	13	♎2	♎11	♐4	♑13	♓5	♈10	26	♋10	♌11	27	♏2
19	26	15	25	19	27	18	23	♊8	22	24	♎10	16
20	♍9	29	♏10	♑3	♒11	♈1	♉8	20	♌4	♍6	24	♐0
21	22	♏13	24	17	25	14	18	♋2	16	19	♏8	15
22	♎5	27	♐8	♒1	♓9	27	30	14	28	♎2	22	♑0
23	19	♐12	23	15	22	♉9	♊12	25	♍11	16	♐7	15
24	♏3	26	♑7	29	♈5	21	23	♌8	24	30	22	♒1
25	17	♑10	21	♓12	17	♊3	♋5	20	♎7	♏14	♑7	16
26	♐1	24	♒4	25	30	15	17	♍2	21	29	22	♓0
27	15	♒8	18	♈8	♉12	26	29	15	♏5	♐13	♒6	14
28	30	22	♓2	20	24	♋8	♌11	28	19	27	21	28
29	♑14		15	♉3	♊6	20	29	♎11	♐3	♑12	♓5	♈11
30	29		28	15	18	♌2	♍6	25	17	26	18	24
31	♒13		♈11		29		18	♏8		♒10		♉7

H A DREHER

TABLE 10 PAGE 138

SIGNS THE MOON IS IN FOR EACH DAY OF THE MONTH GREENWICH TIME EXACT FOR 1890 AND WITHIN 6 DEGREES FOR ALL OTHER YEARS ON 1 LINE ON INDEX TABLE

DATE OF MONTH	JAN	FEB	MAR	APR	MAY	JUN	JUL	AUG	SEP	OCT	NOV	DEC
1	♉19	♋4	♋13	♌26	♍29	♏17	♐24	♒18	♈11	♉17	♋4	♌6
2	♊1	16	24	♍9	♎12	♐1	♑9	♓3	25	♊1	16	18
3	13	28	♌6	21	25	16	24	18	♉9	13	28	30
4	25	♌10	18	♎4	♏9	♑0	♒9	♈3	22	26	♌10	♍12
5	♋7	22	♍0	17	23	15	24	17	♊5	♋8	22	24
6	19	♍4	13	♏0	♐7	30	♓9	♉0	18	20	♍4	♎6
7	♌1	16	25	14	21	♒15	23	14	♋0	♌2	16	18
8	13	28	♎8	27	♑5	29	♈7	26	12	14	28	♏1
9	25	♎11	21	♐11	20	♓13	21	♊9	24	26	♎10	14
10	♍7	24	♏4	25	♒4	27	♉4	21	♌6	♍8	23	27
11	19	♏7	17	♑9	18	♈11	17	♋3	17	20	♏6	♐11
12	♎1	20	♐1	23	♓2	24	29	15	29	♎2	19	25
13	14	♐4	14	♒7	16	♉7	♊12	27	♍11	15	♐3	♑10
14	27	18	28	21	♈0	20	24	♌9	23	27	16	24
15	♏10	♑2	♑12	♓6	14	♊2	♋6	21	♎6	♏10	♑0	♒9
16	24	17	26	20	27	15	18	♍2	18	23	14	23
17	♐9	♒2	♒11	♈4	♉10	27	30	14	♏1	♐7	28	♓8
18	23	17	26	19	23	♋9	♌12	26	13	20	♒12	22
19	♑8	♓2	♓10	♉1	♊6	21	23	♎9	26	♑4	27	♈6
20	23	16	25	15	18	♌3	♍5	21	♐10	17	♓11	20
21	♒9	♈1	♈9	28	♋1	15	17	♏4	23	♒1	25	♉3
22	24	15	23	♊10	13	27	29	16	♑7	16	♈9	16
23	♓9	29	♉6	23	25	♍8	♎12	29	21	♓0	23	29
24	23	♉12	20	♋5	♌6	21	24	♐13	♒5	14	♉7	♊12
25	♈7	24	♊2	17	18	♎3	♏7	27	20	29	20	25
26	20	♊7	15	28	♍0	15	20	♑11	♓5	♈13	♊3	♋8
27	♉3	19	27	♌10	12	28	♐4	26	20	28	16	20
28	16	♋1	♋9	22	25	♏12	18	♒11	♈5	♉12	29	♌2
29	28		21	♍4	♎7	25	♑2	26	19	25	♋12	14
30	♊10		♌2	17	20	♐9	17	♓11	♉3	♊8	24	26
31	22		14		♏4		♒2	26		21		♍8

H A DREHER

TABLE 11 PAGE 139

SIGNS THE MOON IS IN FOR EACH DAY OF THE MONTH GREENWICH TIME. EXACT FOR 1891 AND WITHIN 6 DEGREES FOR ALL OTHER YEARS ON 1 LINE ON INDEX TABLE

	JAN	FEB	MAR	APR	MAY	JUN	JUL	AUG	SEP	OCT	NOV	DEC
1	♍20	♏4	♏13	♑2	♒10	♈3	♉12	♋2	♌18	♍21	♏6	♐9
2	♎2	17	26	15	24	18	26	14	♍0	♎3	18	22
3	14	30	♐9	29	♓8	♉2	♊9	27	12	15	♐0	♑5
4	26	♐13	22	♒14	23	16	22	♌9	24	27	13	18
5	♏9	27	♑6	28	♈7	29	♋5	21	♎6	♏9	25	♒2
6	22	♑11	20	♓13	22	♊13	18	♍3	18	21	♑8	15
7	♐5	26	♒4	28	♉6	26	♌0	15	30	♐3	21	29
8	19	♒11	19	♈13	21	♋9	13	27	♏12	15	♒5	♓13
9	♑3	26	♓4	28	♊5	22	25	♎9	24	28	18	27
10	18	♓12	20	♉12	18	♌5	♍7	21	♐6	♑11	♓3	♈12
11	♒3	27	♈5	27	♋1	17	19	♏3	19	25	17	26
12	18	♈11	20	♊10	14	29	♎1	15	♑2	♒8	♈1	♉10
13	♓3	26	♉4	23	27	♍11	13	27	15	23	16	25
14	18	♉10	18	♋6	♌9	23	25	♐10	29	♓7	♉1	♊9
15	♈2	23	♊2	19	21	♎5	♏7	23	♒14	22	16	23
16	16	♊6	15	♌1	♏3	17	19	♑7	29	♈7	♊0	♋6
17	♉0	19	28	13	15	29	♐2	21	♓14	23	15	20
18	13	♋1	♋10	25	27	♏11	15	♒6	29	♉8	29	♌3
19	26	13	22	♍7	♎9	24	29	21	♈15	22	♋12	16
20	♊9	25	♌4	19	21	♐7	♑13	♓6	30	♊7	25	28
21	22	♌7	16	♎1	♏3	21	27	21	♉14	21	♌8	♍10
22	♋4	19	28	13	16	♑4	♒12	♈6	28	♋4	20	22
23	16	♍1	♍10	25	29	18	27	21	♊12	17	♍2	♎4
24	28	13	22	♏7	♐12	♒3	♓12	♉5	25	30	14	16
25	♌10	25	♎4	20	25	17	26	19	♋8	♌2	26	28
26	22	♎7	16	♐3	♑9	♓1	♈11	♊3	21	24	♎8	♏10
27	♍4	19	28	16	23	16	25	16	♌3	♍6	20	22
28	16	♏1	♏10	29	♒7	♈0	♉9	29	15	18	♏2	♐5
29	28		23	♑12	21	14	23	♋12	27	30	14	17
30	♎10		♐6	26	♓5	28	♊6	24	♍9	♎12	26	♑1
31	22		19		19		19	♌6		25		14

TABLE 12 PAGE 140

SIGNS THE MOON IS IN FOR EACH DAY OF THE MONTH GREENWICH TIME EXACT FOR 1892 AND WITHIN 6 DEGREES FOR ALL OTHER YEARS ON 1 LINE ON INDEX TABLE

DATE OF MONTH	JAN	FEB.	MAR	APR.	MAY	JUN	JUL	AUG	SEP	OCT	NOV	DEC
1	♑28	♓20	♈14	♊7	♋14	♍21	♎3	♏17	♑1	♒5	♓25	♉3
2	♒12	♈5	29	21	27	13	15	29	14	19	♈10	18
3	26	19	♉14	♋5	♌10	25	27	♐11	27	♓3	25	♊3
4	♓10	♉3	28	18	22	♎7	♏9	23	♒11	17	♉10	18
5	24	17	♊12	♌1	♍5	19	21	♑6	25	♈2	25	♋3
6	♈8	♊1	25	13	17	♏1	♐3	19	♓9	17	♊11	18
7	23	15	♋8	26	29	13	15	♒3	24	♉2	25	♌2
8	♉7	28	21	♍8	♎11	25	28	16	♈8	17	♋10	16
9	20	♋11	♌4	20	22	♐7	♑11	♓0	23	♊2	24	29
10	♊4	24	16	♎2	♏4	19	24	15	♉8	17	♌7	♍12
11	18	♌7	29	14	16	♑2	♒7	29	22	♋1	20	24
12	♋2	20	♍11	25	28	15	21	♈13	♊7	15	♍3	♎6
13	15	♍2	23	♏7	♐10	28	♓5	28	21	28	16	18
14	28	14	♎5	19	22	♒11	19	♉12	♋4	♌11	28	♏0
15	♌11	26	17	♐1	♑5	24	♈3	26	18	24	♎10	12
16	24	♎8	28	13	18	♓8	17	♊10	♌1	♍6	22	24
17	♍6	20	♏10	25	♒1	22	♉1	24	14	19	♏3	♐6
18	18	♏2	22	♑8	14	♈6	15	♋7	27	♎1	15	18
19	♎0	14	♐4	21	27	20	29	21	♍9	13	27	30
20	12	26	16	♒4	♓11	♉4	♊13	♌4	22	25	♐9	♑12
21	24	♐8	29	17	25	19	27	17	♎4	♏6	21	25
22	♏6	20	♑12	♓1	♈10	♊3	♋11	♍0	16	18	♑3	♒7
23	18	♑3	25	16	24	18	25	13	28	♐0	15	20
24	30	16	♒8	♈1	♉9	♋2	♌8	25	♏9	12	28	♓3
25	♐12	♒0	23	16	24	16	22	♎7	21	24	♒10	17
26	25	15	♓7	♉1	♊9	♌0	♍4	19	♐3	♑6	23	♈0
27	♑9	29	22	16	24	13	17	♏1	15	18	♓6	14
28	22	♓14	♈7	♊1	♋8	26	29	13	27	♒1	20	28
29	♒6	29	23	16	22	♍9	♎11	25	♑9	14	♈4	♉12
30	21		♉8	30	♌5	21	23	♐7	22	27	19	27
31	♓5		23		18		♏5	19		♓11		♊12

H A BREHER

TABLE 13 PAGE 141

SIGNS THE MOON IS IN FOR EACH DAY OF THE MONTH GREENWICH TIME. EXACT FOR 1893 AND WITHIN 6 DEGREES FOR ALL OTHER YEARS ON I LINE ON INDEX TABLE

DATE OF MONTH	JAN	FEB	MAR	APR	MAY	JUN	JUL	AUG	SEP	OCT	NOV	DEC.
1	♊27	♌18	♌27	♎14	♏17	♑1	♒5	♓23	♉14	♊23	♌16	♍23
2	♋11	♍2	♍10	26	29	13	17	♈6	28	♋8	30	♎6
3	26	15	23	♏8	♐11	25	♓0	20	♊12	22	♍13	18
4	♌10	28	♎6	20	22	♒8	13	♉3	27	♌6	26	♏1
5	24	♎10	18	♐2	♑4	20	26	17	♋11	19	♎9	13
6	♍7	22	♏0	14	16	♓3	♈9	♊1	25	♍3	21	25
7	20	♏4	12	26	29	16	23	16	♌9	16	♏4	♐7
8	♎2	16	24	♑8	♒11	29	♉7	♋0	23	29	16	19
9	15	28	♐6	20	24	♈13	21	15	♍7	♎12	28	♑0
10	27	♐10	18	♒2	♓7	27	♊6	30	20	25	♐10	12
11	♏8	22	30	15	20	♉12	21	♌14	♎4	♏7	22	24
12	20	♑4	♑12	28	♈4	27	♋6	28	17	19	♑4	♒6
13	♐2	17	24	♓12	19	♊12	21	♍12	29	♐1	15	18
14	14	29	♒7	26	♉3	27	♌5	25	♏11	13	27	♓0
15	26	♒12	20	♈10	18	♋12	20	♎9	23	25	♒9	13
16	♑8	26	♓4	25	♊4	27	♍4	21	♐5	♑7	22	26
17	21	♓9	18	♉10	19	♌12	17	♏4	17	19	♓4	♈9
18	♒4	23	♈2	25	♋4	26	♎1	16	29	♒1	17	22
19	17	♈7	17	♊10	18	♍9	13	28	♑11	13	♈0	♉6
20	♓0	21	♉1	25	♌3	22	25	♐9	23	26	14	21
21	14	♉6	16	♋9	16	♎5	♏8	21	♒6	♓9	28	♊6
22	27	20	♊0	23	♍0	17	19	♑3	18	22	♉13	21
23	♈11	♊4	15	♌7	13	29	♐1	15	♓1	♈6	28	♋6
24	25	18	29	20	26	♏11	13	28	14	20	♊13	22
25	♉9	♋2	♋13	♍3	♎8	23	25	♒10	28	♉5	28	♌7
26	23	16	26	16	20	♐5	♑7	23	♈12	20	♋13	21
27	♊7	30	♌10	29	♏2	16	19	♓7	16	♊4	28	♍6
28	21	♌13	23	♎11	14	28	♒2	19	♉10	19	♌12	19
29	♋6		♍6	23	26	♑10	14	♈3	25	♋4	26	♎2
30	20		19	♏5	♐8	23	27	16	♊9	18	♍10	15
31	♌4		♎2		19		♓10	♉0		♌2		28

M A BREHER

TABLE 14 PAGE 142

SIGNS THE MOON IS IN FOR EACH DAY OF THE MONTH GREENWICH TIME EXACT FOR 1834 AND WITHIN 6 DEGREES FOR ALL OTHER YEARS ON 1 LINE ON INDEX TABLE

DATE OF MONTH	JAN.	FEB.	MAR.	APR.	MAY	JUN.	JUL.	AUG.	SEP.	OCT.	NOV.	DEC.
1	♏10	♐24	♑2	♒16	♓19	♉7	♊15	♌9	♎1	♏7	♐23	♑26
2	22	♑6	14	29	♈2	22	30	24	16	20	♑6	♒8
3	♐4	18	26	♓11	15	♊6	♋15	♍9	29	♐3	18	19
4	16	♒0	♒8	24	29	21	♌0	23	♏12	16	30	♓1
5	27	12	21	♈7	♉13	♋6	16	♎7	25	28	♒11	13
6	♑9	24	♓3	21	28	22	♍0	21	♐8	♑10	23	25
7	21	♓7	16	♉5	♊12	♌6	15	♏4	20	22	♓5	♈8
8	♒3	19	29	19	27	21	28	17	♑2	♒4	17	20
9	15	♈2	♈12	♊3	♋12	♍5	♎12	29	14	16	♈0	♉4
10	27	15	25	17	26	19	25	♐11	26	28	13	17
11	♓10	28	♉9	♋1	♌11	♎2	♏8	23	♒8	♓10	26	♊1
12	22	♉12	22	16	25	15	20	♑5	19	22	♉9	16
13	♈5	25	♊6	30	♍8	28	♐2	17	♓2	♈5	23	♋1
14	18	♊9	20	♌14	22	♏11	14	29	14	18	♊7	16
15	♉1	24	♋4	28	♎5	23	26	♒11	26	♉1	22	♌1
16	15	♋8	19	♍12	18	♐5	♑8	23	♈9	14	♋6	15
17	29	23	♌3	25	♏1	17	20	♓5	22	28	21	30
18	♊14	♌8	17	♎9	14	29	♒2	17	♉5	♊12	♌5	♍14
19	29	23	♍2	22	26	♑11	14	29	18	26	19	28
20	♋14	♏7	16	♏5	♐8	23	26	♈12	♊1	♋10	♍3	♎11
21	29	21	30	17	21	♒5	♓8	25	15	24	17	25
22	♌15	♎5	♎13	♐0	♑3	17	20	♉8	29	♌8	♎1	♏8
23	29	19	26	12	15	29	♈2	21	♋13	23	14	21
24	♍14	♏2	♏9	24	26	♓11	15	♊5	28	♍7	28	♐3
25	27	14	22	♑6	♒8	23	28	19	♌12	21	♏11	16
26	♎11	26	♐4	18	20	♈6	♉11	♋3	27	♎5	24	28
27	24	♐9	16	♒0	♓2	19	25	18	♍11	18	♐7	♑10
28	♏6	21	28	12	15	♉2	♊9	♌2	25	♏2	19	22
29	18		♑10	24	27	16	23	17	♎10	15	♑2	♒4
30	♐0		22	♓6	♈10	♊0	♋8	♍2	24	28	14	16
31	12		♒4		23		24	17		♐11		28

TABLE 15 PAGE 143

SIGNS THE MOON IS IN FOR EACH DAY OF THE MONTH GREENWICH TIME EXACT FOR 1895 AND WITHIN 6 DEGREES FOR ALL OTHER YEARS ON 1 LINE ON INDEX TABLE

DATE OF MONTH	JAN	FEB	MAR	APR.	MAY	JUN.	JUL	AUG.	SEP	OCT	NOV.	DEC
1	♓10	♈25	♉4	♊24	♌2	♍25	♏4	♐23	♒9	♓11	♈26	♉30
2	21	♉7	17	♋7	16	♎9	17	♑5	21	23	♉8	♊13
3	♈3	20	30	21	♏0	23	♐0	18	♓3	♈5	21	26
4	16	♊4	♊13	♌6	15	♏7	13	30	14	17	♊4	♋10
5	28	18	27	20	29	20	26	♒12	26	29	17	24
6	♉12	♋2	♋11	♍5	♎13	♐14	♑9	24	♈8	♉12	♋0	♌8
7	25	17	26	19	27	17	21	♓6	20	24	13	22
8	♊9	♌2	♌10	♎4	♏11	30	♒3	17	♉2	♊7	27	♍6
9	24	17	25	18	25	♑12	15	29	14	20	♌11	20
10	♋9	♍2	♍10	♏3	♐8	25	27	♈11	27	♋3	25	♎4
11	24	18	25	17	21	♒7	♓9	23	♊10	16	♍9	18
12	♌9	♎2	♎10	♐0	♑4	19	21	♉5	23	♌0	23	♏2
13	24	17	25	13	17	♓1	♈2	18	♋7	14	♎8	16
14	♍9	♏1	♏9	26	29	12	14	♊1	21	29	22	♐0
15	24	14	22	♑9	♒11	24	27	14	♌5	♍14	♏7	14
16	♎8	27	♐5	21	23	♈6	♉9	28	20	28	21	27
17	21	♐10	18	♒3	♓4	18	22	♋12	♍5	♎13	♐5	♑10
18	♏5	22	♑1	15	16	♉1	♊5	26	20	28	19	23
19	18	♑4	13	27	28	14	19	♌11	♎5	♏13	♑2	♒6
20	♐0	16	25	♓8	♈11	27	♋4	27	20	27	15	18
21	13	28	♒7	20	23	♊11	18	♍12	♏5	♐11	28	30
22	25	♒10	18	♈2	♉6	25	♌3	27	19	24	♒10	♓12
23	♑7	22	♓0	15	19	♋10	18	♎12	♐3	♑7	22	24
24	19	♓3	12	27	♊3	24	♍3	26	16	20	♓4	♈5
25	♒1	16	24	♉10	16	♌9	18	♏10	29	♒2	16	17
26	13	27	♈6	23	♋0	23	♎2	24	♑12	14	28	29
27	25	♈9	19	♊7	15	♍8	17	♐7	24	26	♈10	♉12
28	♓6	22	♉1	20	29	22	♏0	20	♒6	♓8	22	25
29	18		14	♋4	♌13	♎6	14	♑2	18	20	♉4	♊8
30	♈0		27	18	27	20	27	15	29	♈2	17	21
31	12		♊10		♍11		♐10	27		14		♋5

TABLE 16 — PAGE 144

SIGNS THE MOON IS IN FOR EACH DAY OF THE MONTH GREENWICH TIME. EXACT FOR 1898 AND WITHIN 6 DEGREES FOR ALL OTHER YEARS ON 1 LINE ON INDEX TABLE

DATE OF MONTH	JAN.	FEB.	MAR.	APR.	MAY	JUN.	JUL.	AUG	SEP.	OCT.	NOV	DEC.
1	♋19	♍11	♎5	♏28	♑4	♒21	♓23	♉7	♊21	♋26	♍16	♎25
2	♌3	26	20	♐12	17	♓3	♈5	19	♋4	♌9	♎1	♏9
3	18	♎11	♏5	26	♒0	15	17	♊1	17	23	16	24
4	♍2	25	19	♑9	13	27	29	13	♌1	♍7	♏1	♐9
5	16	♏9	♐3	22	25	♈9	♉11	26	15	22	16	24
6	♎1	23	17	♒4	♓7	21	23	♋9	29	♎8	♐1	♑9
7	15	♐7	30	16	19	♉3	♊5	23	♍14	23	16	23
8	29	20	♑13	28	♈0	15	18	♌7	29	♏8	♑1	♒6
9	♏13	♑3	25	♓10	12	27	♋1	21	♎14	23	15	19
10	26	15	♒7	22	24	♊10	15	♍6	29	♐8	28	♓2
11	♐10	28	19	♈4	♉6	23	28	20	♏14	22	♒11	14
12	23	♒10	♓1	16	18	♋6	♌12	♎5	28	♑6	24	26
13	♑6	22	13	27	♊1	19	26	19	♐12	19	♓6	♈8
14	19	♓4	25	♉9	13	♌2	♍10	♏4	26	♒2	18	20
15	♒1	16	♈7	22	26	16	25	18	♑9	15	30	♉2
16	14	28	19	♊4	♋9	30	♎9	♐2	22	27	♈12	14
17	26	♈10	♉0	16	22	♍14	23	16	♒5	♓9	23	26
18	♓8	22	12	29	♌5	28	♏7	29	18	21	♉5	♊8
19	20	♉4	25	♋12	19	♎12	21	♑12	30	♈3	17	20
20	♈1	16	♊7	25	♍3	26	♐5	25	♓12	15	29	♋3
21	13	28	19	♌9	17	♏11	19	♒8	24	27	♊12	16
22	25	♊10	♋2	23	♎1	25	♑3	21	♈6	♉8	24	29
23	♉7	23	16	♍7	16	♐9	16	♓3	18	20	♋6	♌12
24	20	♋7	30	21	♏1	23	29	15	30	♊2	19	25
25	♊2	21	♌13	♎6	15	♑7	♒12	27	♉11	14	♌2	♍8
26	15	♌5	28	21	♐1	20	24	♈9	23	27	15	22
27	29	20	♍13	♏7	14	♒3	♓7	21	♊5	♋9	28	♎6
28	♋13	♍5	28	22	29	16	19	♉3	18	22	♍12	20
29	27	20	♎13	♐6	♑12	29	♈1	15	♋0	♌5	26	♏5
30	♌12		28	20	26	♓11	13	27	13	18	♎10	19
31	27		♏13		♒8		25	♊9		♍2		♐4

TABLE 17 PAGE 145

SIGNS THE MOON IS IN FOR EACH DAY OF THE MONTH GREENWICH TIME EXACT FOR 1897 AND WITHIN 6 DEGREES FOR ALL OTHER YEARS ON 1 LINE ON INDEX TABLE.

DATE OF MONTH	JAN	FEB	MAR	APR	MAY	JUN	JUL	AUG.	SEP	OCT	NOV	DEC.
1	♐18	♒9	♒18	♈4	♉7	♊22	♋26	♍14	♏6	♐16	♒8	♓14
2	♑2	22	♓1	16	19	♋4	♌8	28	21	♑0	21	27
3	17	♓5	13	28	♊1	16	21	♎12	♐5	14	♓4	♈9
4	♒0	17	26	♉10	13	29	♍4	26	19	28	17	21
5	14	30	♈8	22	25	♌11	17	♏10	♑3	♒11	30	♉3
6	27	♈12	20	♊4	♋7	24	♎1	24	17	24	♈12	15
7	♓10	24	♉2	10	19	♍7	15	♐8	♒1	♓7	24	27
8	22	♉6	14	25	♌1	20	23	22	14	20	♉6	♊9
9	♈4	18	26	♋10	14	♎4	♏13	♑7	28	♈3	18	21
10	16	29	♊7	22	27	19	28	21	♓11	15	♊0	♋3
11	28	♊12	13	♌5	♍11	♏4	♐13	♒5	24	27	12	15
12	♉10	24	♋2	18	25	18	27	19	♈6	♉10	24	27
13	22	♋6	14	♍2	♎9	♐3	♑12	♓2	19	22	♋6	♌9
14	♊4	19	27	16	24	16	26	15	♉1	♊3	18	21
15	16	♌3	♌10	♎1	♏3	♑3	♒10	28	13	16	30	♍4
16	29	16	24	16	25	18	24	♈11	25	27	♌12	16
17	♋11	♍0	♍8	♏1	♐10	♒2	♓7	23	♊7	♋9	24	30
18	24	14	23	16	25	16	20	♉5	19	21	♍7	♎13
19	♌8	29	♎7	♐1	♑10	29	♈3	17	♋1	♌3	21	27
20	21	♎13	22	16	24	♓12	15	29	13	16	♎4	♏12
21	♍5	28	♏7	♑1	♒8	25	27	♊11	25	29	19	27
22	19	♏12	22	15	21	♈7	♉9	23	♌8	♍12	♏4	♐12
23	♎3	26	♐7	29	♓4	19	21	♋5	21	26	19	27
24	17	♐11	21	♒12	16	♉1	♊3	17	♍4	♎11	♐4	♑12
25	♏1	24	♑5	24	28	13	15	♌0	18	26	19	27
26	15	♑8	19	♓7	♈10	25	27	13	♎3	♏11	♑4	♒12
27	30	22	♒2	19	22	♊7	♋9	26	17	26	19	26
28	♐14	♒5	15	♈1	♉4	19	22	♏10	♏2	♐11	♒4	♓9
29	28		27	13	16	♋1	♌5	24	17	26	17	23
30	♑12		♓10	25	28	13	17	♎8	♐1	♑10	♓1	♈5
31	25		22		♊10		♍1	22		24		18

TABLE 18. **PAGE 146**

SIGNS THE MOON IS IN FOR EACH DAY OF THE MONTH GREENWICH TIME. EXACT FOR 1898 AND WITHIN 6 DEGREES FOR ALL OTHER YEARS ON 1 LINE ON INDEX TABLE

DATE OF MONTH	JAN.	FEB.	MAR.	APR.	MAY	JUN	JUL.	AUG	SEP.	OCT.	NOV.	DEC.
1	♉0	♊14	♊22	♌6	♍9	♎28	♐6	♑29	♓22	♈27	♊13	♋16
2	12	26	♋4	18	22	♏12	21	♒14	♈6	♉10	26	27
3	24	♋8	16	♍1	♎6	27	♑6	29	19	23	♋7	♌9
4	♊6	20	28	14	20	♐12	21	♓14	♉2	♊5	19	21
5	18	♌2	♌10	28	♏4	28	♒6	28	15	18	♌1	♍3
6	30	15	23	♎11	19	♑13	21	♈11	28	30	13	15
7	♋11	27	♍6	26	♐4	28	♓5	24	♊10	♋11	25	28
8	24	♍10	19	♏10	19	♒12	19	♉7	22	23	♍7	♎10
9	♌6	23	♎3	25	♑4	26	♈3	19	♋4	♌5	20	24
10	18	♎7	17	♐9	18	♓10	16	♊2	15	17	♎3	♏8
11	♍1	20	♏1	24	♒3	23	28	14	27	29	16	22
12	13	♏4	15	♑8	17	♈6	♉11	25	♌9	♍12	♏0	♐7
13	26	18	29	22	♓0	19	23	♋7	21	25	14	22
14	♎10	♐2	♐13	♒6	14	♉2	♊5	19	♍4	♎8	29	♑7
15	23	16	27	20	27	14	17	♌1	17	22	♐13	22
16	♏7	♑1	♑11	♓3	♈9	26	29	13	29	♏6	28	♒7
17	21	15	25	17	22	♊8	♋10	25	♎13	20	♑13	21
18	♐6	29	♒9	30	♉5	20	22	♍8	26	♐4	27	♓6
19	21	♒14	23	♈13	17	♋2	♌4	20	♏10	18	♒11	19
20	♑6	28	♓7	25	29	13	16	♎3	24	♑2	25	♈3
21	20	♓12	20	♉8	♊11	25	28	16	♐7	16	♓9	16
22	♒5	25	♈4	20	23	♌7	♍11	29	21	♒1	23	29
23	20	♈8	17	♊2	♋5	19	23	♏13	♑5	15	♈6	♉12
24	♓4	21	29	14	16	♍1	♎6	27	20	29	19	24
25	17	♉4	♉12	26	28	14	19	♐11	♒4	♓12	♉2	♊6
26	♈1	16	24	♋7	♌10	26	♏2	25	18	26	15	19
27	14	28	♊6	20	22	♎9	16	♑9	♓2	♈10	27	♋0
28	26	♊10	18	♌2	♍4	23	♐0	24	16	23	♊10	12
29	♉8		30	14	17	♏7	15	♒8	♈0	♉6	22	24
30	20		♋12	28	♎0	21	30	23	14	19	♋4	♌6
31	♊2		24		14		♑14	♓7		♊1		18

TABLE 13 :

PAGE 147

SIGNS THE MOON IS IN FOR EACH DAY OF THE MONTH GREENWICH TIME EXACT FOR 1899 AND WITHIN 6 DEGREES FOR ALL OTHER YEARS ON 1 LINE ON INDEX TABLE

DAY OF MONTH	JAN	FEB	MAR	APR.	MAY	JUN.	JUL.	AUG	SEP	OCT	NOV	DEC
1	♌30	♎16	♎26	♐16	♑24	♓18	♈26	♊14	♋29	♍1	♎16	♏20
2	♍12	23	♏9	30	♒9	♈2	♉9	26	♌11	13	29	♐3
3	24	♏12	22	♑13	23	15	22	♋8	23	25	♏12	17
4	♎6	25	♐5	28	♓7	29	♊4	20	♍5	♎8	25	♑1
5	19	♐9	19	♒12	21	♉12	17	♌2	16	20	♐8	15
6	♏2	23	♑3	26	♈5	25	29	14	29	♏2	21	29
7	16	♑8	17	♓11	19	♊8	♋11	26	♎11	15	♑5	♒14
8	♐0	23	♒2	25	♉2	20	23	♍7	23	28	19	28
9	15	♒8	16	♈9	16	♋2	♌5	19	♏5	♐11	♒3	♓12
10	29	23	♓1	23	29	14	17	♎1	18	25	17	26
11	♑15	♓8	16	♉7	♊12	26	29	14	♐1	♑8	♓1	♈10
12	30	23	♈1	20	24	♌8	♍10	26	14	22	15	24
13	♒15	♈7	15	♊3	♋6	20	22	♏9	28	♒6	30	♉8
14	♓0	21	29	16	18	♍2	♎4	21	♑12	20	♈14	21
15	15	♉5	♉12	28	♌0	14	17	♐5	26	♓5	28	♊5
16	29	17	26	♋10	12	26	29	18	♒11	20	♉12	18
17	♈13	♊0	♊8	22	24	♎8	♏12	♑2	26	♈5	26	♋0
18	26	12	20	♌4	♍6	21	26	17	♓11	19	♊9	13
19	♉9	24	♋3	16	18	♏4	♐10	♒2	26	♉4	22	25
20	21	♋6	14	28	♎0	18	24	17	♈11	18	♋5	♌7
21	♊3	18	26	♍10	13	♐1	♑9	♓2	25	♊1	17	19
22	16	30	♌8	22	26	16	24	18	♉10	14	30	♍1
23	27	♌12	20	♎5	♏10	♑0	♒9	♈3	23	27	♌12	13
24	♋9	23	♍2	18	23	15	24	17	♊6	♋10	24	25
25	21	♍6	14	♏1	♐7	♒0	♓9	♉1	19	22	♍5	♎7
26	♌3	18	27	15	22	15	24	15	♋2	♌4	17	19
27	15	♎0	♎9	28	♑6	30	♈8	28	14	16	29	♏2
28	27	13	22	♐12	21	♓14	22	♊11	26	28	♎12	15
29	♍9		♏5	26	♒5	28	♉6	23	♌8	♍9	24	28
30	21		19	♑10	19	♈12	19	♋5	19	21	♏7	♐11
31	♎3		♐2		♓4		♊1	17		♎4		25

1

ASTROLOGY AS A SCIENCE is the Mother of all science. It is the deepest, the most profound, and if thoroly understood, the most beneficial of all science. Yet there are educated biggots and ape like followers who declare it is an exploded theory, but they have never told us who exploded it. This is largely due to the, would be, wit thrown at astrology, or the pridictions of astrology by the press. This has caused many to suppose astrology is a superstition or a fake game of fortune tellers, and that no intellegent self respecting person would engage in ; and sti ll with this use ge from the press they wonder why we do not advertise more.

To get the truth before the public in a proper manner and free from contemptuous slur, we have been compeled, at great expens e, to publish magazines and phamplets. It is true there are fake astrologers as there are fakes in every thing and the greatest advertiser, in any thing is, generally, the greatest fake; becaus the enormous advertising bills must be paid by hook or by crook. An honest astrologer could not do work enough to pay such enormous bills, if he got the work to do. My work has brought me all the work I can do, without advertising, except the little I do in my book announcements. Even at a dollar no man can get rich casting horoscopes. I do more writing than any lawyer would do for ten dollars. This is to say nothing of the mathematical labor or the stationary necessary.

ASTROLOGY AS A SCIENCE.

Astrology is a science that few can understand and practiee successfully, and is generally followed by old men, and more often than otherwise, they are investigators and literary people and do not practio to any great extent, or if they do it is more in the intrest of study than for the money there is in it.

It is true astrologers make mistakes, but no more than do other proffessionals. "It is human to error."

Professer Chaney, who died in Chicag in 1903 was 82 years old. Way back in 1877 he predicted his own death and that it would take place at the age of 82, and that a tempest would be rageing at the time. All of which took place.

Dr. Broughton of N. Y. who died six yeasrs ago, was upward of seventy.

The late Ernest S. Green. of Calafornia, was nearing the 80 mark when he died.

Professor Hatfeild was known so long in the astrological world as to stamp him an old man.

Professor Loren Chadwick, of Battle Creek, Mich. made researches in astrology, for over 40 years, for the benefit of agriculture, which of course shows he was a very old man.

Charles Taylor, of Detroit Mich. died at the age of 70.

I Lyman E. Stowe, the writer of these lines, am

64 years old, and have been in Commercial business for many years. Was a soldier during the great rebellion, am the author of many books, some of which are advertised here.

I here mention a few of the astrologers of my aquaintance.

Mr. Hodges, as his picture shows, is well along in years, but hale, hearty, and as straight as an arrow. His writings, in his magazine, show a thotful, sound and brilliant mind. He jokeingly said "Do not tell my age." He, probably; reasoned, that since one of our prominent physicans has sent forth the idea that a man should be strangled at 45, or in other words has lost his usefulness; thus reversing the old adage "Old men for council, young men for war." Prehaps he would send the old men to war to get rid of them.

Mr. Hodges is one of Detroit's successfull business men, often called a millionair. The Hodges, Building has been an ornament to our city for years. Mr. Hodges is also extensivly engaged in varyous enterprises. If a millionair it would be a blessng to our country if we had more like him. I speak of this matter to let the public see the kind of people that are interested in astrology. But, what interests us most is that Mr. Hodges edited and published the five great astrological volumes, "Science and Key of Life." These works are unique, of great value to the casual reader and almost indsipensable to the deep student of astrology.

HENRY CLAY HODGES.

Mr. Hodges is also Editor of the Stellar Ray magazino, one of the very best magazins published for a dollar a year. We will take orders for any of the books here mentioned.

Here is MR. HODGES GREAT QUESTION.

"SOME are born to honor, and others to dishonor; some to wealth and others to want; some in the midst of crime, ignorance and sorrow, others e vironed in happy conditions. When and where is the Law of Compensation applied to epualize these condtions, or why should these things be?"

MR. WHITE, of Crystal Bav, Minn. is a judge and the Editor of the Adept. A boy or a fake could not hold such positions.

Dr. Mac Donald, of Binghampton N. Y., is a well known physician and is the author of "Secrets of Astrology Revealed." This book contains one article on the roundity of the Earth, which is worth many times the price of the book. We will furnish the book for a dollar, or it may be had of the author.

Walter H. Lewis, of Manchester N. H., is a well known musician, a composer of music and musical director of Opera companies. Also the creator of the Luck Dial. We will mail this dial for a dollar or it may be had of the author.

Sullivan, of Yonkers, N. Y., must be over fifty.

Ormsby, of Chicago is a well known author, editor and publisher, and I understand once a Government Astronomer. I have heard he is over 50.

Butler, now of California, published that, wonderful book Solor Biology, [We can furnish this book for $5. and no family should be without it,] 20 years ago and his pictur showes him, then, to be at least 50 years of age.

James Cross, better known as Raphael, author of the English Ephemries, I am told is over 70.

Al n Leo, editor, author and publisher of London England. is well along in years, and so I might go on and show that astrologers of note are

are men of years of experience, philosophers and men of thot, and not likly to be superstitious.

FREDRICK WHITE,

Mr. White is a resident of Crystal Bay, Minn. is the Editor of the Adept and publisher of the American Ephemeries. which is equal to, if not better than the English ephemeries. He is also the author and publisher of many valuable works on astrology, also teacher of the science. He also fills all orders for books on Occult matters. This is not a paid add, but is for the purpose of showing the class of men who interest them selves in the great science. Look at the intelligenc, manifest in the picture here presented, and compare with those of any class of professional men. Are these not the the faces of inteligent searchers after truth?

Mr. White was born in Norton Mass, 3 oo P. M. Friday May 11 th 1866. He is a typical Uranian, consequenly, must take to astrology. He is of American stock, light complexion, medium build, a graduate of the Boston Latin School. He served three years apprentic ship as light machenest, finally became an electrician. During the panic of 1893 he found himself stranded, in Chicago, here he became interested in astrology. On finding the public apreciated his work in this line he plunged deeper in the study of the occults, spending large sumes of money in search of truth. Believing Minnapoiis offered the best field for his labors he settled there and laid the foundation of his publishing business. Finally moveing to his present abiding place. Here he quickly won the confidence of the people, and tho a rank socilist he was elected Justice of the Peace, in a smart Republican town. This is certianly a good record for an astrologer or any other person.

'See in our cataloge books mentioned in these biographical sketches.

THE STORY OF THE ZODIAC. 8

A J MAC DONALD, M. D., Ph. D. Of Binghamton. New York.

Dr.Mac Donald is an astrologer that nearly every person has heard something about. He is a man of unusual intelligence, as his picture here

denotes. By the name one would, alamost, think the Dr. is fresh from Scotland, but his long line of American ancestry. of Scotch and Holand descent, as given in his Autobiogrophy' dispells that illussion, and shows you he is one of those enterprising men, who derives his superior intllect and energy from a mixed race of people.

The Doctor's experience in the Occults dates back to childhood and he has been a great student ever since. He has, at great expense, investigated every branch of the science, not only this but the has done what every doctor aught to do, he has applied astrology to his medical profession.

I am sorry the want of space forbids my giving the whole of his autobiography and discription of his wonderful book "Secretsof Astrology Revealed" but pshaw, what is a dollar if you are really seeking knowlag? He or any other good astrologer paid out hundreds for what htey give you for a treifle. He also publishes the Plnetary hour Indicator, send for it. price one dollar.

ONE OF THE BEST AND MOST EARNEST INVESTIGATORS of astrology in this country is Walter H. Lewis of Manchestetr N. H. He is the inventor of the Luck Dial, which is a revolving disk on a bed piece of peculiar design. This dial is for the purpose of getting the proper hours of the day in whi- ch to be succesful

WALTER H. LEWIS.

in any undertaking. It is not only a thing of beauty but it is a joy for ever, and a thing of great utility and he predictes that it will, eventually, be found on every business man's table, as an indespensable article. We can furnish it or it may be had direct from Mr. Lewis,

Any person, of good judgment. can readly see, by the picture that Mr. Lewis is a man of great intelligence. He is a musican of national reputation, so he does not depend upon astrology for a living, but he is fascinated with it, because of the debth, as well as the antiquity of the science.

A FEW TESTIMONIALS.

I have never done much advertising in the line of Astrology, because I did not have to. My work has braught me all I could do without advertising. Astrologers do not get very rich writing horoscopes for a dollar each. I do more writing for a dollar than any lawyer would do for $10. I present these testimonials, not to advertise, but to show the effect of the science. I have had hundreds of fine testimonials sent me without asking. I give the following because they are all short and to the point:

Detroit, Mich., Nov. 16th, 1905.

In August, 1900, I called on Prof. Stowe for a reading. He told me I had better get my husband's life insured as he could not live to exceed seven years and was likely to die at any time.

My husband was then a strong, fleshy man, but I got his life insured, which I should not have done only for Mr. Stowe's advice.

My husband died of cancer of the bowels on Oct. 19th, 1905.

MRS. G. BELAND,
1497 Helen Ave., Detroit, Mich.

908 Union St.,
Manchester, N. H., Nov. 10, 1905.

Prof. Lyman E. Stowe,
133 Catherine St., Detroit, Mich.

My Dear Brother Stowe:

It must interest you to know how accurately your prophetic skill proves itself, so I write you to tell you that the first I knew of you was when I sent to you for your most excellent book, "The Universe," in answer to which you wrote me, in the first of 1901, that I would soon be called west on a very important matter, of which I had not the slightest thought. On May 6th, 1901, I went west, being telegraphed for, and I afterwards met the very persons whose names you had given me, in a very strange and beneficial way.

Many of your prophecies yet remain to be fulfilled so I have future pleasant things to write you when time brings into my life.

With best wishes for the continuance of your success in Prophecy, I am ever

Yours cordially,

WALTER H. LEWIS.

Detroit, Mich., Aug. 3rd, 1906.

In 1899 I called on Prof. Lyman E. Stowe and he gave me advice I thought erroneous; and like King Charles of England, with Lilly the Astrologer, I disobeyed, and it cost me $10,000. Two years later I did the same thing again and lost again, and today ask advice I intend to follow.

W. N. MISHLRE.

Reading, Pa., 11-1-1905.

My Dear Friend Stowe:

I find the correct date of party is * * * He has been all that you warned me he would be. How marvelous that I should again be warned by you as late as July 24 about this very matter. * * * Please tell me the right and best thing to do. It is confidential, between you and me.

Your firmest friend,

C. H. MOLLY.

I answered and soon received the following:

Reading, Pa., Nov. 8th, 1905.

Prof. Lyman E. Stowe,
133 Catherine St., Detroit, Mich.

Dear Professor:

Your findings are most wonderfully correct. Of course they should be and always must be with one well versed in the science, for if the Astronomer can figure the movements of the planets accurately enough to foretell the eclipse, the Astrologer should be able to figure their influences quite as readily.

I assure you I am much pleased to find that your work is very reliable and that I can depend on what you advise me, for your work satisfies me that though you do it for pay, you nevertheless put your conscience and your honor into all you do in this wonderful science. May the day soon dawn when men will live and do business more by the same, for with such directions as you are able to give them from accurate mathematical calculation *the great percentage of failures should be greatly lessened.*

Wishing you and the cause every progress,

Yours very truly,

C. F. MOLLY.

In 1901 I received an order for a horoscope of Mr. George Halsey Tuthill, of Brooklyn, N. Y. In the horoscope I told him he was about to fall heir to a large fortune.

He wrote back saying he thought the horoscope a good one, except for the idea of his falling heir to anything, as he was 70 years old and everybody dead who could leave him anything.

I wrote back: "Please let me know when you get it."

This he promised to do and it brought on a strong friendship and correspondence between us, and finally an acknowledgment that he had been notified of a small inheritance.

In November, 1905, I received the following:

"October 30, 1905.

"Dear Friend—I have received my inheritance all O. K. and it is an inheritance too far beyond my expectation. I shall go home in a few days, if assisted by other interested parties.

"Yours hastily,

"GEORGE HALSEY TUTHILL,

"169 Flatbush Ave., Brooklyn, N. Y.

Detroit, Mich., Aug. 4th, 1906.

I had a horoscope cast by Prof. L. E. Stowe which I consider very accurate, but a business matter on which I should have called for advice but which I neglected until after I had made the investment. He then told me I "let the horse be stolen and then locked the barn." Both members of the firm being in an evil cycle, they could not succeed and I have since sadly regretted that I made the investment.

MARY L. RANDALL.

WHAT IS A HOROSCOPE?

I am often asked "What is a horoscope?"

A horoscope is a delination of character, it lets you see your self as others see you. No it does not pretend, to tell you every thing that is to take place in the future. If it did it would show you to be nothing but a machine, while the real purpose of the horoscope is to tell you what will come to you, what you should avoid and what you should take advantage of. What better can the father do for the child than to complete his education, by showing him his own nature, his good and evil periods, how to take advantage of them, and what locality, and what business he would be most successful in, and what occupation he is best adapted for.

Look at the time wasted by great men before they discovered what they were best fitted for.

A. T. Stewart was educated for the ministry; he made a failure then tried school teaching, but failed in that, then by accident he learned his proper vocation, and became one of the greatest merchant princes the world has ever known.

J. Gould failed as a storekeeper, tanner, surveyor and civil engineer, before he learned his place and became a great railroad king. Grant failed as a tanner, a farmer, merchant and banker but was one of the most successful soldiers the world ever knew. John Adams failed as a shomaker but made a brilant statesman. Josh Billings tried farming, auctioneering, and Newspaper work before he lerned that comic literature was his forte. Barnum tried fourteen different occupations before he learned he was a born showman. Paul Borghese had fourteen trades, yet starved to death.

The wealth of Rockefeller, the success of Wanamaker, the triumphs of Edison attract and dazzle the public eye. Change positions of these men and they would prove utter failures. They met success becaus they found the business they were best adapted to. Effort or intelligence must always fail, unless applied in the proper time and place.

Now look at Ecclesiastes III-1 to 8.

1. "To every thing there is a season, and a time to every purpose under the heaven.

2. "A time to be born, and a time to die; a time to plant, and a time to pluck up that which is planted.

3. "A time to kill, and a time to heal; a time to break down, and a time to build up.

4. "A time to weep, and a time to laugh; a time to mourn, and a time to dance.

5. "A time to cast away stones, and a time to gather stones together; a time to embrace, and a time to refrain from embracing.

6. "A time to get, and a time to lose; a time to keep, and a time to cast away.

7. "A time to rend, and a time to sew; a time to keep silent, and a time to speak.

8. "A time to love, and a time to hate; a time of war, and a time of peace."

This writer was an Astrologer. If every man understood Astrology, he would know when he is likely to meet with misfortune, and so to keep still or avoid the rending, and thus avoid the mending.

In my Astrological Periodicity I show any man how to know the most of his good and evil periods, so he may take advantage of them, and by nothing his periods of the past, if they are correct, he cannot help admitting the truth of those of the future.

There never was a book writen that gives so much value for $2.00 as this wonderful guide to doctors, officers of the law, or all kinds of professional men, business men and farmers, as well as to the masses of the people. It is the result of many years of hard labor.

Who would not take advantage of the knowledge which would benefit him, if he knew it?

The commercial reports claim that 95 per cent of all business men fail, sooner or later, and I will wager I can tell any man the years which his misfortune came upon him, or the years of the greatest evils of his life, as soon as I get his date of birth. Anyone sending me his place and date of birth, including the hour, if possible, with his address and $1.00 to pay my typewriter and other expenses, I will give him his characteristics, nature, what locality and occupation will be best for him, together with his good and evil periods. Shakespeare says:

"There is a tide in the affairs of man which, if taken at its flood, leads on to fortune."

Then why not take advantage of it?

ASTROLOGY AS A SCIENCE. 16

TO KNOW YOUR GOOD AND EVIL PERIODS IS TO BE FOREWARNED AGAINST EVIL.

Mark ten questions and send date and place of birth, state whether married or single, your present address, and mail with one dollar, and know what the stars say for you.

Address as below.

Send ten cents for each additional question.

These questions are only to make you think, you do not have to ask these questions nor need a person ask any questions, but we cannot write a horoscope covering every event, for a dollar, so we might write a volume and not touch just the things you would like to know about, hence by asking questions you get nearer to what you desire to know.

If you mark any of the questions in the rhyme give dates of the following numbers:

5. When started or desire to start.
6. Date of his birth if possible.
16. Male or female when born.
17. Date of loved one's birth.
18. When was it lent?
24. Give date of his or her birth.
29. Near what time dreamed?
32. When earned or due.
34. Give date of person's birth and when imprisoned.
37. Give date of birth and when went away.
39. Give date when lost or stolen.
41. Give date of birth.
42. Whose property or who is to sell it?

WHAT THE ASTROLOGER HEARS.

BY PROF. LYMAN E. STOWE,

1[illegible] Catherine Street, Detroit, Mich.

1. Will my fortune, true be told?
2. Will my life be blessed with gold?
3. Will my luck be very great?

4. Will I own much real estate?
5. Will my enterprise pay well?
6. Will my friend the secret tell?
7. Will I meet with a surprise?
8. Will I take time as she flies?
9. Will I ever cross the sea?
10. Will I ever married be?
11. Will I marry more than one?
12. Will I ever have a son?
13. Will I have children one or more?
14. Will sorrow often reach my door?
15. Have I rivals, one or two.
16. Will the promise be kept true?
17. Will my loved one soon repent?
18. Will I get back what I lent?
19. Shall I go and make amends?
20. Am I soon to lose my friends?
21. Will my love prove true and kind?
22. Will I ever lose my mind?
23. Is my marriage to be blessed?
24. Will the one in mind prove best?
25. Will I get a job ere long?
26. Will a person do me wrong?
27. Will my honor be assailed?
28. Will the lie be quickly nailed?
29. Will evil come out of my dream?
30. Does luck upon my future beam?
31. Will I have good luck to-day?
32. Will I soon receive my pay?
33. Will my wishes granted be?
34. Will the prisoner go free?
35. Shall I toil with my hands?
36. Will I live in foreign lands?
37. Will the absent soon return?
38. Will death cause me soon to mourn?
39. Shall lost or stolen be returned?
40. Is the lesson got well learned?
41. Does the party love me well?
42. Will the property soon sell?
43. Will news come to me to-day?
44. Are letters to me on their way?
45. Am I doing as I should?

46. Will the thought in mind prove good?
47. Is there more I'd like to know?
48. If there is then tell me so.
49. Oh! have I enemies and why?
50. Tell me when I'm going to die.

REARKES.

The more information we can get the more accurate the reading will be, because our work depends on mathehatical calculations, from certain causes.

A nativity gives a sketch of your character, nature and points of destiny. Periods the heart affections are stirred, all through life whether you are married or single.

It tells the number of times you are likely to marry.

The number of children.

About travel.

The best locality for you.

Occupation, best fitted for.

What month your love should be born in.

Your good and evil dyas, years and cycles and many other things too numerous to mention.

This costs $1.00.

If you ask questions concerning another person you should give their date of birth.

A yearly horoscope costs $1.00 and deals with the events likely to take place during the year.

Where a person is about to enter into now business and with new partners, as much information as possible should be given, including the date and if possible even the hour of the day the first thought came; also date of birth of parties interested, if possible. This costs $5.00, and is money well spent.

FORM.

Name of applicant..................................

Where born ....

The year ....

Month and day of...................................

The hour if possible, if not a personal description, weakest point of illness..........................

....

Male or female.....................................

Married or single..................................

Complexion and color of eyes.......................

Present address ....

....

REMARKS.

THE CHART OF DESTINY.

What is the Chart of Destiny?

Ans.—1st. It is a chart that at once shows the position and meaning of the fixed stars.

2nd. A clock of the heavens.

3rd. The subject to be judged in each sign.

4th. The degrees of the Zodiac corresponding with the days of the month.

5th. The planets ruling each decan of each sign.

6th. The dignities of the planets, or where each planet is strong in a sign.

7th. A complete Heliocentric Ephemris.

8th. The degrees each sign in the Zodiac occupies.

9th. The signs in which planets exalt, rule or fall.

10th. This chart, together with a perpetual calendar, places and phases of the Moon.

11th. What it is to be born at different days of the age of the Moon.

12th. The day of the week any time in eternity.

13th. The farmer's guide.

14th. Astrology and successful chicken raising.

15th. A simple method of preserving eggs so they will hatch in two years.

16th. There never was so much useful Astrological information boiled down into so small and comprehensive a manner as is found in Stowe's Guide and Chart of Destiny. Mailed free for $1.00.

For convenience of shipping, the chart is printed on calendar paper and folded in each book, together with a hand, eyelt and flexible rivet. The chart should be pasted on heavy cardboard and the hand attached, though it can be used without.

Address

ASTROLOGICAL PUBLISHING CO.,
131-133 Chestnut St., Detroit, Mich.

ADVERTISMENT PAGE NO 1

THE SOLAR BIO-SCOPE.

is a chart of the Zodiac, with a revolving disk representing the earth's divisions, under zodical names; also descriptions of signs and mundane houses; and was first designed to be used to ascertain the relative positions of mundane houses to the signs of the Zodiac or celestial mansions. But upon using it for that purpose we discovered a simple system for astrological reading so perfect and so accurate that we determined to give it to the public; especially so as we find the great interest of the public displayed in their search for knowledge along the lines of psychic phenomena, and as astrology as taught by the old masters is too intricate to be understood by the masses, this new system will be a god-send to the hungry after knowledge of that kind, and with a little explanation a child may be able to use the system, and write horoscopes not only for amusement, but for profit.

We send a set of printed blanks with every Bio-scope, and we furnish the operator with printed blanks for one dollar per hundred. We furnish the Bio-scope for $5, but only on condition that the agent purchases his blanks of us. But the Bio-scope remains our property, to be recalled by us if the agent does not buy his stock of blanks of us. And one dollar for a hundred blanks, for which he gets a hundred dollars for, is certainly not much. No one expects to get a horoscope for less than one dollar, and everybody nowadays wants a horoscope. No intelligent person will go groping his way through the world when he can learn his attributes, what best adapted for, his unlucky days and years, his weakest physical point, by merely investing one dollar.

The blanks spoken of are the necessary printed forms together with attributes given by the signs, so the greater portion of the work is already done.

Few people have the opportunity thrust upon them of entering a profitable business by the investment of five or six dollars, to say nothing of the amusement of being able to write your own and your friends' horoscopes.

The Bio-scope may be used in both Northern and Southern temperate zones, but when used in a southern temperate zone it must be reversed and sunrise taken from the right side as Libra.

AN OFFER TO THE INTELLIGENT WHO ARE SEEKING A PROFITABLE BUSINESS.

"Knowedge is Power."

To him who can read the future, uncertainties cease to exist.

Become your own ASTROLOGER by the use of our new and simple system of ASTROLOGY.

No long study and expensive lessons necessary. as the tedious calculations are already made.

THE SOLAR BIO-SCOPE

is absolutely necessary for quick work in getting the positions of houses for the old method, and is so improved and elaborated that it is an ASTROLOGER in itself

FOR GETTING THE HOUR OF BIRTH, where it is not known, that system with the SOLAR BIO-SCOPE is the best yet devised. No student, no astrologer, no person who tryes to fathem the mystries of astrology can aford to be without it. The price, $6. with 100 blanks, in colors or $5. in one color is in no comparison to its value.

Instead of the colord charts spoken of, where we retain a right to the revolving chart, we now furnish 100 better and more comprehinsive charts, in one color, with the Bio-scop, mailed free all your property for five dollars. This is a more recent arrangment than that mentioned of the colord charts, yet cost us less to print so we give the custimer the benifit of it.

SCIENCE BETTER THAN LUCK. NO 1.

ADVICE GENERALLY GIVEN TO BUSINESS MEN IS "If you find yourself in hard lines, push your business all the harder."

This may or may not be right. Commercial statistics show 95 per cent of all business men fail sooner or later.

The reason may be generally traced to a restless desire to push business, during an evil cycle or year. When successful is the time to push business, when unsuccessful rest and enjoy life. If you know your good and evil periods you can do this. Show me a man who has failed in business and I will show his downfall began in a period when he should have been most cautious, but was the least so. Get your horoscope cast and you will know at what time of life your good and evil periods come in.

If the higher organisms have power over the lower ones, through vibrations, you should at once commence the study of Astrology to learn this great secret.

If you are interested, I would advise you to get my "Universe," 50c; "What is Coming," 50c; and "Poetical Drifts of Thought," $2.50.

Remember, discordant vibrations will have their effects, learn what those effects are on you.

The blow that breaks a limb may be visable, but it is no more certain in its effects than an invisable vibration that causes the knot on yonder tree, or the crook in yonder limb. Astrology lets us know how to take advantage of these vibrations. By telling us

SCIENCE BETTER THAN LUCK, NO 2.

what we are best fitted for, what part of the world is best for us.

Diseases, we should guard against most earnestly, our fortunate and unfortunate days, months, years and cycles. Who to choose as friends or partners, and who to avoid. Whether we are fortunate or unfortunate. Every man, woman and child should have their horoscope cast. Inclose $1, with place of birth, year, day of month and hour, if possible, whether male or female, married or single, together with four questions you desire to know most about.

Address

If you are in trouble, or wish advice in any matter, get Prof. Stowe's advice. He may save you from a fit of sickness, from loss of a loved one, or separation, divorce or law suits. He is a man of years of great 'experience and judgment' and unsurpassed as an Astrologer. His advice is sought by all classes, the wealthy as well as the poor. He can how vast numbers of testimonials. All matters strictly confidential.

CHILDREN coax your parents to have your horoscope cast that you may know what is best for you to do in life.

PARENTS do not neglect your children. Have one child's horoscope cast and you will see the benefits and have horoscopes for the rest.

If married get a horoscope to know how to get along well together. If not married get your horoscope to know how to choose the one best fitted to you.

SCIENCE BETTE THAN LUCK. NO. 3.

If you wish to be put in communication with one born in the proper sign to make you a good companion it will cost you one dollar to register on our books, and when we have others fitted for you, registered, we will put you in communication. But remember this is no swindling matrimonial bureau. No charges are made for trying to make people happy.

Try once and you will come again.

Do not go into any enterprise, travel, marry, or make changes until you learn whether or not you are in a good or an evil cycle. As an evidence of what we can tell of the future we will tell of some of the evil periods of the past free of charge.

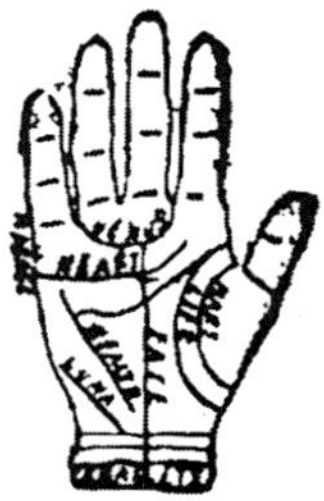

TELL YOUR OWN FORTUNE. THE SECRETS OF PALMISTRY is the only book on Palmistry worth having. Gives secrets never before published! People who thought they could never learn Palmistry are making money by its practice. Mailed free on receipt of 50c. Address Astrological Publishing Co., 133 Catherine St., Detroit, Mich.

"MY WIFE NELLIE AND I" is one of the sweatest little books cf poems you ever read, ro high folution trash but pleasing rhymes for ready readers. Mailed free for 25 cts. The "Joak in rhyme" alone is worth more thn 25 c'ts.

PROF. LYMAN E. STOWE,
133 Catherine St.,
Detroit, Mich.

We furnish the book that is so much called for, entitled "How to Succee or Secrets of Astrology Revealed." By Prof. J. McDonald. Postpaid on receipt of publisher's price, $1.

"WHAT IS COMING." By Lyman E. Stowe. A marvel of foresight. Postpaid, in paper, 50 cents; in cloth, $1.00.

"MY WIFE NELLIE AND I." By Lyman E. Stowe. Excells all poetical pastime. Postpaid, 25 cents.

We furnish you with 100 Horoscope blanks, printed in colors, for $1.00, which you will get $100.00 for.

OUR SOLAR BIO-SCOPE with 12 lessons and 100 blanks, a simplified system of Astrology, only $6.00.

FULL COURSE of lessons in Astrology, $10.

FULL COURSE of lessons in all branches of Occult Science, $25, including hypnotism.

SECRETS OF PALMISTRY is the only book printed that gives the whole secrets of palmistry so plain and comprehensive that a child can understand it. It is just the size to carry in the pocket, and consists of 12 lessons in palmistry, including the SECRETS of palmistry, 50 cents. If you take the least interest in palmistry you cannot afford to be without this book. People may conceal their disposition under a mask of deception in the face, but they cannot change the shape and lines of the hand.

EVERYONE should study palmistry. The intelligent can make and save money by it.

To those who purchase the book, SECRETS OF PALMISTRY, at the office—a reading free with the book for 50 cents.

Intelligent, energetic agents can make money at this business.

ASTROLOGICAL PUBLISHING CO.,
133 Catherine st., Detroit, Mich.

Why people have bad luck.

Dear Friend:

You will probably find this letter of interest to you. Did you ever ask the question, "Why is it that at one time you may start a journey, make a garment or start an enterprise and everything works like clock-work and runs smooth, pleasant and profitable, and at another time, seemingly under just as favorable conditions, everything goes wrong, everyone looks cross, you loose at every turn?" Nearly everybody has noticed these things and wondered why it is so.

Would it not be profitable to know why, that you might take advantage of it? Well, it has been found out and proven that the planets rule the days of the week and the hours of the day, and that your success in any enterprise depends upon planetary influences and the hour you start the enterprise or journey. Or even the durability of a garment bought at a good or evil hour or the success of any other important event in life. Even one may tell where the conversation is likely to drift by the hour one starts for or arrives at a destination. What benefit must be derived from this knowledge, which can be found in a cheap little book entitled "Right Hours to Success," together with a revolving disk for the purpose of selecting the best hours of the day for any purpose, the two mailed free for $1.00. This is a small risk for such great possibilities, yet there are people who will take greater business risks every day who will feel tempted to delay sending for this outfit. Do not delay; for your own good fill out this order at once, mail with $1.00 to the

Remember this is not the ordinary hour book, as this gives the signs of the Zodiac ruling the hours, as well as the planets, and no other hour book does that.

[Over.]

OUR PUBLICATIONS.

The UNIVERSE. A book of condensed thought. Making brief, clear and plain, world building. Evolution and the atomic soul theory, which clears up the mysteries of ghosts, apparition, thought transferance, dreams, trances, spirit manifestations, hypnotism, insanity, vibratory powers; together with the clearest treatise on astrology yet published. By Lyman E. Stowe. Paper 50c; cloth $1.00.

BIBLE ASTROLOGY. The marvel of the ages; makes those passages of the Bible plain and clear which the most gifted theologians have stumbled over. Tells the Free Mason more about his order than he knows of, and why it and the church were antagonistic. No student of the Bible or of astrology, or of Free Masonry can afford to be without this work. Written by Lyman E. Stowe. Illustrated; bound in leatherette. Price, mailed free, $1.00.

THE GREAT ASTROKABALA, OR WORLD'S WONDER. Intuitive astrology; only a few left and we have no plates. Those seeking literary curiosities should apply quickly. Written by Lyman E. Stowe. Mailed free for $1.00.

RIGHT HOURS TO SUCCESS. Getting the right hours for success for every kind of business, which also includes the right sign of the zodiac, with revolving disks, which makes it handy. The best hour book published. Written by Lyman E. Stowe. Price $1.00.

ASTROLOGICAL PERIODICITY is the most practical work on astrology for the casual reader ever published. It contains too many features to mention here, but its chief purpose is to make plain the good and evil periods of a person's life, that the physician may study the case of his patient to better advantage, the judge to understand the criminal, the detective to read nature, and the business man to judge his good and evil periods that he may not be one of the 88 per cent who fail. A book of nearly 400 pages, with revolving charts, $5.00 Written by Lyman E. Stowe.

OUR PUBLICATIONS, 2.

THE SOLAR BIOSCOPE is a chart on heavy board, 9x14 inches, with a revolving chart, and a book of instructions for getting the ascending sign and thereby the hour of birth, where the hour is not known; also how to write a horoscope by the effects of the signs of the Zodiac without the tedious work of figuring out the planetary aspects. Also showing where to look for marks and moles caused by the rising sign. There is 100 assorted blanks with book, when filled out should be worth $1.00 each or $100, and each one a better horoscope than is generally given for a dollar. This is actual value and a benefit to every person who owns the work. Old Astrologers will find this work a tremendous help. By Lyman E. Stowe. Price, with blanks, $5.00; without blanks, $4.00.

SECRETS OF PALMISTRY. Vest pocket edition; a great aid to getting hour of birth. Contains matter heretofore secret with the palmist. By Lyman E. Stowe. Price 50c.

STOWE'S HANDY KEY TO ASTROLOGY. The influence of planets in signs and houses always before you. Very handy. Price 25c.

STOWE'S HELIO CENTRIC EPHEMRIES, with chart of destiny which shows at a glance the degree of birth of what we judge in each sign and house. The dignities of the planets, thus if a planet be in 10 degrees of any sign look to that degree on the map and it tells you the decan, part or dignity where strong or weak, at a glance, where a planet rules, exalts, detriment or fall. These ephemries also contain a perpetual calendar. Chart and book $1.00. Those having Stowe's Astrological Periodicity will have this work and chart.

STOWE'S ASTROLOGICAL FORTUNE TELLING CARDS. A pack of 56 cards, also explanations how to use them and how to read in a tea cup and why it is possible to read the future with cards or tea cup. Price $1.00 per pack. Send for discriptive circular and testimonials. These cards are a great curiosity.

OUR PUBLICATIONS, a.

STOWE'S PRIVATE LESSONS IN THE ATOMIC Soul Theory and Concentration of Power, and Private Lessons in Hypnotism, together with Private Correspondence in the same. Price $5.00.

WHAT IS COMING. This is a work on finance that should be read by every person who is interested in the welfare of the human race, and that he may judge of what is near by for the human race. A history of the money question from Solomon to the present, and the Bible commands concerning it, together with two large illustrations in explanation of the meaning of the GREAT RED DRAGON. The Mother of Harlots and her daughters and what comes of them. The Beasts or Daniel's vision now about to be fulfilled, the setting up of the abomination that maketh desolate, and other things spoken of in the book, written in 1895 and now taking place. Mailed free. Paper, 50c; cloth, $1.00.

POETICAL DRIFHTS OF THOUGHT. Octavo 300 pages in prose and verse. Illustrated. Bound in green and gold. By Lyman E. Stowe. A beautiful book for the table. Price $.200.

MY WIFE NELLIE AND I. A little gem in prose and verse. Illustrated. By Lyman E. Stowe. This little book is just the thing for a few hours' pastime. Paper, 50c; board, 75c.

FREDERICK WHITE'S EASY LESSONS IN GEOCENTRIC ASTROLOGY. Just the thing for the beginner. No. 1, 50c; No. 2, 50c. Private lessons in directions, 50c. WHITE'S GEO-EPHEMERIES, as good as the E nglish, for 25c each year.

INSTRUCTIONS FOR MONTHLY READINGS.

Since the book was published, having discovered this process of giving monthly forecasts or trend of the months, I produce these instructions.

A wonderful horoscope may be written by this system alone. First, by giving the influence of the sign of the Zodiac, and if you have the effects of the exact degree, which I have written but not yet published, you can get much nearer. This should be mixed with the effects of the rising sign, then with the effects of the sign the Moon is in.

Now, to get the effects, at birth or any year after, or of an event to transpire any year after, you judge it as explained in the book, by first noting the cycle a person is passing through, then look for the year. For instance, the 41st birthday to 43rd birthday is evil, but depends on the cycle one is passing through.

Now, to get an evil month, you start with the month between 41 and 42, which in this case is a Scorpio month, good for money but bad for headth and for other matters except for money matters. Being about the 13th degree of Aries, this would run to May 2nd, thence to the 2nd of each month, and you will judge each month from the date the sign starts to 30 degrees or days ahead, just as you would judge the years, only not so strong.

Aries, restless, active, but prosperous.

Taurus is a good money month, year or cycle. Sometimes other troubles may arise, because it is right opposite the worst sign, Scorpio. You must note the year, cycle or month opposite to any sign.

Gemini is always a nervous cycle, year or month, and generally brings nervousness, change or travel.

A Cancer year or month is a rather unfriendly month or year, bringing sorrows, deaths, parting of friends as well as other worries, though often brings thoughts of home, children and quietude.

Leo generally brings harmony, love, pleasures, activity, and often inventive trend of the mind.

Virgo is a good period for money, though it may bring ill health; it is a good cycle, year or month.

Libra is a nervous, restless period; often brings love, partnership, change and letters, yet often sort of melancholy feelings; not a good time to start new business.

Scorpio is apt to bring any looked for trouble, quarrels, expected law suits or sickness. Though a good time to push old business, is not good to start new business.

Sagittarius is an excellent cycle, year or month, a good time for money, almost sure to bring travel and change, or nervous desire to do so.

Capricornus year, cycle or month is a very fine period to start new work; almost sure to get a new business offer, or at least to lay new plans for business, though it often brings death, or separation of friends. Must be judged by other positions.

Aquarius: This brings many friends, or quarrels and separations from friends.

Pisces is called a bad cycle, year or month; often brings sickness, sorrow or enemies, though sometimes good luck in business or money, because of being opposite to Virgo.

Remember to judge the cycle strong, the year a little less strong, and the month still less, or merely the trend of the months.

Example.

A person born April 2nd, 1843, was 67 years old last April, hence in his Capricornus cycle—his Virgo year; a good cycle for business, a good year for business, but not ery good for health, especially in June and December.

The trend of each of the twelve months will be about as follows, from the 2nd of one month to the 2nd of the next:

April—In this case is an Aries-Virgo-Capricornus month. Capricornus being a business cycle, and Aries representing activity, the month will be an active business month. Virgo being fortunate, yet representing health, it will be fortunate in money but not in health, because it represents a Virgo year. Had it fallen in Leo, Scorpio or Taurus the health would be good also.

May—A Taurus-Leo-Capricornus month.

The mind is on business, and successful, and expresses much anxiety for loved ones, liable to visits of loved friends, also the making of new friends. The young may court or marry.

June—In this case a Gemini-Cancer-Capricornus month. This is a nervous, restless, worrisome month, and possibly loss or illness. Possibly unpleasantness in the home.

July—In this case July is almost a repetition of June, as it is the same combination, except Gemini and Cancer are reversed in position, which fills the mind with a desire to travel, but is apt to defer travel into August (and this did do so for this person this very year).

August—A Leo-Taurus-Capricornus year. Business, activity and success is the judgment.

September—A Virgo-Capricornus-Aquarius month. Notice when the months run past the mother cycle or cycle one is passing through, you mix slightly the effects of the next cycle. Thus the judgment of September is a very active month, will pay well, with a slight ill-health, strongly literary or good for letters, etc., etc.

This is sufficient to show how the work is done. The combination is as great as that of any system of astrology and far more reliable.

Events can be figured down to the hour by using the hour dial. Figuring an evil event to come during an evil year in an evil cycle, an evil months and an evil day of the week and a Mars or Saturn hour of the day and a good thing to take place during good periods, and as the periods become mixed so will the effects become mixed. Of course much depends upon the wisdom and judgment of the reader.

Notice the signs of the Zodiac stand for cycles, years and months. Thus the 68th year is an Aries month, because it starts in April, Capricornus because the prson is in his Capricornus cycle. Virgo because between 67 and 68 is a Virgo sign, hence the month will partake of the Aries, Capricornus and Virgo nature, and May will partake of the Aries, Capricornus and Leo nature and so on through the twelve months.

MISTAKES.

It is impossible to publish a book without making mistakes.

It was said some years ago that our guide book, Webster's Dictionary, contained thirty pages of errors, if all put together.

Some years ago a London publishing house declared they would have one perfect book, when first published. They paid twenty-five of the best proofreaders that could be found to proofread the work, and then felt so sure of perfection that they offered $500 for a mistake, and before the ink was hardly dry on the paper twenty mistakes were pointed out, and one of those in the large type on the title page.

All my life I have had to work under difficulties few men can understand. My thought has run so far in advance of my fellow man it is unpopular, and I cannot get publishers to take hold of my works, and I have had to publish them myself.

The evidence of this will be found in the illustrations in my Poetical Drifts of Thought, published in 1884, and shows I am practically the inventor of the present aeroplane or flying machine, and other modern improvements; yet much is made of every one of my little mistakes, as if I had committed a crime or was unworthy of notice.

In the description of Heavenly bodies, in Periodicity the error is made of saying the star Syres is found in the constellation Scorpio, whereas it is in Cancer. No credit is given to the fact that the list of fixed stars on the accompanying charts puts Syres in Cancer. I have made the awful mistake of saying it will be found in Scorpio. Of course I have made other mistakes. I am not a practical printer, nor did I receive a complete college education. Neither did any of the greatest thinkers of the world. Besides, I have committed the terrible crime of being an old man subject to error, but hope intelligent people will overlook such errors, and they will be corrected as soon as possible.

Published by

Facsimile Publisher
Ashok Vihar, Delhi-110052 (India)
Website: www.facsimilepublishers.com

Distributed by

Gyan Books Pvt. Ltd.
5, Ansari Road, Daryaganj, New Delhi-110002 (India)
E-mail: books@gyanbooks.com, Website: www.gyanbooks.com

9 789361 581328